Adobe Photoshop® Lightroom® Classic

for **dummies**®
A Wiley Brand

Adobe Photoshop® Lightroom® Classic

3rd Edition

by Rob Sylvan

A Wiley Brand

Adobe Photoshop® Lightroom® Classic For Dummies®, 3rd Edition

Published by: **John Wiley & Sons, Inc.**, 111 River Street, Hoboken, NJ 07030-5774, www.wiley.com

Copyright © 2025 by John Wiley & Sons, Inc. All rights reserved, including rights for text and data mining and training of artificial technologies or similar technologies.

Media and software compilation copyright © 2025 by John Wiley & Sons, Inc. All rights reserved, including rights for text and data mining and training of artificial technologies or similar technologies.

Published simultaneously in Canada

For general information on our other products and services, please contact our Customer Care Department within the U.S. at 877-762-2974, outside the U.S. at 317-572-3993, or fax 317-572-4002. For technical support, please visit https://hub.wiley.com/community/support/dummies.

Wiley publishes in a variety of print and electronic formats and by print-on-demand. Some material included with standard print versions of this book may not be included in e-books or in print-on-demand. If this book refers to media that is not included in the version you purchased, you may download this material at http://booksupport.wiley.com. For more information about Wiley products, visit www.wiley.com.

Library of Congress Control Number is available from the publisher.

ISBN 978-1-394-28461-0 (pbk); ISBN 978-1-394-28463-4 (ebk); ISBN 978-1-394-28464-1 (ebk)
SKY10100992_032825

Contents at a Glance

Table of Contents

PART 3: WORKING IN LIGHTROOM CLASSIC'S DIGITAL DARKROOM

Introduction

t's been over 16 years since I wrote the first edition of this book on what was then Lightroom 2. Saying that a lot has changed since then is a bit of an understatement. At the end of 2017, Adobe released two similar, but distinctly different, versions of Lightroom with the goal of addressing two similar, yet different, digital photography workflows. I've structured this book to help you understand the differences between these versions of Lightroom — one now called Adobe Photoshop Lightroom Classic and a new one now just called Adobe Photoshop Lightroom — so that you are prepared to choose the right one for your needs. Just be sure to read all of Chapter 1 to get a handle on that aspect. That said, the primary focus of this book is on how to get the most out of Lightroom Classic. A few chapters can help a Lightroom Classic user get started with the new Lightroom on the mobile platform, but if you're using only the new Lightroom on all your devices, you'll want to check out a different book.

Back in 2007 when Lightroom 1.0 was released, it was considered a paradigm shift in the way photographers managed and edited their digital photos. Today we are witnessing a new paradigm shift, thanks to the rise of the smartphone as digital camera with always-connected Internet (which is why this new Lightroom version was released). Although paradigm shifts offer new ways of doing things and the potential of improved workflows, they can sometimes be disorienting and frustrating to come to terms with at first. That's why Adobe still offers the original version, which is now called Lightroom Classic. My hope is that this book can serve as a resource to keep you out of trouble, on task, and moving forward as you take your photos from camera to storage to output, over and over again.

About This Book

I am more than just a user of both versions of Lightroom. Through my roles on the KelbyOne.com Lightroom Help Desk, as an educator, as an author, and from my participation in various Lightroom groups, workshops, and forums, I've worked with tens of thousands of fellow Lightroom users over the past decade. I've tried to understand the problems they faced as I've helped them find solutions. I wrote this book with the intention of preventing you from encountering the same problems that others have stumbled over while also sharing the collective wisdom I've gained to make your workflow as efficient as possible.

I've organized this book with the larger Lightroom Classic workflow in mind, but each chapter — and even the sections within a chapter — represent all the smaller workflows that make up the larger whole. So, although there's something to be gained from following the structure I lay out in the book, if you're new to Lightroom Classic, my hope is that you can pick up this book when you need it and jump right to the place in your workflow that you want to learn more about.

Because of the existence of two different versions of Lightroom, I've also structured the book with the goal of minimizing confusion about which version I'm talking about. I explicitly refer to Adobe Photoshop Lightroom Classic as *Lightroom Classic* (as cumbersome as that is to read over and over again) and refer to the new Adobe Photoshop Lightroom as just *Lightroom* (along with references to it being cloud-based or part of an ecosystem) within a given chapter.

Note that until the middle of 2019, both versions had the initials *CC* (for Creative Cloud) appended to the end of their respective names. Now that it's possible to license any version of the Lightroom family of products only through a Creative Cloud subscription, Adobe dropped the *CC* from the ends of both product names. For the sake of clarity, what was Lightroom Classic CC is now just Lightroom Classic, and what was Lightroom CC is now just Lightroom.

Lightroom Classic is a workflow tool by design, and within the macro workflow of capture to output, there exist countless smaller workflows that cover all the micro tasks every photographer needs to complete. The very concept of a workflow implies that there is both a natural beginning and a finite end. I mean, you can't start editing a photo if you haven't first pressed the shutter, right?

Conventions Used in This Book

Lightroom Classic is wonderfully identical on both the Windows and Mac operating systems. I use both operating systems, but I create the majority of screen captures on the Mac because that's what I use most. However, I do include Windows captures where needed to highlight the few places where there are minor differences in the interface or dialog boxes, and I've added a few captures from mobile devices where needed.

In the case of keyboard shortcuts (and there are many), I lead off with the Mac shortcut and always include the Windows shortcut in parentheses afterward. All the shortcuts that don't require an additional modifier key are the same on both platforms. When I give an instruction for opening a contextual menu, I use the term *right-click* even though you may not be using an input device with a right-click button. For the Mac, right-clicking is the same as Control-clicking an onscreen element to open the contextual menu, though you may have a mouse for the Mac that has a right-click button, too.

With regard to menu commands, I use the convention of separating each menu command with this cute arrow: ➪. To quit, for example, I tell you to choose Lightroom Classic➪Quit Lightroom (File➪Exit on Windows). You can also quit the program by pressing ⌘+Q (Ctrl+Q on Windows).

Icons Used in This Book

Scattered throughout this book you find some nifty little icons that point out bits of information that are especially useful, important, or noteworthy.

TIP

You see this icon the most. I include many tips to help you get the most benefit from each aspect of the program.

WARNING

You won't see many of these icons (fortunately). I use them only when there's a chance you might lose data if you aren't careful.

REMEMBER

Whenever a certain piece of information isn't particularly intuitive — but vital to keep in mind — I add this icon to help it stand out.

TECHNICAL STUFF

This icon indicates a heads-up for those few places where I need to explain some of the more technical aspects of the software.

Beyond the Book

Like every *For Dummies* book, this one comes with a free Cheat Sheet that brings together some of the most commonly needed information for readers struggling with Lightroom Classic. Turn to this sheet for a handy list of shortcuts, a close-up of what's included around image thumbnails, all the tools available on the Library Toolbar, and suggestions for what to do when things go wrong. To get the Cheat Sheet, head for www.dummies.com and, using the Search box, search for *Adobe Photoshop Lightroom Classic For Dummies Cheat Sheet.*

Where to Go from Here

If you're just starting out, my advice to you is to visit Part 1 sooner rather than later. Beyond that, this book is intended to be a reference that you can rely on when you find yourself stuck or that you can use proactively to avoid the most common pitfalls before you go in.

Be sure to check out my website, at `https://Lightroomers.com`, and my weekly Lightroom blog, at `https://LightroomKillerTips.com`, for the latest news, tips, and tutorials on both Lightroom Classic and Lightroom.

1

Getting Started with Lightroom Classic

Chapter **1**

Getting to Know Adobe Photoshop Lightroom Classic

When I wrote the first edition of this book, the only product available was Adobe Photoshop Lightroom, and the iPhone had just been introduced. The intervening years have brought a boon to camera technology, mobile technology, software capabilities, and the Internet. Adobe has responded to these advances by spinning off a new version of the original Lightroom (while adding Classic to the old version) in a way that leverages the ubiquity of mobile devices, cloud storage, and always-connected Internet. This has resulted in more choice but also a bit of confusion.

In this chapter, I aim to clarify the key distinctions between the two versions of Lightroom to help you choose the version that is right for you. I encourage you to go back and read the book's Introduction to get a big-picture view of how this book is organized and clarity on how I refer to the two versions of Lightroom throughout the book. To get some historical context on the evolution of Lightroom, I encourage you to read my blog post on Adobe's original announcement of the new version: `https://lightroomkillertips.com/new-lightroom-whole-new-ecosystem`.

The Two Versions of Lightroom

At the time of this writing, Adobe provides two separate but similar programs with the name *Lightroom* in the title. In a nutshell, the key differences are that

» **Lightroom Classic** uses a catalog (more on that later) that is stored on your computer, which references photos that can be stored on your computer, an external drive, a network-attached storage device, or any combination of those local storage options. It has been evolving since 2007 and will feel most familiar to anyone who has used a previous version of Lightroom. Lightroom Classic is the main focus of this book.

» **Lightroom** stores everything (photos, information about the photos, and all adjustments) in the *cloud* (storage that is accessible only through an Internet connection and paid for through your Adobe Creative Cloud subscription), and by virtue of everything being stored in the cloud, you can access all your work from any device (laptop, desktop, tablet, or smartphone) that runs Lightroom (available for the macOS, Windows, iOS, and Android platforms). Because everything is stored in the cloud, you can even access your Lightroom photos from a web browser. Lightroom has fewer features than Lightroom Classic (although Adobe adds more all the time) and is designed for use in our always-connected mobile world. I introduce you to Lightroom in Part 5, where I explore how Lightroom on a mobile device can be a useful companion to Lightroom Classic.

This book focuses on Lightroom Classic because this version is the most mature of the two versions, has the most features, and doesn't require an Internet connection to access your photos. In my view, Lightroom Classic is the most powerful version of Lightroom and makes the most sense for most people looking to manage a growing photo library over time. It also provides the greatest variety of output possibilities (prints, books, slideshows, web galleries, and more). Lightroom Classic is what I use, and I will continue to use it into the foreseeable future.

I don't want you to think that I am not a fan of the new Lightroom; I am very excited about the opportunities it offers people who don't need everything Lightroom Classic offers, who want a simpler interface, and who place a premium on being able to access their photo library from any laptop, desktop, or mobile device. In fact, I devote three chapters at the end of this book to Lightroom to help you see its potential. That said, if you want to use just Lightroom on all your devices, this is not the book for you. Because Lightroom is new and simpler and has far fewer features than Lightroom Classic, you can get by just fine using the web-based training from Adobe: `https://helpx.adobe.com/lightroom-cc/tutorials.html`.

Just about all of Adobe's software has moved from a pay-one-price perpetual license model to a new subscription-based model, which Adobe calls the Creative Cloud (often shortened to CC). Both versions of Lightroom are available only through a subscription plan. Let's dive into this topic a little deeper.

Understanding the Creative Cloud

Adobe coined the name Creative Cloud in 2011, but the term took on new meaning in 2013 when Adobe moved away from the old Creative Suite of products and made its flagship products (like Photoshop) available for licensing only through a monthly or annual subscription. All programs are still installed locally to your computer and function in the same way they always had; the only difference with the Creative Cloud (CC) is how you pay for the software.

While paying monthly or annually for the use of software may seem like a drag, Adobe has made it pretty affordable for photographers through the CC Photography Plan (more on that in the next section). The subscription model offers a few benefits, including the following:

>> Access to the latest version of included software the moment Adobe releases it, without additional cost

>> Periodic updates, which include new features as well as new camera support and bug fixes

>> Able to be installed on as many computers as you own, although you can be logged into only two at a time

>> Cross-platform compatible, so no special hoops to jump through if you have both a Mac and a Windows computer

REMEMBER

The Creative Cloud subscription model provides a few benefits. Notably, Adobe frequently releases updates that include new features, new camera support, and bug fixes. With the subscription service, you can access these features immediately instead of waiting 18 to 24 months to see new features added.

There are a few CC plans to choose from, and due to the somewhat fluid nature of how these plans evolve, I'm going to direct you to Adobe's website to read up on what's included and the various prices. Head over to `https://blog.adobe.com/en/publish/2024/12/15/all-new-photography-innovations-pricing-updates` to learn more.

Considering the Creative Cloud Photography Plan

Within the various subscription options, the plan that makes the most sense for photographers who are new to Adobe subscriptions is the 1TB Photography Plan, which goes for $19.99/month and includes the latest versions of Lightroom Classic, Lightroom, and Photoshop, 1TB of online storage, and more (like a free online portfolio), so check the link in the preceding section to get the full understanding of recent changes to plan options.

TIP

Adobe Photoshop is the prime tool to complement Lightroom Classic and Lightroom. It gives you the most power and offers the greatest functionality and tightest integration with both versions of Lightroom. In fact, when you consider all the features in Lightroom Classic, you may find you don't need anything else for most of your work.

Adobe also offers a Lightroom plan, which as of January 2025 is $11.99/month (or prepaid annually for $119.88/year to save $24 over paying monthly), and includes Lightroom and Lightroom Classic (but it doesn't include Photoshop) and 1 terabyte (TB) of online storage (which is enough for hundreds of thousands of JPG photos). If you don't ever plan on using Photoshop this could be a good option for using Lightroom Classic and Lightroom together.

From here, I assume that as a reader of *Adobe Photoshop Lightroom Classic For Dummies,* with a focus on Lightroom Classic, you have (or will be using) either plan that includes Lightroom Classic.

Figuring out whether Lightroom Classic is right for you

If you have used any older version of Lightroom in the past ten years, you will feel the most comfortable in Lightroom Classic. Due to its maturity as a software product, Lightroom Classic has substantially more features and capabilities than Lightroom, and this alone may be the deciding factor for some people. For example, Lightroom Classic has an entire module devoted to printing, and Lightroom has no local print function.

Lightroom Classic is best used if you have a high volume of photos stored in your library and plan to continue adding photos to that library. Lightroom Classic stores all your photos locally, so this is a much more affordable option for anyone with over 1TB of storage. Hard drives are relatively cheap, so adding more space to store more photos is affordable and easy.

Lightroom Classic plays nicely with third-party plug-ins. Let's face it, you can find lots of outstanding photo editing programs out there from companies like On1, Topaz, DxO, and more. You can configure Lightroom Classic to send copies to these editors (and to Photoshop, too!) and have those copies automatically added back to Lightroom Classic.

If you like to create photo books, you will enjoy using Lightroom Classic's Book module. If you need to create slideshows, check out Lightroom Classic's Slideshow module. Lightroom Classic supports a high-volume workflow, so it has a greater array of output options for when you need to create copies for any reason.

Lightroom Classic and Lightroom share the same powerful editing tools used to make your photos look awesome, so there is no real compromise there. So, what makes Lightroom compelling? Read on!

Deciding whether you need the new Lightroom

If I had to sketch out the type of photographer who would be the best fit for using Lightroom (at the time of this writing), I would think of someone who primarily shoots with a smartphone and/or digital camera set to JPG mode, has a photo library that's less than 1TB of total data, and has no inkjet printer. That's not to say that someone who only shoots raw (refer to Chapter 3 for more on file formats) with a DSLR/mirrorless and prints every photo can't use Lightroom, but considering Lightroom's current set of features and cost, the raw DSLR/mirrorless shooter could find using Lightroom frustrating and expensive. I'm sure this situation will evolve.

Lightroom's greatest asset is that it makes all your photos available on all your devices, and it does that by storing the full-resolution photos in the cloud. This is an amazing feature! However, as I discuss in the section "Understanding the Creative Cloud," earlier in this chapter, the Lightroom plan is currently $11.99/month for 1TB of storage. If you have less than 1TB of total storage needs, this is a pretty affordable way to have all your photos backed up, accessible, and combined with a state-of-the-art photo editor (and mobile camera app) with easy access to sharing on social media.

WARNING

Each additional terabyte of storage costs an additional $9.99/month. If you have a photo library that requires 3TB of storage, you are looking at $29.97/month to store that in the cloud in perpetuity. That's $359.64 per year, and I don't know many photographers willing to pay that much per year to store their photos in the cloud. Depending on how you purchased your current plan, you may need to contact Adobe support for assistance in upgrading to a plan with a larger storage amount.

Now don't get me wrong; I love the direction Lightroom is heading, and I think it is a great match for people who fit well within its current feature set, but it just isn't for everyone. That said, who knows how things will change and evolve in the next ten years? Nothing is static in the world of digital photography. However, keep in mind that Lightroom is also included with the CC Photography Plan with Lightroom Classic and Photoshop (and 1TB of storage), and in Chapters 16 through 18, I discuss how to use Lightroom Classic and Lightroom together.

If you're intrigued about Lightroom, jump ahead to Part 5 of this book for an introduction to using it on your mobile device. The remaining sections of this chapter look at the interface of the focus of the book, Lightroom Classic.

Introducing the Lightroom Classic Interface

Adobe built Lightroom Classic using a *modular* architecture, which means that Lightroom Classic comprises a set of unique applications that share a common interface and access a common database (or *catalog,* as it is called). Each of the applications is referred to as a *module,* and Lightroom Classic has seven modules.

REMEMBER

None of these modules can function outside of Lightroom Classic. Although tightly integrated, they each have a set of unique menus, panels, and tools tailored to the specific function each module is designed to handle.

I drill down into the specific panels, tools, and menus in the chapters ahead, but for now, I'm going to do the overview thing by taking a stab at what makes each module unique and then showing you how to get the most out of the common interface.

Getting what makes each module unique

Lightroom Classic has seven modules — but the beauty of modular construction is that the potential exists for more to be added. Adobe has opened only limited aspects of Lightroom Classic's guts to third-party developers, and the outcome has been quite positive.

The potential for extending Lightroom Classic's functionality in the future is something to look forward to, but there's already plenty of power under the hood. Here are the seven modules you find in Lightroom Classic:

>> **The Library module:** Your organizational hub, the Library module (see Figure 1-1), is where many of your Lightroom Classic sessions start and end. Common Library module tasks include

- Keywording and metadata entry.
- File moving, deletion, and renaming.
- Finding, sorting, and grouping.

FIGURE 1-1: The Library module.

>> **The Develop module:** The bulk of your image processing takes place in the Develop module. Armed with a powerful array of image-adjustment tools, shown in Figure 1-2, common Develop module tasks include

- Setting white balance and tonal adjustments.
- Adjusting contrast and color.
- Reducing noise and adding sharpening.
- Cropping and adjusting crooked horizons.
- Making selective adjustments and removing distractions.

FIGURE 1-2:
The Develop
module.

>> **The Map module:** Shown in Figure 1-3, the Map module is for finding photos with embedded geolocation information on the map, or for manually placing photos on the map. The tools in this module allow you to

● See photos with geolocation data appear on the map.

● Manually place photos on the map.

● Use the geolocation data in the photo to apply location information (city, state, country) to its metadata.

FIGURE 1-3:
The Map
module.

» **The Book module:** Shown in Figure 1-4, the Book module is for creating book layouts that you can upload to be printed through Blurb.com. The tools in this module allow you to

- Adjust book page layouts.
- Create a cover for the book.
- Add text to individual pages.

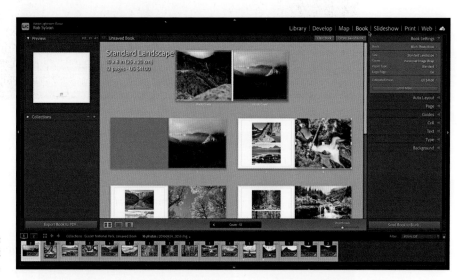

FIGURE 1-4:
The Book
module.

» **The Slideshow module:** The aptly named Slideshow module, shown in Figure 1-5, is for creating presentations of your photos. The tools in this module allow you to

- Adjust slideshow layout.
- Adjust slide transitions.
- Set the show to music.
- Export a slideshow as a video, PDF, or series of JPGs.

» **The Print module:** If you print photos, you'll soon find the Print module, shown in Figure 1-6, to be a valuable addition to your printing workflow. Here you find controls for

- Creating layouts and print packages.
- Using output-specific color profiles to ensure the best-looking prints.
- Printing to a local printer or to a JPG file.

FIGURE 1-5:
The Slideshow
module.

FIGURE 1-6:
The Print
module.

>> **The Web module:** Getting your photos online in some capacity is a require-
ment these days. The Web module, shown in Figure 1-7, allows you to manage
your web presence by letting you

- Choose from various photo gallery styles.

- Configure the look and feel of your web gallery.

- Upload directly to your web server.

FIGURE 1-7:
The Web
module.

What the Lightroom Classic modules have in common

Having all modules share parts of a common interface might make it harder (at first glance) to tell which module is which, but don't worry too much about that. Clarity will reign supreme when you have Lightroom Classic up and running. Think of it this way: A common interface is in fact one of Lightroom Classic's greatest strengths because keeping the same interface means you don't have to spend time learning seven different interfaces. The interface behaves the same and has the same basic structure no matter what you're using Lightroom Classic to accomplish.

Check out Figure 1-8 to see what I mean. The Library module shown there sports the following standard interface components that each module shares:

» **The Title bar:** Provides an at-a-glance view of the name of the catalog and the module you're in.

» **The Menu bar:** The go-to place for all the commands needed for each module's tasks.

» **The Module Picker:** An easy method to pick the module you want to work with. This area of the interface is also home to the identity plate on the left, which you can customize to insert your own graphic, as well as the progress meter that appears whenever Lightroom performs a task. (For more on the identity plate, check out Chapter 5.)

» **The Left Panel group:** Although the content varies with each module, the panels to the left of the interface are generally functions that involve accessing, grouping, and previewing photos and templates.

>> **The Right Panel group:** The panels to the right of the interface also vary with each module, but this is where you find controls for adjusting and tweaking.

>> **The Toolbar:** Each module has its own set of tools, but the Toolbar that appears under the main content area is a staple of every module.

>> **The Filmstrip:** At the bottom of each module, you find the Filmstrip, which displays thumbnails of the image grouping you are working with. It also is home to a row of tools right there along the top that put many items at your fingertips, no matter what module you are in:

- *Main and Second Window controls:* Click and hold either of these window icons to access a number of shortcuts for controlling each window (more details on the second window function later in this chapter).

- *Jump to Grid View icon:* No matter where you are in Lightroom, one click takes you to Grid view in the Library module.

- *Go Back and Go Forward buttons:* These buttons allow you to navigate between previously selected image groupings (folders, collections, searches) you have been viewing.

- *Filmstrip Source Indicator:* This item provides an at-a-glance view of the current image grouping and active photo. Click the drop-down arrow at the end for quick access to the special collections found in the Catalog panel as well as a list of recently visited folders, collections, and favorites.

- *Filters:* When clicked, the Filter label expands to reveal ways to filter the current image grouping by flag, rating, or color label. The Custom Filter drop-down menu provides quick access to all Library Filter bar options. The last button on the right toggles filtering on and off.

FIGURE 1-8: The Lightroom Classic interface components.

Controlling the Lightroom Classic interface

Lightroom Classic's interface has a number of options for reducing and simplifying the workspace. Here's an example: My publisher had me capture the images of Lightroom Classic shown in this book at a screen resolution of 1600 x 900, so things are looking a little cramped. No way would I work at this resolution — I'd naturally bump it up to the highest resolution my monitor supports so that I can have as much space to work with as possible. However, sometimes there's just not enough room for everything the interface has to offer — usually, those times when you really just want to give as much screen real estate to your photos as possible. Imagine trying to work on a project in your shop and being forced to lay all your tools in neat rows on the workbench — I guess it's handy, but you surely won't have as much space as you would like for the project you're working on. Lightroom has some pretty clever ways of tweaking how your tools are displayed so that you can maximize the size of your workspace.

The simplest way to maximize space is to take advantage of working in Full Screen mode. Just like with any application you currently use, you're just a keystroke combo away from maximizing Lightroom Classic to fill the available screen. The neat thing about Lightroom Classic, though, is that it takes this maximizing business a step further by providing two separate Full Screen modes in addition to the Normal Screen mode (refer to Figure 1-8 to see Normal) for working:

>> **Full Screen with Menu bar:** With this option, Lightroom Classic expands to fill the screen and hide its title bar to gain more space. The Menu bar is at the top of the screen. Note that the standard Minimize, Maximize, and Close buttons vanish from the top of the window in this mode.

>> **Full Screen:** With this option, Lightroom Classic expands to take over the screen completely. The Menu bar disappears, and the Dock (Taskbar in Windows) isn't accessible.

>> **Normal (shown in Figure 1-8):** All options are visible, and the Lightroom Classic interface can be resized and moved by grabbing the edge of the window, just like in any other application.

TIP

To switch between the three screen modes, press Shift+F to jump from one view to another. Keep in mind, though, that if it appears as though you "lost" the Minimize, Maximize, and Close buttons at the top of the window (the horror!), what's really happened is that you've simply entered one of the Full Screen modes. (I can't tell you how many panicked emails I have received from folks who believe they've somehow lopped off said buttons by mistake, asking whether I could please help them get back their buttons.)

If you just want to see your photo full-screen on a black background with no interface cluttering things up, press (only) the F key to toggle Full Screen Preview — useful for putting a photo front and center for evaluation. You can even use the arrow keys to move between photos. Press F again to exit the preview.

If you still want more space, you can take advantage of the collapsible nature of the Module Picker, Panel groups, and Filmstrip. Refer to Figure 1-8 — do you see the small arrow in the center of the outer edge of each side of the interface? Clicking an arrow once causes that panel to "hide" from view. Now move your cursor away and then back over any part of that edge, and the hidden panel returns, giving you access to the contents of the panel until you move the cursor away again. This is called Auto Hide & Show. Right-click an arrow, and the following options appear:

>> **Auto Hide:** When enabled, that panel automatically hides when you move the cursor away from it, but it won't show again until you click the arrow. I personally like this option because having the Auto Show kicking in every time I venture too close to the edge tends to drive me nuts.

>> **Manual:** Nothing automatic. If you click an arrow to hide, and it stays that way until you click again.

>> **Sync with Opposite Panel:** When selected, the Auto Hide/Manual settings you choose will also be applied to the panel on the opposite side.

I find a more convenient method for showing and hiding these screen elements is the keyboard shortcuts:

>> **F5:** Show/hide the Module Picker.

>> **F6:** Show/hide the Filmstrip.

>> **F7:** Show/hide the Left Panel group.

>> **F8:** Show/hide the Right Panel group.

>> **Tab:** Show/hide both the Left and Right panel groups.

>> **Shift+Tab:** Show/hide all four screen elements at once.

>> **T:** Show/hide the Toolbar.

When it comes to clearing the clutter and focusing on your photos, Lightroom Classic has one further cool trick up its sleeve. It's called Lights Out mode and has three states:

>> **Lights On:** This is the normal operating condition, where everything is visible.

>> **Lights Dim:** In this mode, your selected photos remain unchanged but the surrounding interface dims. Although dimmed, the interface is accessible and functional (if you know where things are).

>> **Lights Off:** Taking the dim view to the extreme, the entire interface is blacked out and only your photos are visible — the ultimate way to reduce clutter!

TIP

You can jump through each Lights Out mode by pressing the L key. You set the amount of dimming and the color the screen dims to in the preferences. (I cover all the preference settings in Chapter 3.)

Using Lightroom Classic's secondary display view

The ultimate way to gain more screen real estate is to add another screen! Lightroom Classic's approach to dual monitor support is the addition of a second window that you can move to your second monitor. The result is that you have the same primary Lightroom Classic window on one monitor (this is where you access all the modules and do your work), and then the secondary display window provides additional ways to view the photos you are working on. (Although it's possible to enable the secondary window on a single monitor system, it is limited in its usefulness because it competes for the same screen real estate as the primary window.)

The secondary display window functions in the same manner with all Lightroom Classic modules. Here are the options available in the secondary window:

>> **Grid:** Essentially extends the Filmstrip to the second window so that it provides greater access to all the thumbnails of the current group of photos. The secondary window Grid view functions the same as Grid view in the Library module (see Chapter 5 for more information on Grid view).

>> **Loupe:** Allows for viewing a single image in its entirety or zoomed in close within the second window. Loupe has three options:

- *Normal:* Always displays the active photo selected in the primary window

- *Live:* Continually displays the photo under the cursor as you move over photos in the main window

- *Locked:* Allows you to choose one photo to display continuously in the second window while you view a different photo in the primary window

>> **Compare:** Allows you to compare two or more photos side by side. The secondary-window Compare view functions the same way as Compare view in the Library module. (See Chapter 6 for more information on Compare view.)

>> **Survey:** Allows you to view multiple photos side by side within the secondary window. The secondary-window Survey view functions the same way as Survey view in the Library module. (See Chapter 6 for more information on Survey view.)

>> **Slideshow:** Available only when you have the secondary window set to Full Screen (not possible on a single monitor system). This option allows you to run the slideshow on the secondary display.

One other cool option related to the secondary window is called Show Second Monitor Preview. (It works only when the secondary window is in Full Screen mode.) When enabled, it provides a small preview window showing what's being displayed in the secondary window. Huh? It's intended for situations where you might have your secondary monitor facing away from you and toward an audience. This way, you can be showing photos to an audience on the secondary display while you work on the primary display, and the preview window lets you have a peek at what your audience is seeing.

TIP

You can enable and disable the second window by clicking its icon on the Filmstrip or choosing Window ⇨ Secondary Display ⇨ Show from the main menu.

Getting Up and Running

I'm sure you're champing at the bit for the opportunity to roll up your sleeves and start putting Lightroom Classic through its paces. I don't blame you! You're gonna love it. However, if you take the time to lay the groundwork so that you get all your ducks in a row, you're sure to start on the right foot. (Could I cram in any more metaphors?)

Preparing for installation

Don't think of an application installation as being a tiresome chore. Rather, think of it as a perfect excuse to do a little hard drive housekeeping. What better time to do tasks like the following:

>> Free up disk space by deleting unused files, clearing caches, moving files to another disk, and emptying the Trash.

>> Uninstall unused applications.

>> Close all programs and reboot to start fresh.

The best reason to clean house before installing is that it might just prevent problems that you'd likely blame on the new application you just installed.

Meeting the requirements

I assume you've confirmed that your system meets the posted minimum requirements before you purchased your subscription, but generally, it's always in your best interest to exceed the minimum whenever possible for best performance. Here's what matters most:

>> **RAM:** Maximizing the amount of installed RAM will probably give you the most bang for your buck. It's more than likely that you'll be running other applications alongside Lightroom Classic, so the more RAM you have, the better for everyone.

>> **Processor:** Processing large volumes of huge files takes horsepower. Lightroom Classic is able to take advantage of multi-core processors, so if an upgrade is in your future, put that under consideration.

>> **Disk space:** When working with digital images, you just can't have enough disk space. If you're shooting raw on a 12-, 24-, or 45-megapixel camera, you don't want to worry about running out of storage space. Beyond storage, you need ample free space on your start-up drive so that all your applications and your operating system have enough elbow room to function. I like using external drives with more than 2TB of storage because they are relatively inexpensive and easy to add and remove.

>> **Monitor:** You might think you're looking at your photos, but you are in fact looking at your monitor. (I actually don't want to think about how many hours in a day I spend basking in its glow.) For the benefit of your eyes and the quality of your editing, consider a monitor upgrade in your future. Unfortunately, the monitors that typically come bundled with most computers are better suited to word processing, web browsing, and email. This is probably a good time to call in a friend to help you shop if you're unsure where to start, but here are a few factors to keep in mind:

- *Price:* Quality in a monitor doesn't come cheap. At the high end, you could look at models from Eizo and LaCie, although many people I know are quite happy on the higher end with Dell and Apple. The technology is improving, and prices are falling.

- *Size:* Bigger is usually better. Your monitor is your desk space. The bigger your desk, the easier it is to work. The 24- to 30-inch monitors are pretty typically used for photo work.

- *Resolution:* A monitor's resolution is expressed by how many pixels across by how many pixels down it can display (such as 2560×1440). The larger the number, the more pixels will be displayed, which means the more room you have to work.

- *Graphics card:* This is the part of your computer that drives the video display. You need to have a graphics card powerful enough to run your monitor at its native size. You don't want to cart home a monitor your system can't handle. Have all your computer's specifications with you when you shop, and be sure to ask for help.

You can read the minimum requirements here:

- ❯❯ **Lightroom Classic:** `https://helpx.adobe.com/lightroom/system-requirements.html`

- ❯❯ **Lightroom:** `https://helpx.adobe.com/lightroom-cc/system-requirements.html`

After you determine which version of Lightroom is best for you and install it, you are ready to take a closer look at this catalog thing that Lightroom Classic uses, which, as it turns out, is pretty important.

TIP

I've made all of the Figures in the book available as a PDF you can download so you can zoom in and see details more clearly: `https://lightroomers.com/L4D/LCFD-Figure-Rerference.pdf`

IN THIS CHAPTER

» **Understanding the catalog concept**

» **Backing up and optimizing your catalogs**

» **Working with regular previews versus Smart Previews**

» **Getting a handle on what *metadata* means**

» **Transferring data across multiple catalogs**

Chapter **2**

Working with Catalogs

W hen you install Lightroom Classic, it automatically creates an empty catalog file at the default location as part of the installation process. In fact, Lightroom Classic can't even function without one. You can open Microsoft Word without having a document open, and you can open Photoshop without having an image open, but you can't open Lightroom Classic without opening a catalog. The catalog is integral to Lightroom Classic's operation.

This chapter shows you how to work with the Lightroom Classic catalog. You will see where on your system the catalog is located, how to keep it backed up, and how to keep it optimized. You'll also learn the role of the associated preview cache files and even how to transfer data between two catalogs.

Understanding How the Catalog Works

A key factor separating Lightroom Classic from a pixel editor like Adobe Photoshop and a file browser like Adobe Bridge is Lightroom Classic's use of a catalog file. The *catalog* in Lightroom Classic is essentially a database, and as such it is simply the repository for everything Lightroom Classic "knows" about your photos. Luckily, you don't need to know much about databases to use Lightroom Classic, but if you understand how this particular database fits into the big picture, you can work smarter when managing, organizing, processing, outputting, and safeguarding your photos.

The great thing about a database is that it can (unlike my own brain) recall everything you enter into it. Equally important to note, however, is that a database knows *only* what you enter into it. To ensure that the catalog remains in the know, you should always use Lightroom Classic for basic file maintenance tasks, such as moving, deleting, and renaming your imported photos (which I cover in Chapters 5 and 6).

WARNING

So rather than use Windows File Explorer, macOS Finder, or Adobe Bridge for file maintenance of your imported photos (use whatever program you want before they're imported), use Lightroom Classic to ensure that your catalog remains up-to-date with the changes you make. If you perform file maintenance tasks outside of Lightroom Classic, the catalog isn't updated as you move, rename, or delete files on your computer, and as a result, the locations of your photos within the catalog will be out of sync with the locations of your photos because they're actually stored on your computer. When this happens, your photos are considered missing or offline by Lightroom Classic, and you won't be able to edit in Develop or export copies until they're reconnected to the catalog. Take a moment to read an article I wrote about how to reconnect the catalog to missing or offline files (in case it happens to you): https://lightroomkillertips.com/when-photos-go-missing

One catalog to rule them all

Before we go any further, I want to discuss the question of how many catalogs you should have. Ideally, and recommended by Adobe (and me), you would have only one catalog that serves as the master go-to location for accessing all your photography. After all, the catalog is nothing more than a database, and the more data (information about your photos) you put in it, the more you can leverage that database to find and organize your photo library over time. Lightroom Classic sets no hard limit on how many photos a catalog can hold, but performance can be impacted over time by having a very large catalog on a computer that's lacking in horsepower (see Chapter 1 for minimum requirements). My own master catalog exceeds 200,000 photos, and I don't have a problem.

That said, I know of other photographers who feel that having multiple catalogs is the best solution for their workflow. They may feel that having one catalog per year or per decade or per event or whatever grouping fits their shooting style and way of thinking is fine, as long as it works. The thing you need to keep in mind about having multiple catalogs is that, because you can't search across catalogs, you need to create an external system to organize your photo library so that you know which catalog you need to open to find a specific photo. Having one catalog per year sounds appealing until a few years go by and you can't remember which year you took a certain photo. My suggestion is to stick with one catalog unless you have a compelling reason not to do so and you have a good system for staying organized.

Knowing where the catalog is located

By default, the catalog is stored in a folder named `Lightroom` within the `Pictures` folder. Inside the `Lightroom` folder, you find the catalog file, which has the `.lrcat` file extension, and the file that holds all the previews of your imported images (called the *preview cache*), which has the `.lrdata` file extension. These two files work together to make Lightroom Classic operational. I cover the cache files contained in this folder in the section "Managing the preview cache files," later in this chapter. Note the new file with the `.lrcat-data` extension for storing data related to the improved Masking functionality (see Chapter 9).

TIP

To store your catalog at a location other than the default (if your default drive is low on free space, for example, or if you prefer to keep all your photo-related files in a different location), use your computer's file management app to move the entire `Lightroom` folder to a new location on your computer. The catalog works fine from any (non-network-connected) location — you just have to help Lightroom Classic find the catalog in its new location the first time you access it. More on that in a bit.

Here are a couple of things to keep in mind regarding where a catalog can live happily:

>> **Local drive:** The catalog has to be kept on a locally connected drive (external drives are fine). Lightroom Classic can't access a catalog stored on a network drive (though it can access photos stored on a network drive).

>> **Free space:** Be sure to place the catalog on a drive that has a large enough amount of free space to store your work (as in hundreds of available gigabytes or more). The size of your database and its companion preview caches (more on preview caches in the later section "Managing the preview cache files") need room to grow as you import new images and process them.

REMEMBER

Chapter 4 covers where on your drive to store your photos in the sections that cover importing files. For now, keep in mind that photos are not physically stored "inside" the catalog file; they're stored, rather, on a drive of your choosing outside of Lightroom Classic. The catalog refers, or points, to the actual storage location of each imported photo.

If you move your catalog, you have to help Lightroom Classic find that catalog the next time you want to open it. Here's how that's done:

1. **Launch Lightroom Classic.**

   If Lightroom Classic can't immediately locate the catalog, it displays the dialog shown in Figure 2-1.

2. **Click the Choose a Different Catalog button.**

   The Select Catalog dialog appears (see Figure 2-2). You may or may not see other catalog files listed there. If you see the one you want to open, select it and click Open. If you don't see the desired catalog, move to Step 3.

3. **Click the Choose a Different Catalog button in that dialog.**

FIGURE 2-1:
The Confirm dialog; the Lightroom Classic catalog wasn't found.

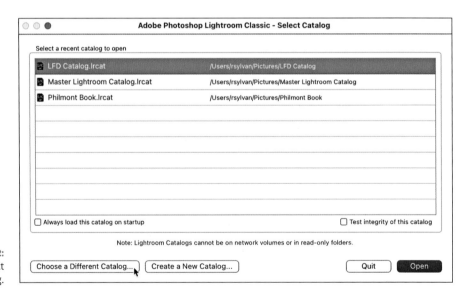

FIGURE 2-2:
The Select Catalog dialog.

4. **In the new file browsing dialog that appears, navigate to the location you chose as the new home for your catalog, select the** .lrcat **file, and then click Choose.**

You return to the Select Catalog dialog, and the path to the catalog you selected appears prominently in the Catalog Location field.

5. **Click the Open button (or Select on Windows).**

Lightroom Classic launches with the catalog at this new location.

Choosing which catalog to open

Lightroom Classic stores the location of your catalogs in its Preferences file. You can configure which catalog Lightroom Classic opens at launch by going to Lightroom Classic ⇨ Preferences (or Edit ⇨ Preferences on Windows) and clicking the General tab, as shown in Figure 2-3. The Default Catalog drop-down menu reveals the following choices:

» **Load most recent catalog:** This is the default option. Lightroom Classic simply opens the last catalog that was used.

» **Prompt me when starting lightroom:** The Select Catalog dialog box (refer to Figure 2-2) appears when Lightroom Classic is launched. From here, you can choose to open any catalog or even create a new one.

» **Other:** You can configure a specific catalog to always open when Lightroom Classic is launched.

TIP

Set Lightroom Classic to use a specific catalog when starting up so that it opens the same catalog every time you launch the program — even if you have only one catalog now (which is the best option for most people, as I recommend earlier in this chapter). This will make your life simpler down the road because you will know that opening Lightroom Classic always means opening that specific catalog. It's easy enough to switch to another catalog using the File ⇨ Open Catalog or File ⇨ Open Recent command. In fact, you can even force the Select Catalog dialog to open by holding Option (or Ctrl on Windows) and launching Lightroom Classic.

FIGURE 2-3:
The Default
Catalog
preference
setting.

Caring for the Catalog

You initially enter information about your photos into the catalog with the help of Lightroom Classic's Import function. As each photo is imported, Lightroom Classic writes its metadata and its location on your hard drive into the catalog. While you continue to work in Lightroom Classic, everything you do with your photos is automatically saved in the catalog in real-time (Lightroom Classic has no Save command). When I say *everything*, I mean everything — from keywords and ratings to exposure adjustments to collection membership and virtual copies.

REMEMBER

Because of this design feature, Lightroom Classic is referred to as a *metadata editor*, meaning that when you edit your photos with Lightroom Classic, you don't edit the pixels in your source photos. This feature is also referred to as *nondestructive editing* because all the adjustments you perform in Lightroom Classic are stored only as a set of metadata instructions — in the catalog, of course — that Lightroom Classic uses to create its internal preview files and to create copies of your original files during output (such as when exporting copies, books, slideshows, and prints). People who shoot raw might be more familiar with this concept, but it's a huge paradigm shift for those who shoot JPG, or who are used to editing JPG, PSD, and TIF files in an image editor such as Photoshop. Take a moment to let that statement sink in because it will make your life much easier moving forward. In light of this, the catalog *must* be well cared for and protected.

Lightroom Classic has a catalog control panel (of sorts) that displays important information and provides tools for its care. It's called the Catalog Settings dialog, and you can see it in Figure 2-4. Choosing Lightroom Classic ➪ Catalog Settings (or Edit ➪ Catalog Settings on Windows) from the main menu gets you there.

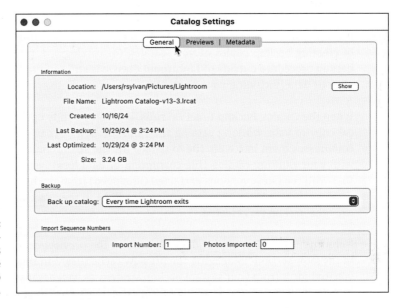

FIGURE 2-4:
The Catalog Settings dialog with the General tab active.

The General tab allows you to control the following:

» **Information:** Displays the catalog's location, name, creation date, last backup date, last optimized date, and file size. Click the Show button to open the folder containing the catalog in the Mac's Finder or Windows File Explorer.

» **Backup:** Configures the frequency with which the catalog backup function is run.

» **Import Sequence Numbers:** Used with certain filename templates.

Any longtime user might remember there was an optimize option on that panel. It has since moved to the menu under File ⇨ Optimize Catalog. Clicking the Optimize Catalog option performs a little database housekeeping on the catalog to reduce its size and improve performance, which is generally most helpful on very large catalogs (more on this in the later section "Optimizing your catalog"). Backing up and optimizing are important enough topics to warrant their own sections, so I do the smart thing and provide them next.

Backing up your catalog

Lightroom Classic's backup function does *not* back up your photos (because your photos are never in the catalog), but it can help protect you against data loss (meaning all the work you do in Lightroom Classic) by automating the process of creating backup copies of your catalog (or catalogs). A full computer system backup procedure outside of Lightroom Classic is still required in order to protect all your data (including your photos).

When the Catalog Backup function runs, it creates a fully operational and identical copy of your working catalog file (and the new .lrcat-data file), and then compresses them into a Zip file to reduce the file size. Should you have a problem with your working catalog (file corruption or data loss), you must swap the bad files with the latest versions extracted (unzipped) from the backup. The next time you launch Lightroom Classic, your work will be in the exact state it was in at the time the backup was created.

Note that Lightroom Classic doesn't back up the preview caches (more on these in the later section "Managing the preview cache files") in this process. I suggest you exclude it from your system backup strategy as well because the cache file will grow quite large as you continue to import new photos (I'm talking gigabytes of space here). If you ever "lose" your preview cache, Lightroom Classic automatically creates a new one for you.

Thankfully, you can automate the catalog backup process so that you don't have to think about it. In the Catalog Settings dialog, click the Back up catalog drop-down menu to see your scheduling choices, which range from Never to Every time Lightroom exits, as shown in Figure 2-5. The first thing you might notice is that the backup can run only when Lightroom Classic exits. If you want to force a backup after a good day's work, set the backup to run Every time Lightroom exits; then close Lightroom Classic when you finish working to trigger the backup.

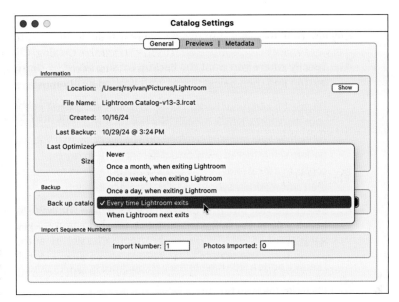

FIGURE 2-5:
The Back Up
Catalog drop-
down menu.

TIP

When considering the frequency with which to schedule a backup, just imagine what would happen if your catalog went kerflooey. You want your backup catalog to be as fresh as possible, right? Setting it to run once per day is a safe choice. I personally have mine set to Every time Lightroom exits. It may seem like overkill, but the backup dialog you see on exit is equipped with a Skip this time button. The result is that I see a reminder to back up every time I quit Lightroom Classic and see the option to skip if I haven't done much work since the last time I backed up. This setting also makes it easy to force a backup by simply closing the program after a big work session.

The next time you exit Lightroom Classic in the period for the backup function to run, you're greeted with the Back Up Catalog dialog, shown in Figure 2-6.

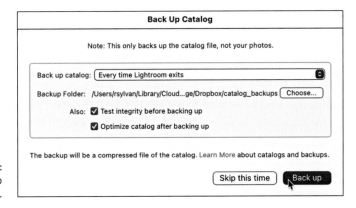

FIGURE 2-6:
The Back Up
Catalog dialog.

Here's how you handle the Back Up Catalog dialog:

1. **Specify where you want the backup catalog saved by clicking the Choose button and then navigating to your desired location.**

   I suggest having your backup saved to a different drive (if possible) than where your working catalog is located. The reason is that if you lose the drive containing your working catalog, you'll be very glad that you had a recent backup safely tucked away on a different drive. In my case, I save the backup copies to a local folder in my Dropbox account (refer to Figure 2-6), which is then automatically synced to a cloud storage location.

2. **Select the Test integrity before backing up and Optimize catalog after backing up boxes to have the backup process check for corruption in the database.**

   I know it adds a little time to the backup process, but it's time well spent.

3. **Click the Back up button to begin the process.**

   If you change your mind and just want Lightroom Classic to exit, click the Skip this time button to bypass the backup. Note that you can change the backup schedule in this dialog as well.

REMEMBER

Each backup function creates a new copy without touching the existing backup files. It's up to you to manage the backup files so that they don't fill the destination hard drive. If you run your backups regularly without clearing the old ones, you might just have several gigabytes of hard drive space waiting to be recovered! I periodically delete all but the most recent two or three backup copies.

Figuring out the Import Sequence Numbers

"But wait, Rob — what's this Import Sequence Numbers section doing at the bottom of the General tab of Catalog Settings?" you might ask. Okay, this section's inclusion here might be Lightroom Classic's version of a non sequitur — at least in the context of talking about catalogs. However, because it's here and you're obviously looking at it (and no doubt wondering what it's all about), let me tell you:

>> **Import Number:** This is where Lightroom Classic tracks the number of imports for use in filename templates when renaming files during import using the Import# token. It increments only when that particular filename token is being used to rename files. You can change the number before importing to set it at a different value.

>> **Photos Imported:** This is where Lightroom Classic tracks the number of photos for use in filename templates when renaming files during import using the Image# token. It increments only when that particular filename token is being used to rename files. You can change the number before importing to set it at a different value. The main use of this value is for when you want to number files incrementally across multiple imports.

I guess they had to put these two guys somewhere. Just keep them in mind when I discuss file-naming in Chapter 4.

Optimizing your catalog

I mention the File ⇨ Optimize Catalog command earlier in this chapter and now just want to provide a little more detail. If you have a large catalog and notice that it seems sluggish, an Optimize operation might give it a performance boost. The Optimize command organizes the data in the catalog and removes unused space, which can result in a smaller and faster catalog file.

Choosing the Optimize Catalog command opens a dialog displaying the last time the operation was run and gives you the option to proceed by clicking Optimize or bail out by clicking Cancel. If you choose Optimize, it runs the housekeeping functions on the catalog and then displays a confirmation dialog saying that it has finished. Then just click OK (Lightroom Classic restarts) and enjoy the results.

TIP

The whole Optimize process was originally put in place by Lightroom Classic's designers to speed up slowpoke catalogs, but I've seen circumstances where Optimize has corrected problems ranging from catalog exports to identity plates, so I regularly include this as a troubleshooting step for people with strange catalog behaviors. If you're new to Lightroom Classic, you probably won't need this for a while, so just file it away for the future.

Renaming your catalog

A brand-new option in Lightroom Classic 14 is the ability to rename the catalog from within the program (which you used to have to do manually outside of Lightroom Classic). The need to rename a catalog is entirely a human one and completely optional. Lightroom Classic doesn't care what the filename of the catalog happens to be, but you might. In the past, installing a new version of Lightroom Classic required the upgrading of a copy of your current catalog to work in the new version (this is still true), but in so doing, it often ended up appending numbers into the catalog filename, making it long and, possibly, confusing. If you're happy (or indifferent) about the current name of your catalog file, feel free to file this information away and skip ahead. If you want to rename your catalog, here's how:

1. Go to File ➪ Rename Catalog to open the Rename Catalog dialog box.

2. Enter the desired name for the catalog in the New Name field and click the Rename button.

As soon as you click Rename, Lightroom Classic closes and then, behind the scenes, renames the catalog and its associated cache files and then displays a prompt informing you that the renaming process is complete. Clicking OK in that prompt reopens the newly named catalog back into Lightroom Classic.

Managing the preview cache files

When you make your way through the options in the Catalog Settings dialog, you notice the Previews tab (formerly named File Handling) to the immediate right of the General tab. The Previews tab (shown in Figure 2-7) has options to help you manage the size and quality of the standard preview files that Lightroom Classic creates for all your imported photos, as well as a running tally of the size of the cache for the optional Smart Previews (which I cover in the upcoming section "Smart Previews"). Lightroom Classic also has a new control for managing the cache size.

FIGURE 2-7:
The Previews tab of the Catalog Settings dialog.

Previews

Before I get into what the controls do, I'd like to talk about what previews are and what they do. I was once asked a great question by a new user who was trying to understand how previews work: "If my photos are never altered and never in Lightroom Classic, then what am I looking at when I'm working?" What a great question! The answer, of course, is preview files. You encounter two types of preview files in all modules except Develop (Develop needs to access the actual photos for its on-the-fly preview when you edit):

>> **Standard:** These are what you see in all modules except Develop. The size and quality of these previews are determined by the settings you choose on the Previews tab.

>> **1:1:** These previews match the pixel dimensions of your source files. These are used when you view images at 1:1 view in the Library.

Therefore, you're almost always looking at a cached preview of your photos. While you make adjustments in Develop, Lightroom Classic re-renders previews on the fly to show you the effect of the adjustments (but never applies changes to the original photos). All these previews are stored in the Preview cache alongside the catalog file. Because Lightroom Classic renders the previews as needed, they aren't essential files and aren't included in the backup process. However, because they're rendered for every photo you import, they can require a significant chunk of disk space over time. This brings the discussion back to the Previews tab of the Catalog Settings dialog (refer to Figure 2-7).

You can tweak your preview cache settings in two ways:

>> **Standard Preview Size:** Use this drop-down menu to choose a pixel size that best matches the resolution of your monitor, or let Lightroom Classic do it for you and just leave it set to the default of Auto. Lightroom Classic uses standard-sized previews when you view the image at Fit Screen, meaning you see the entire image onscreen. Because of this, you don't need to generate a standard-sized preview that's greater than the resolution of your monitor. If space is an issue, choose a smaller size to help keep the cache smaller.

>> **Preview Quality:** This drop-down menu allows you to determine the amount of JPG compression applied to the standard-sized previews. The default setting of Medium is a good compromise between quality and file size.

Over time, the settings you choose here will impact how large the preview cache grows as you import new photos. You can put additional limits on the cache size in the new section named Preview Storage Management (see Figure 2-7). You can choose only one of the following two options:

>> **Automatically Discard 1:1 Previews:** Use this drop-down menu to configure how long to keep the 1:1 previews in the cache. Because they're high-quality, pixel-for-pixel copies of your source files, such preview files can be quite large, so you might not want them lying about on your hard drive for too long. Lightroom Classic, of course, re-renders them if they're needed after having been discarded, but then you have to wait for the render to complete. Leaving the setting to After One Week is a good balance between maintaining performance and keeping a damper on the growing size of the cache.

>> **Limit Preview Cache Size:** This new option puts a hard limit on how large the preview cache can grow. If free space on your drive is tight, you might consider using this option instead to ensure that the cache never grows larger than the value you enter. Click the Learn More link to go to Adobe's Help page on this topic.

TIP

You can force Lightroom Classic to delete 1:1 previews at any time by going to Library ⇨ Previews ⇨ Discard 1:1 Previews.

Smart Previews

Okay, if those are regular previews, what are Smart Previews? Another good question. *Smart Previews* are basically a smaller version (2560 pixels on the long side) of the original that preserves many of the qualities of a raw file that make it useful for editing. This smaller version is saved as a special DNG file (I cover DNG in more depth in Chapter 7), which allows for a type of compression to make the file size in bytes smaller as well.

The original reason for the introduction of Smart Previews was to have a way to store a smaller, yet still editable, version of the original photo alongside the catalog file so that you could still perform tasks in the Develop module even if the original photo was inaccessible due to being offline. For example, I keep the majority of my photos on an external hard drive, which isn't always connected. By creating Smart Previews of my photos (when needed), I can still edit them in the Develop module because Lightroom Classic is smart enough to refer to the Smart Preview when the original isn't available, and then smart enough to switch back when I plug that drive back in. This has turned out to be a useful compromise because it just wouldn't be possible to keep my external drive plugged in all the time.

REMEMBER

The Develop module is a special case where it needs to access the original photo to be able to perform edits. If the original is offline, a Smart Preview, if created, can stand in to keep your workflow moving forward.

On a related but side note, the compact yet editable package of the Smart Preview became the key to keeping photos synced through the Adobe cloud when syncing with the new Lightroom ecosystem of apps for Mac, Windows, iOS, and Android (see Chapter 16).

Because not everyone needs Smart Previews all the time, or even at all, their creation is completely optional. You can create them from the Import process covered in Chapter 4, or afterward, in the Library module, accessed via the Library ⇨ Previews ⇨ Build Smart Previews menu. For now, you can see a running tally of how much space the cache is taking up on this tab of catalog settings. As with the 1:1 previews, you can manually remove them via the Library ⇨ Previews ⇨ Discard Smart Previews menu command.

Exploring the Metadata options

Metadata is basically data about the data about your photos. It includes the data that comes from your camera (called *EXIF data*), the data you enter (such as copyright, location, and keywords), and all the settings for the adjustments you make when developing your photos — otherwise known as *Develop settings*). This metadata is stored in the catalog file and can be viewed on the Metadata tab of the Catalog Settings dialog (see Figure 2-8).

FIGURE 2-8:
The Metadata tab in the Catalog Settings dialog.

Here are the options that appear on the Metadata tab of the Catalog Settings dialog:

» **Offer suggestions from recently entered values:** While you enter various metadata (such as keywords, titles, and captions), Lightroom Classic tries to help you by offering autocomplete suggestions after you type a few characters that resemble a previous entry. Uncheck the box to turn off this feature. Click the Clear All Suggestions Lists button if you want to keep the feature enabled but want to reset it.

» **Include develop settings in metadata inside JPEG, TIFF, PNG, and PSD files:** Okay, this setting and the next one are related. By default, Lightroom Classic stores only the work you do in the catalog. However, you might also want Lightroom Classic to write that information into each photo's own metadata as a form of redundancy. Leave this box checked if you want to include the Develop settings with all other metadata when you tell Lightroom Classic to write to each of these non-raw file type's metadata. If unchecked, the Develop settings reside only in the catalog file for non-raw photos even if you enable the Automatically write changes into XMP setting. One benefit of writing Develop settings to the file itself is that if that file is imported into another Lightroom Classic catalog, the settings carry over. The next setting in this list is for automating the process of writing from the catalog to each photo's metadata, but you can also do it manually by selecting photos in Grid view of the Library and going to Metadata ⇨ Save Metadata to File.

» **Automatically write changes into XMP:** When this box is checked, Lightroom Classic writes to each photo's XMP metadata space automatically and keeps it in sync with the catalog file. (XMP is short for Adobe's Extensible *M*etadata *P*latform, which simply defines how the data is stored in the file.) However, certain things cannot be written to XMP, such as collection memberships, virtual copies, and stacking (all of these are covered in Chapter 5), and develop histories (see Chapter 9). The benefit of writing to XMP is not only that you keep key metadata and settings embedded in the original photo's metadata space (or a sidecar .xmp file for raw photos) but the information is also accessible to programs outside of Lightroom Classic (Adobe Bridge and Camera Raw, for example). The downside is that the automatic process can include a performance hit (on slower systems) because Lightroom Classic works behind the scenes to write to each file.

» **Write date or time changes into proprietary raw files:** This setting comes into play only if you make a change to the capture date/time of a raw file (see Chapter 3 for more on file types). If the box is checked, Lightroom Classic changes the capture date/time inside the actual raw file. Some people prefer to keep their raw files completely unaltered, so if the box is unchecked (the default state), Lightroom Classic writes the change only to the associated XMP file, leaving the source raw file unchanged.

TIP

If you're noticing a drag on performance with the Automatically write changes into XMP option enabled, you can disable it and then manually tell Lightroom Classic to write to each file's XMP metadata by selecting the file(s) in Grid view and going to Metadata ⇨ Save Metadata to File or pressing ⌘+S (Ctrl+S for Windows). The result is the same, but you get to control when it occurs. The downside is that it's up to you to remember.

REMEMBER

Although Lightroom Classic doesn't change the pixels in your source photos, these options do present an opportunity to have it change each photo's metadata (think of it as text stored within or alongside the original photo). Aside from performance issues related to using the Automatically write changes into XMP option, you might not want Lightroom Classic writing to each photo's metadata at all, in which case, leave those options unchecked.

Chapter 7 covers the Face Detection option.

Working with Multiple Catalogs

I often am asked about the circumstances under which it makes sense to employ a multiple catalog approach to working with Lightroom Classic. There's no absolute right answer, but if you understand the limitations of catalogs, you can make the best decision for your circumstances (however, for most people, having just a single catalog works best).

WARNING

The single most important factor when considering the use of multiple catalogs is that Lightroom Classic cannot search across multiple catalogs. From a management perspective, if you want to access all your photos, it's far simpler to have them in a single catalog, which allows you to leverage all the power of Lightroom Classic's database to find, gather, and work with your photos. It's terribly inefficient to develop a manual (human) system for managing your catalogs just so you know which catalog is responsible for which photos.

That said, if you have unique circumstances where groups of photos are so discrete that you might want or need to keep them separate from each other (for example, having a separate catalog for each client or job), a multicatalog approach might make more sense. You still need a system for managing all these catalogs so that you can get your hands on the right image when you need it, though.

Some people are concerned about the size of a single catalog as a limiting factor, seeing that as a reason to have many smaller catalogs. However, your system components are a bigger limiting effect on performance when working with large catalogs. Generally, maximizing your system's RAM, maintaining ample free space on your startup disk (an SSD drive here is also a good idea), and using fast multicore processors all improve the performance of working with very large catalogs.

I can imagine one scenario, though, where multiple catalogs might make sense: when you're working with a laptop on the road and away from your desktop (and master catalog). Because this set of circumstances is probably common, I think it makes sense to look at what's involved in transferring information between two catalogs.

Transferring data between catalogs

Okay, in this scenario you have a desktop computer and it contains your master catalog. You do most of your image processing and printing from this workstation. The catalog on this computer is the hub through which all your work passes. However, as the saying goes, you can't take it with you, so you also have a laptop for working offsite (or while watching TV).

Pretend you're leaving home for a week of shooting at some exotic location (hey, you're imagining, so you may as well enjoy it). You need to be able to import and process the photos on your laptop while on location and then get all that work into your master catalog upon your return. In this circumstance, you must

>> Import and process new photos into the laptop while on the road.

>> Transfer all the work from the laptop to the desktop (and master catalog) upon returning.

Is this possible? Yes, by using Lightroom Classic's catalog Export and Import functions. The next two sections give you the blow-by-blow.

Exporting a catalog

Okay, you've returned from the trip with a laptop full of photos and the laptop's catalog full of data. The first part of your (imaginary) process is to transfer these photos and the catalog data from the laptop to the desktop computer. Here are the steps for one way to do it:

1. **Open Lightroom Classic on the laptop.**

    This opens your temporary working catalog from the trip.

2. **Expand the Catalog panel in the Library module and click All Photographs.**

   For this example, you'll want to export all the photos in the laptop catalog, and this is the easiest way to gather them. You'll see the thumbnails of all imported photos appear in the content area.

3. **Choose File ⇨ Export as Catalog from the main menu.**

   Doing so launches the dialog shown in Figure 2-9.

FIGURE 2-9:
The dialog that appears when exporting a catalog on Mac. In Windows, the dialog box looks like a File Explorer window but functions the same.

4. **Choose the location where you want the exported catalog and photos to be saved.**

   The goal is to get the data from the laptop to the desktop. High-speed external drives are helpful for data transfers of this size. You can export across a network, but a high-speed external drive may be faster if you're moving a lot of data. I like using external drives so that I can do the export before I get home and then simply connect the external drive to the desktop for transfer. The choice is yours.

5. **Enter a name in the Save As field.**

6. **Configure the check boxes at the bottom.**

   Figure 2-9 shows I am exporting a catalog with 105 photos and two virtual copies (more on virtual copies in Chapter 5). By clicking All Photographs in Step 2, I told Lightroom Classic I wanted to export everything, so I don't want to select the Export selected photos only option (this option appears only if one or more photos were selected before invoking the menu). The Export negative files option means that Lightroom Classic will include a copy of every imported photo along with the exported catalog, so that needs to be selected. (This is how you move the photos from the laptop to the desktop.) Including available previews isn't required, but it enables you to see the thumbnails when you import this catalog into the master catalog. There isn't a need to create Smart Previews now, so leave that unchecked.

7. **Click Export Catalog.**

    Your export begins.

When the progress meter is complete, a copy of your catalog has migrated to the new location you chose. It's a fully functional catalog containing all the data the master catalog has on those exported photos. Look in the exported folder, and you see the folders containing the photos alongside the catalog file. (You can even open it into Lightroom Classic to verify its contents, if you want.) Phase 1 is done — time to connect that catalog to the one on your desktop computer.

Importing from a catalog

Now that you have a folder containing your exported catalog as well as copies of your photos, you need to make it accessible to the desktop computer. In my example, I used an external drive that I moved from the laptop to the desktop computer. Here are the steps to import from a catalog:

1. **Connect the external drive to the desktop computer.**

2. **Open the desired Lightroom Classic catalog on the desktop computer.**

    This opens the catalog to which you want to import the data from the other catalog.

3. **Choose File ⇨ Import from Another Catalog.**

    A file browsing window appears.

4. **Navigate to the exported .lrcat file on the external drive, select it, and then click Choose (or Open on Windows).**

    Doing so launches the Import from Catalog dialog, shown in Figure 2-10. **Note:** The name of the .lrcat file you're importing from is shown on the Title bar of the dialog.

    If your photos aren't visible in the Preview section, select the Show Preview check box.

TIP

FIGURE 2-10:
The Import
from Catalog
dialog.

5. **Choose the Copy new photos to a new location and import option from the File Handling drop-down menu.**

The goal is to copy files from the external drive to the internal drive and store them with all your other photos.

6. **For the Copy To field, click the Choose button, navigate to a folder on the desktop computer drive where the photos can be saved, and then click OK.**

The selected location is entered into the Copy To field.

7. **Click Import.**

The import process kicks off. The data from the .lrcat file on the external drive is copied into the .lrcat file on the desktop computer. The photos are copied from the external drive to the desktop computer as well.

Once the progress meter is complete, you'll have successfully transferred a group of photos (and all the work that has been done to them) from the laptop to the desktop computer. (Time to congratulate yourself.) By using Lightroom Classic to perform the data handoff, you ensure that the program never loses track of the source photos and that all your work makes it back home.

Note the option for importing edits made to existing photos under Changed Existing Photos. If you include photos from your master catalog when you first leave on your (imaginary) trip and then edit them on the road, you can import the changes back to the master catalog. In this case, I didn't have any existing photos, so there wasn't anything to import.

The other thing to keep in mind in this scenario is that once you have everything safely transferred to the master desktop catalog (and backed up), you should delete the temporary catalog and photos from the laptop and external drive used in the transfer to avoid confusion and duplication down the road.

TIP

Chapter **3**

Lightroom Classic Basics That You Should Know

B eyond the all-important catalog are a number of topics, from key preference settings to color spaces, that every Lightroom Classic user should know before diving in too deep. I also want to clarify what is meant by "the cloud" in the context of the Lightroom world. Let's start with the nitty-gritty preference settings you'll want to know.

Configuring Lightroom Classic Preferences

Lightroom Classic's default preference settings are good for getting you up and running, but that doesn't mean you can't make a few tweaks to better suit your workflow. You adjust the seat or mirrors in your car every now and then, right? You'll probably want to do the same here.

To see what's what with your default settings, first open the Preferences dialog by choosing Lightroom Classic ⮕ Preferences (Edit ⮕ Preferences in Windows) from the main menu. The Preferences dialog appears onscreen in all its glory, as shown in Figure 3-1. What you see here are *global* preference settings — these preferences are in effect regardless of which catalog you have open. Although many of these preferences are self-explanatory (I'll skip those), a few are worth digging into. I do the digging for you in the next few sections.

FIGURE 3-1:
The Preferences dialog, set to General.

General preferences

The General preferences tab is kind of like the catchall drawer in the kitchen: It contains all the stuff that didn't fit neatly anywhere else:

>> **Default Catalog:** I cover this topic in Chapter 2, but it's important enough to repeat that you should choose a specific catalog instead of Load most recent.

>> **Import Options:** You can control some actions that happen at import:

- *Show import dialog when a memory card is detected:* If you find it convenient to have the Import dialog open automatically, keep this option selected; otherwise, deselect it.

- *Select the Current/Previous Import collection during import:* If you like to start an import and then select another folder or collection to work on while the import happens in the background, deselect this check box; otherwise, when the import begins, Lightroom Classic shifts your view to this special collection found on the Catalog panel. I leave this option selected because I like to see the new photos appear.

- *Ignore camera-generated folder names when naming folders:* Some cameras can be configured to create folders on the memory card. Select this check box to ignore them.

- *Treat JPEG files next to raw files as separate photos:* Anyone shooting raw+JPG who wants to see both photos side by side in Lightroom Classic should select this check box. By default (deselected), Lightroom Classic treats the JPG as a sidecar file and you see only the raw.

- *Replace embedded previews with standard previews during idle time:* Chapter 4 describes the import dialog options. In those options, you'll find a setting for previews called Embedded & Sidecar, which tells Lightroom Classic to use the embedded preview at first. This preference setting here tells Lightroom Classic to go ahead and replace those embedded previews with standard previews when you aren't working.

- *Show parent folder during import*: When selected, and if the Folders panel is expanded, the folder containing newly imported photos is visible in the Folders panel while the photos are being imported. The idea is to help make it easier to see where your photos are being stored.

» **Completion Sounds** (Optional)**:** Configure the sounds you want the program to make when it completes those tasks.

» **Prompts:** These are the warning dialogs that pop up when you attempt to do things like move photos or folders. Some prompts have a Don't show again option to disable them from appearing in the future, which is useful when you find that the warning prompts slow you down. However, they can help keep you out of trouble, so if you change your mind and want to enable them again, click the Reset all warning dialogs button to bring them back.

The Presets preferences

The Presets tab is one-stop shopping for all the settings that pertain to Lightroom Classic's default presets and templates, and is broken into five sections, as follows (I recommend leaving all default settings alone at first, so I didn't include a figure):

» **HDR Defaults:** This new check box, when selected, automatically enables HDR editing for new HDR (high dynamic range) photos in the Develop module (see Chapter 7 for more on HDR).

» **Raw Defaults:** Adobe revamped the process for customizing the default settings applied to all raw photos (visit the following link to see how it works). This gives you the power to define the starting point for your raw photos (non-raw photos have no settings applied by default) if you choose to take advantage of this feature. There's nothing wrong with using the Adobe default when you're just getting started.

Check out my article on customizing your default settings: `https://lightroomkillertips.com/customizing-camera-raw-defaults-in-lightroom-classic`.

>> **Visibility:** A *partially compatible* preset is a preset that contains some settings not applicable to a specific type of photo. For example, perhaps you include a camera-specific profile along with other settings in a preset, so as a result, that preset will be only partially compatible with photos that are not from that specific camera. When it's deselected, you don't see presets in the Presets panel that are not fully compatible with the photo you're editing.

>> **Location:** By default, Lightroom Classic stores all your presets in a central location that's accessible to any catalog you might have open at the time (as well as the Camera Raw plug-in for Photoshop). This makes the most sense for most Lightroom Classic users. However, if you'd prefer to store your presets folder within the same folder as your catalog file, you can select this box, and Lightroom Classic will copy the default presets to the new location. Click the Show Lightroom Develop Presets button for quick access to your preset files.

>> **Lightroom Defaults:** This collection of buttons serves a single purpose, which is to set each type of preset collection back to its default state. If presets ever seem to go missing, come back here and click the button that corresponds to the type of missing preset.

The External Editing preferences

If you have Photoshop installed, you'll see, as shown in Figure 3-2, that it's configured as your primary external editor. You can also configure other applications to have additional editors. However, if you don't have Photoshop installed, you'll only be able to configure the Additional External Editor option, because the first slot is reserved exclusively for Photoshop.

The purpose of this dialog is to configure the default settings Lightroom Classic uses when you send a copy of a photo with adjustments to an external editor for additional work. Remember that Lightroom Classic doesn't alter your source photos, so if you want to take all the work you have done in Lightroom Classic and apply it to a file so that you can continue working in a different application, Lightroom Classic first has to create a copy of that photo. These are the settings Lightroom Classic uses to create that copy. You'll also configure what applications (if any) you want to use as an additional editor in this dialog.

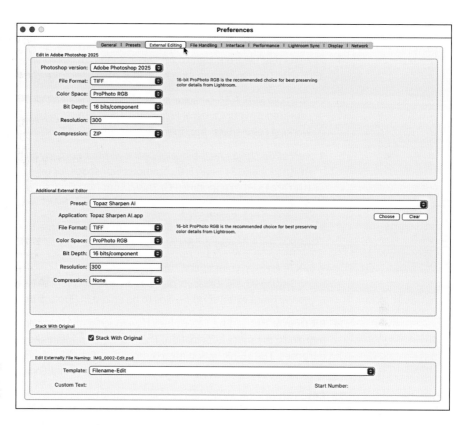

FIGURE 3-2:
The External
Editing
preferences.

All external editors have the same basic file-setting options (File Format, Color Space, Bit Depth, Resolution, and Compression) to be configured. You do need to configure both editors independently, but this gives you the opportunity to set up each editor differently. The options you choose are determined by your own needs and the type of editor you're using. After giving you a closer look at the file options, I go over the steps for adding additional editors. Here are the file options:

>> **File Format:** You have two file format options to choose from — TIFF and PSD. (JPEG is also an option for the additional external editors.) Both formats support layers, 16-bit files, and available color spaces. PSD is Photoshop's native file format, but it's a proprietary format and not as widely supported outside the Adobe family of applications. In light of this, my preference is to use TIFF, but there's no wrong choice here.

>> **Color Space:** You can find out more about color spaces in the "Understanding color spaces" section, later in this chapter, but in a nutshell, a *color space* is a way to define a range of colors so that those colors can be accurately reproduced on different systems. Lightroom Classic has an internal color space that contains all the colors your camera can capture. Any time

Lightroom Classic creates an actual rendered copy of your source files, it converts that file from Lightroom Classic's internal color space to the output color space you've chosen. You have four color spaces to choose from:

- *ProPhoto RGB:* A 16-bit color space capable of holding all the colors captured by your camera, ProPhoto RGB is similar to Lightroom Classic's working color space, and therefore I recommend this setting.

- *AdobeRGB (1998):* An 8-bit color space without as many colors as ProPhoto RGB, AdobeRGB (1998) is a common color space for digital photographers who are used to shooting JPG. This is your best choice if you choose 8 bits from the Bit Depth drop-down list.

- *Display P3:* A newer 10-bit color space that has become the standard wide-gamut display profile on Apple devices.

- *sRGB:* An 8-bit color space, but with fewer saturated colors than Adobe RGB or Display P3, sRGB has its place as an output color space, but it isn't a good choice when sending files to be edited in Photoshop.

>> **Bit Depth:** This setting determines how much data is contained in a file. The more bits, the more information. The more information, the better for editing purposes. The 16-bit option is recommended if you're working with raw originals; 8-bit is recommended if you're working with JPG originals.

>> **Resolution:** Ultimately, the resolution setting comes into play only when you're printing. In this context, it simply sets the resolution tag in the new file's metadata. It doesn't affect the number of pixels in the file whatsoever. You'll see 240 as the default setting; however, if your workflow requires that files have a different resolution setting (such as 300), you can enter it here.

>> **Compression:** This option is available only when TIFF is selected as the file format. ZIP is a lossless compression format. With 16-bit files, your choices here are to use no compression (None) or apply compression (ZIP). If you opt for 8-bit TIFF then LZW appears another compression option, which works as well as ZIP. Certain other applications have trouble handling compressed TIFFs, so if you want a more compatible choice, choose None. If you want to save a bit of disk space, choose ZIP.

Setting up additional external editors

In a nutshell, you choose an editor, configure its settings, and then save those settings as a preset. You can create as many presets as you need. Here are the steps:

1. **In the Additional External Editor section, click Choose.**

2. **Navigate to and select the application you want to use as an editor.**

   On Mac, look in the Applications folder. In Windows, look in the Program Files folder. After you select them, you see the name of the chosen application listed next to Application back in the Preferences dialog box.

3. **Configure all the file-setting options for the type of files you want to send to that editor.**

4. **Choose Save Current Settings as New Preset from the Preset drop-down menu.**

5. **Give the preset a name and click Create.**

   You see this name listed under the Photo ⇨ Edit In on the menu, so make it descriptive of both the application and file settings.

TIP

You can repeat these steps for any additional editors or multiple configurations of settings for the same editor.

When Lightroom Classic renders a copy to send to Photoshop, it appends an –Edit suffix to the saved copy by default. You can customize this suffix in the Edit Externally File Naming section at the bottom of the dialog, but I'd say, unless you have a real need to change the suffix, the default works just fine.

The File Handling preferences

Figure 3-3 shows the File Handling preference settings. Let's walk through each section and make some sense of what can be done here:

» **Import DNG Creation:** These settings pertain to the Copy as DNG on import. The medium-size JPEG preview is a good compromise on file size. The default conversion method settings are helpful because they preserve the raw data and create a smaller file using lossless compression. The big choice is whether you want to embed the original raw file: You would want to embed the original raw file if you believe there may come a time when you want to extract the original raw file so that you can process it in software that doesn't support DNG. The downside to embedding the original raw file is that you double the file's size because you will have the converted raw data (this is what Lightroom Classic will use) and then add the entire original unaltered file as well (which just sits untouched in case someday it's needed). I prefer to leave this option deselected. Keeping Embed Fast Load Data selected can help improve performance in the Develop module when editing DNG files with this information.

>> **Reading Metadata:** It's possible to create structure or hierarchies in your keywords (that is, you might have a keyword *Animal* and then, under it, you would nest all the types of animals in your photos). No single standard exists for what character must be used to separate hierarchical keywords when they're written into a file's metadata. Lightroom Classic automatically recognizes the pipe (|) character between two words as a means to denote structure, but if you use other programs that use either a dot (.) or a slash (/) as a keyword separator, select the respective boxes in the preferences; Lightroom Classic respects your choice during import so that your keyword structure is maintained.

>> **File Name Generation:** Different operating systems and even different applications can have problems with certain characters being used within filenames. The settings in the File Name Generation section allow you to configure how Lightroom Classic responds to these characters when it encounters them in a filename. Here's what I recommend for creating a consistent and bombproof approach to dealing with problematic filenames:

- Choose the largest set of characters to treat as illegal.

- Choose either Dashes or Underscores to be used as a replacement character whenever an illegal character is encountered.

- Don't sweat spaces in filenames (Leave As-Is).

FIGURE 3-3: The File Handling preferences.

At the bottom is a new check box for automatically adding keywords to Enhanced images (see Chapter 7), which can be helpful for finding and filtering those photos down the road.

The Interface preferences

Although some of the Interface preferences, as shown in Figure 3-4, are entirely cosmetic, other settings in this panel are truly useful:

>> **Panels:** I'll leave the Panels End Marks decision up to your own sense of flair, but whenever this option is enabled, these little decorative icons appear at the bottom of the panel groups in each module. For the most part, you won't notice them after a while (they're set to None by default). In regard to panel font size, if you're finding the panel text a little on the small side, you can try bumping Font Size up a notch (it takes effect the next time you start the program). There's also a new accessibility option that, when selected, swaps the contents of the left and right panels in either just the Develop module or across all of them.

>> **Lights Out:** I go over the Lights Out function in Chapter 1, but here are its configuration settings. The Dim Level option controls how much the Screen Color changes at the first level of dimming (at 80%, you can just make out the interface). The defaults work well, but you can increase or decrease the first dim level amount by changing the percentage, or change the color used to hide the interface to different shades of gray.

>> **Background:** The area around the photo — but not inside the panels — is called the background. The default color is medium gray because that's a neutral color that will have the least influence on how you perceive the colors in your photo. You might try different colors, but I think you'll come back to the default.

>> **Keyword Entry:** Choose to have keywords separated by commas or spaces. My suggestion is to use commas so that you can have multiword keywords (such as *New Hampshire*).

>> **Filmstrip:** When it comes to the Filmstrip settings, I prefer to keep all these options selected. I like being able to see ratings, picks, and badges (small icons that appear if keywords, cropping, or develop settings have been applied to a photo) on the thumbnails in the Filmstrip. The photo info tooltips are a helpful way to see the filename, capture date and time, and _ dimensions; just hover the cursor over an image. The most helpful option is to select Ignore clicks on badges so that you don't inadvertently click a badge when trying to select a photo and end up jumping to the Crop tool or wherever the badge takes you.

TECHNICAL STUFF

>> **Tweaks:** The Tweaks section is the one area of the Interface panel where you see a slight difference between Windows and Mac. On the Mac, you find an option to use typographic fractions, but if you wander over to a Windows machine, you find that such fractions aren't available. Therefore, Mac users can have their shutter speed fractions expressed in a much cuter manner.

Don't take this as an unassailable argument for switching platforms, however; Windows users have a tweak that Mac does not — the Use System Preference for font smoothing option. What it means is that Lightroom Classic, in Windows, applies *font smoothing* (literally making the edges of screen fonts appear smoother and rounder) independently of the operating system. If you intentionally turned off font smoothing at the operating system level (some people don't like the smooth look) and want Lightroom Classic to follow suit, check the Use System Preference for font smoothing box. Not to be outdone, a new option was recently added only to Macs, which is Swipe between images using mouse/trackpad. This makes for one more (very fast) way to scroll the Filmstrip, and hardly one more reason to switch platforms. Deselect if you find the speed too dizzying.

Both operating systems have a setting in common, though: Zoom clicked point to center. When you select this option, Lightroom Classic zooms in and shifts the point you clicked to the center of the screen. I prefer to leave this option deselected because, when I click to zoom in, I want the point I clicked to remain under the cursor. When Zoom clicked point to center is enabled, the point you click instead zooms and shifts to the center. Give it a test drive, but I think you'll agree that deselected is better.

FIGURE 3-4:
The Interface
preferences.

The Performance preferences

One of the most requested areas of improvement in Lightroom Classic has been performance. To that end, Adobe makes pretty regular updates in this regard. Here in the Performance preferences, as shown in Figure 3–5, you can tweak a few settings to get Lightroom Classic working at its best possible performance (be sure to click the More Performance Tips link embedded at the bottom of the panel, too):

>> **Use Graphics Processor:** As long as you have recent hardware and have installed up-to-date drivers for it, you can leave this option set to Auto; but to get the most boost from your computer's GPU in Develop and even when rendering previews in Library, click the drop-down menu and choose Custom. However, if you notice weird-looking display issues or performance slow-downs, set this to Off to see whether it makes an improvement.

>> **Camera Raw Cache Settings:** The intended purpose of any cache is to store (usually, temporarily) frequently accessed data to speed up the processes that require that data to function. In this case, Lightroom Classic shares a cache with Adobe Camera Raw, with the primary purpose of helping Lightroom Classic reopen files in the Develop module faster. Keeping a cache size of 10GB to 20GB strikes a good compromise between size of the cache and benefit from its use. If you have a drive with lots of free space, you can click Choose and select a different disk.

>> **Video Cache Settings:** This setting can be left at the default.

>> **Enable hover preview of presets, history and snapshots in loupe:** You can see a live preview of any preset as you hover the cursor over it in the Presets panel. Some people find it distracting or even a performance hit. Deselect the feature if it bothers you, because the Navigator panel still shows the preview.

>> **Use Smart Previews instead of Originals for image editing:** This is a trade-off between improving performance and image quality when editing. On a high-powered computer, I would leave this deselected, but if your machine seems to be struggling when editing, you might enable this setting to see whether it helps.

>> **Generate Previews in Parallel:** If you have a quad-core CPU (or higher), you can select this check box and have Lightroom Classic create multiple previews in parallel instead of just one at a time. In theory, higher-horsepower machines should see much faster preview rendering.

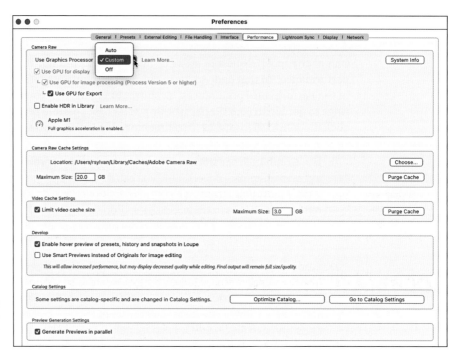

FIGURE 3-5:
The
Performance
preferences.

The Lightroom Sync preferences

The Lightroom Sync panel, shown in Figure 3-6, is used for those times when you use Lightroom Classic and the cloud-based Lightroom together, as covered in Chapter 16. If you're not syncing with the Lightroom ecosystem, you can ignore this panel completely. The main thing to remember is that you can come to this panel and configure where the photos synced back from Lightroom are stored locally on your computer. When sync activities are happening, you can see a live feed at the bottom of the panel.

The Display preferences

If your system uses more than one monitor, you can use this panel to select which display is used for the secondary window (discussed in Chapter 1).

The Network preferences

This panel is used only by people who are in work environments where they need to connect to the Internet via a proxy server. Configuring this panel ensures that your Creative Cloud subscription can be validated properly. If that doesn't describe you, you'll most likely never need to look at it.

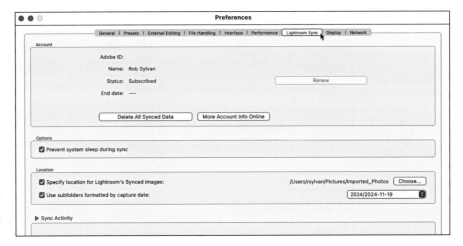

FIGURE 3-6:
The Lightroom Sync preferences.

Local Storage versus Cloud Storage

Let's talk about storage. Our digital photo libraries require an ever-increasing amount of storage. It's just too easy to keep taking more and more photos! Knowing the best place to store them is an ongoing challenge.

Local storage

I think it's safe to say that anyone using a computer or mobile device is already familiar with the concept of local storage because that's the storage that comes with your device. Anyone who has ever owned a mobile phone with only 128GB of storage is acutely familiar with managing local storage. When you're purchasing a new device, the size of the hard drive is usually within the top parameters that affect your decision to buy. Likewise, the size of that storage will affect the price of that device, and although the cost of storage has gone down overall, it's just a fact that the more storage you buy, the more the device will cost. My point is simply that there is a cost associated with storing our digital lives, and that cost increases over time.

Aside from the internal drive within the computer/device you're using, you're likely using additional storage in the form of external drives connected via cable and possibly even a network-attached storage device. No matter which type or combination of these storage options you're using, one thing they all have in common is that they're all under your local control. In other words, you purchased the actual drives, and they may be physically in your presence, or they're available on your local network. Anything that falls into these categories is what I mean when I refer to local storage throughout the rest of this book. Lightroom Classic can be used entirely with only locally based storage. In other words, no cloud storage is needed to use Lightroom Classic. The cloud-based Lightroom ecosystem, on the other hand, has different storage requirements. The following sections discuss the Lightroom ecosystem and its associated cloud storage.

TIP

Adobe often refers to this family of Lightroom apps for each operating system (macOS, Windows, iOS, and Android) pointing to a central cloud-based storage as the *Lightroom ecosystem*. In this book's introduction, I discuss how I refer to the two versions of Lightroom throughout the text.

Cloud storage

In addition to all the local storage options you have at your disposal, you can store data on the Internet, in what has become known as *cloud storage* (think of it as remote storage, maintained by a third party, that you access over the Internet). An ever-growing number of cloud-based storage options are available these days, from services like Dropbox and Google Drive to Microsoft's OneDrive, and so many more. Some types of cloud storage can be free (usually in small amounts), some types may be included as a perk with another service or subscription (like Microsoft's OneDrive), and others are completely integral to the actual service you're paying for, such as is the case with the Lightroom ecosystem run by Adobe.

The main benefit of cloud storage is that you can access the same pool of data from any Internet-connected device (with the correct login information), which makes for a flexible and useful storage solution. I've been a huge fan of Dropbox since 2009 and can't imagine doing business without access to an online storage service. That said, the downside of cloud-based storage is that it isn't under your direct control, which means you need to put your trust in the institution behind the service. In addition, as connected to the Internet as we all are these days, we're still sometimes faced with little or no connection, and in those situations, relying on cloud storage can be problematic. There are trade-offs in all things, and this is no exception.

In this age of always-connected mobile devices, Adobe recognized an opportunity to create a service (now just called Lightroom) that caters to users with large storage needs (such as for photos and videos) but who are using mobile devices with relatively low amounts of local storage. Although the desktop version of the new Lightroom has the option to store copies of photos locally, for all intents and purposes, you can (and should) consider Lightroom to be entirely dependent on cloud storage to work. In a Lightroom-only world, all devices point to the photos in the cloud as the primary storage location.

Though I have been mostly using the word *storage* in this discussion, there's more to Adobe's offering than just a parking place in the cloud for your photos. Because photos imported through Lightroom or synced from Lightroom Classic are sitting on Adobe's servers, Adobe leverages emerging technologies to analyze the contents of your photos to determine the subject matter they contain and then gives you the ability to use that information to more easily find and organize your photos without having to manually add keywords and names to them (refer to Chapter 17). Note that you can use the apps in the Lightroom ecosystem in limited ways while you're offline, but an Internet connection is required for full use.

What if I stop my subscription?

If you're using the latest version of Lightroom Classic or Lightroom, you must have a Creative Cloud subscription. Let me talk briefly about what happens if you cancel your subscription. If you're using Lightroom Classic and you cancel your subscription, you retain the ability to launch Lightroom Classic and access all your photos. You can even still import new photos, as well as export copies of previously edited photos, and make prints, web galleries, and slide shows. What you can no longer do is use the Develop and Map modules or sync to the Lightroom ecosystem. If you decide to renew your subscription at a later date, you get everything back.

If you're using the cloud-based Lightroom and you cancel your subscription, you retain the ability to launch Lightroom and download your original files for one year, and that's about it. Adobe will keep your original files on its server for over a year, but if you're serious about canceling, I recommend that you download them as soon as you can. Should you decide to renew your subscription during that year, you regain all functionality and can pick up where you left off. If you cancel your subscription and need to quickly download all your photos in one go, check out the Adobe Lightroom Downloader tool: `https://lightroom.adobe.com/lightroom-downloader`

Getting Familiar with File Formats

As Adobe says, the Lightroom family of products is intended to be part of "the professional photographer's essential toolbox"; therefore, Adobe assumes its users are already fluent with a certain level of digital-photo-ese. Although that's certainly true for many users, it's been my experience (from helping many professional photographers with this application) that a person can be quite skilled in the art of photography without knowing a bit from a byte or an NEF from a CR3 or a DNG. I can tell you quite confidently that your experience with all versions of Lightroom improves significantly when you increase your working knowledge of a few fundamental digital photography concepts.

Some of these concepts are complex and involve new words and mind-numbing calculations (done by the computer, not by you), and some subjects have entire books devoted to just that topic alone. I'm not going to get that in-depth. What I want to do is introduce you to these fundamentals and explain how they affect your Lightroom experience.

Digital cameras aren't just light-capturing devices, but image-processing computers as well. The act of clicking the shutter release *does* expose the sensor to light through the lens, but after that, the camera's internal computer takes over and creates a digital file. Your camera settings determine the type of file that's created and, depending on the file type, the image processing that happens to that file after it's captured. If you're scanning slides, negatives, or prints, you're using a different capture device (the scanner) to create a digital file. In the end, this digital file can move through Lightroom to any number of output destinations. The file format choice you make has an impact on the amount of information contained in the file, the number and range of colors in the file, and its file size.

Supported file formats

Lightroom is a tool designed specifically for digital photography and as such supports only certain image formats. Image formats are largely known by their file extensions, but don't get too hung up on what the acronyms stand for — just understand the roles they play:

>> **JPEG:** The most common file format available on all digital cameras is JPEG (or JPG), which stands for Joint Photographic Experts Group. The JPEG format is popular because it can be opened in just about any application, and it can be saved at a range of file sizes. It achieves these various file sizes by compressing the original data contained in the file. The upside of this is that the more you compress an image, the smaller the file size becomes and the more pictures your memory card holds, and your camera can write the data to the card faster. The downside here is that the type of compression employed by the JPEG format is *lossy,* which makes files smaller by removing some of the original data. Too much compression results in too much data loss, which results in a degraded image.

>> **PNG:** Originally an alternative to the Graphics Interchange Format (GIF) file format for lossless compression of graphics, PNG (Portable Network Graphics) has emerged as a useful file format for screen captures and other graphics used in a photographic workflow.

>> **AVIF:** This open-source image compression format offers smaller file sizes and higher quality than JPEG.

>> **HEIC:** This is Apple's proprietary version of the High-Efficiency Image File format (HEIF), which is intended to be a better alternative for JPG when it comes to compressing photos to a smaller size and higher quality. HEIC has become the default image file format for mobile capture on Apple devices.

>> **Raw:** This file format is available on many digital cameras. The upside of shooting raw is that the image file contains all the data the camera is capable of capturing, and it's saved without being processed by the camera (hence, raw). The downside is that the image has to be processed by software to be finished. Raw files come in many flavors (NEF, CR3, and ARW, to name a few) based on the camera maker. Lightroom Classic can also convert raw files to DNG (Digital Negative), which retains its rawness but puts it in a more Adobe-friendly container (see Chapter 7 for more on this topic). Adobe releases periodic updates to include support for new cameras after they're released.

>> **TIFF:** Although TIFF (or TIF), which stands for Tagged Image File Format, is occasionally found as an option on some camera models, I don't recommend using it, because the highest-quality JPG setting is almost as good but with a smaller file size. However, TIFF *is* a widely supported and versatile file format that provides either 8 or 16 bits per channel and supports all of Photoshop's features (layers, smart objects, and so on). TIFF can also apply a form of lossless compression (no data is lost) and is a great choice for scanning or for saving processed raw files that will be edited further in Photoshop or other image editors.

>> **PSD:** This is Photoshop's native file format (Photoshop Document). Although it obviously supports all of Photoshop's features, PSD is a proprietary format, so applications outside the Adobe family might not work with files stored in the format. Like TIFF, PSD files can be 8 or 16 bits per channel and are not lossy — they don't lose information, like JPG files do. PSD is a great format when you're working exclusively within the Adobe suite of products. Be sure to save these (and PSB) files in Photoshop with Maximize PSD and PSB File Compatibility enabled to work in Lightroom Classic.

>> **PSB:** If your PSD files end up being bigger than 30,000 x 30,000 pixels or 2GB, you'll need to save them using Photoshop's Large Document format, called PSB. Lightroom Classic supports PSB files up to 65,000 pixels on the long side and a maximum dimension of 512 megapixels (that's a lot of pixels!).

Note that you can import supported video files into Lightroom (for an in-depth discussion of the supported types, see `https://helpx.adobe.com/lightroom/kb/video-support-lightroom.html`), and Lightroom Classic can even perform a limited amount of editing (such as trimming, saving a still, and making color and tonal adjustments). For full video editing, you need to use a program like Adobe Premiere, but Lightroom can at least get the footage off the memory card and copied to your storage.

Understanding color spaces

In the previous section, I mention that both versions of Lightroom deal only with the RGB color model, and I show that the number of gray levels that can be expressed by each channel determines the number of possible colors that can be represented. All useful info, but none of it tells what actual color any combination of red, green, and blue will represent. To do that, the computer needs to know what color space is being represented. A *color space* defines the range of colors (called its *gamut*) an image can contain within a given color model (in this case, RGB) and assigns each color within that range a specific numeric value. You will encounter the following color spaces in camera settings and software when you deal with digital photos:

>> **sRGB:** Contains the narrowest range, or gamut, of colors among these four color spaces. However, this narrow gamut is closest to the range of colors that most display devices are capable of reproducing. sRGB is also the color space best suited for photos being viewed on the web, which means this is most commonly used for JPG files.

>> **Adobe RGB (1998):** Although it possesses the same number of colors as sRGB, Adobe RGB (1998) covers a wider gamut (meaning it has more colors at the more saturated end of the visual spectrum than sRGB has). This color space was created to better match the wider gamut of the offset press. Adobe RGB (1998) is a more common choice for use with 8-bits-per-channel file formats because it contains more of these more saturated colors than sRGB.

>> **Display P3:** A newer arrival on the color space scene, Display P3 was created by Apple as an alternative to sRGB for displays. It contains a wider gamut than Adobe RGB, but where Adobe RGB has more saturated colors (compared to sRGB) toward the blue and green ends of the spectrum, Display P3 contains more toward the yellow and red ends. Newer devices like iMacs, iPads, and even devices in the Surface line from Microsoft have P3 displays.

>> **ProPhoto RGB:** Primarily used with 16-bits-per-channel file formats, the ProPhoto RGB color space contains more colors (more shades of gray per channel) than 8-bits-per-channel files, and it has a significantly wider gamut than either Adobe RGB or sRGB — wide enough to contain all the colors your camera can capture.

2

Managing Your Photos with Lightroom Classic

IN THIS CHAPTER

» **Understanding the import process**

» **Getting to know the Import dialog**

» **Using an import workflow**

» **Setting up an auto import**

» **Shooting tethered**

Chapter **4**

Tackling the Lightroom Classic Import Process

efore you can do anything in Lightroom Classic, you need to introduce your photos to the Lightroom Classic library, which is referred to as *importing* your photos. In this chapter, you get up close and personal with the Import dialog, work through various importing scenarios, and even see how to configure Lightroom Classic to import photos while you capture them with your camera. If you read the entire chapter, you'll have a firm understanding of the import process and be ready to customize this process to meet your needs.

Knowing How the Import Process Works

In the Lightroom Classic context, importing is commonly thought of as "getting your photos into Lightroom Classic," and on the surface, that appears to be what's happening. I use this conversational shortcut as much as anyone does, but it's not a literal description of what happens. What really happens is that Lightroom Classic writes data about your photos into your catalog file. The reason I make this important distinction — apart from its being true — is that it has been a source of confusion for many new users. Some people mistakenly think their photos are stored inside Lightroom Classic; this just isn't the case. With that in mind, the *import process* is where you introduce the catalog to your photos. During this introduction, Lightroom Classic learns everything it can about each photo. The way Lightroom Classic learns is by reading each photo's embedded metadata and copying that information into its catalog.

Based on your import settings and the location of the source files, Lightroom Classic might perform a few other tasks as part of the import process, including copying or moving photos to a new location and renaming them, applying user-generated metadata (such as your copyright), applying keywords, or even beginning the development process by applying a set of adjustments (called *Develop settings*). Importing is a powerful operation that's integral to working with Lightroom Classic. Put another way, you can't work on any photo in Lightroom Classic that hasn't first been through the import process.

Exploring the Import Dialog

Although the name doesn't appear on it anywhere, the dialog shown in Figure 4-1, which I refer to as the *Import dialog*, can be accessed by clicking the Import button on the lower left side of the Library module or by choosing the File ⇨ Import Photos and Video menu command. Depending on your Import preferences (see Chapter 3), the dialog may even open automatically whenever a memory card is detected. Note that, depending on your system and what other software you have installed, some other photo program may open and try to assist with copying the photos from the memory card. You must close any other program that tries to access the memory card, to keep it from interfering with Lightroom Classic.

FIGURE 4-1:
The Import dialog, set up for copying from a memory card.

The Import dialog contains the following sections and controls, starting from the upper left side:

>> **From/Select a Source:** Before you can import photos, you must select the location where the photos you want to import are stored. Lightroom automatically selects your memory card as the source if it's detected (as shown in Figure 4-1). If your computer doesn't have a memory card mounted, you see the text *Select a source* in the upper left instead of *From*. This upper left panel is actually a button you can click to select common sources (like the Pictures folder), but I find it easier to choose a folder for import from the Source panel.

>> **Source panel:** If a memory card is detected, the Devices section appears at the top of the Source panel. Below the Devices section is the Files section, which is the closest thing Lightroom Classic has to a file browser. You can navigate to any folder on your system to select a source, or you can choose a mounted device or memory card, as shown in Figure 4-1. If a memory card is selected, the Eject after import check box appears and is selected automatically. To improve import speed, Lightroom should select the folder on your memory card in the Files section (make sure that Include Subfolders is selected) rather than under Devices, but either method will work.

>> **Center top area:** The four buttons at the top of the Import dialog tell Lightroom Classic what to do with the photos you're importing. It's critical that you make the right choice here:

- *Copy as DNG:* This method works the same as the Copy method, covered in the next bullet, with the extra step of converting any raw photos to DNG after they're copied to the destination and added to the catalog. This increases the amount of time required for the import process, but some people prefer converting to DNG from the start. You can always convert to DNG after import (see Chapter 7 for more on DNG).

- *Copy:* You're most likely to use this method when you're importing from a memory card, but you can use it anytime you want to copy files from one location to another and import at the same time.

  Because you're copying files to a new location, you need to choose a location to copy them to as well as an Organize option for the folders that will be created, which is handled in the Destination panel (more on that later).

- *Move:* The configuration options for the Move method are the same as with the Copy method. The only difference is that Lightroom Classic *moves* the files to the location you choose instead of *copying* them. *Move* means the files are first copied and then deleted from the original location. I don't recommend using Move for this reason. Using Copy is safer, and you can manually delete photos from the original location after you're sure they're safely in the new destination.

REMEMBER

- *Add:* This method simply notes where each photo is stored on your hard disk and adds each photo's metadata to the catalog. If your photos are already stored in the exact location where you want them to remain, choose this method (not available with a memory card, for obvious reasons).

>> **Main content area:** Smack in the center of the Import dialog, you see thumbnails of photos from the selected source. Above the thumbnails is a row of buttons you can use to change how those thumbnails appear. The meaning of All Photos is obvious, as is New Photos. If you choose Destination Folders, the thumbnails are grouped based on the folders they will be placed into (based on the settings you choose in the Destination panel). Below the thumbnails are buttons for switching between Grid view and Loupe view, selecting/deselecting all photos for import, changing the sort options, and sizing the thumbnails. Below that is where you can save your Import settings as a preset.

>> **To:** In the upper right corner of the Import dialog, the To area shows where your photos will be stored at the end of this import operation. For any Copy/Move operation, you see the destination folder. When you use the Add option, however, you see only My Catalog. Like the From/Select a source area in the upper left corner of the Import dialog, the To area is a button you can click to indicate where the photos are copied or moved — though I prefer to do that in the Destination panel.

>> **File Handling:** This panel is home to controls for building previews, building smart previews, preventing the import of (suspected) duplicates, copying the photos to a second location for short-term backup, and adding photos to a collection. Let's dig in:

  - *Build Previews:* Although Lightroom Classic renders previews on the fly as it needs to, you can configure it to begin rendering standard-size or 1:1 previews as soon as the import process is complete by choosing either option from the drop-down menu. The other two options — Minimal and Embedded & Sidecar — cause Lightroom to pull in either the low-quality or full-size previews (respectively) from the raw photos first to show you your photos faster. Lightroom will still eventually render its own previews after import. Embedded & Sidecar does provide the advantage of fastest import because Lightroom doesn't spend time building previews.

  - *Build Smart Previews* (optional): If Smart Previews are part of your workflow (see Chapter 2), you can opt to have them created as part of the import process.

  - *Make a Second Copy To* (optional): The primary function of this option is to provide a means to back up your memory card (in folders based on import date) when you copy and import from a memory card. Ideally, you would select the check box and then choose a backup location on an alternative drive. Then, when the operation is complete, you have your imported files safely copied to two locations at the same time. After you verify that the files are unharmed, you can erase and reuse the memory card in good conscience. Once your photos are included in your full system backup, you can delete this temporary second copy.

- *Add to Collection* (optional): You can add all imported photos to a collection by selecting the Add to Collection check box and then choosing or creating the desired collection.

» **File Renaming:** When copying or moving files during import, you're given the ability to rename the photos. If you don't want to change the filenames, deselect Rename Files. This panel doesn't appear when the Add option is selected.

» **Apply During Import:** With every type of import, you have the option to get a head-start on editing, personalizing, and keyword-tagging your photos. Keep in mind that any information you choose to apply at this stage is applied to all imported photos. These settings are also *sticky,* which means the choices you make today will become the default for the next import, so always double-check every field! Here are the options:

- *Develop Settings:* You can apply a Develop preset (saved Develop module adjustments) to all imported photos. You don't need to apply a preset during import, but it can come in handy if you want to apply some Develop settings to all photos. I normally leave this option set to None and edit later in the Develop module.

- *Metadata:* Even if it means adding only your copyright information, you'll do yourself a favor by including the metadata for your photos with every import. Click the drop-down menu to create a Metadata preset or apply an existing one (see Chapter 6 for more on creating a Metadata preset).

- *Keywords:* Add only relevant keywords to all the photos you're importing. After import, you can add additional keywords relevant to specific photos as needed. You might apply the keyword *beach* to all photos taken at the beach, but keywords like *ice cream* or *sandcastle* might not apply to all photos from that shoot. You can add *beach* during import and the more specific keywords later in the Library module.

» **Destination:** This is the most important panel on the Import dialog to consider when you copy or move photos. The location you choose here is where your photos will be saved. You have to be in the driver's seat for this choice; otherwise, Lightroom Classic uses the Pictures folder by default. I review all the choices in the next section.

After you configure the options in the Import dialog to suit your needs, click the Import button to begin the process. At this point, the Import dialog closes, and the import process, based on your settings, begins. Clicking Cancel closes the Import dialog without importing any photos.

Importing Your Photos into Lightroom Classic

Okay, time to introduce Lightroom Classic to some photos! Unless you just happened to pick up this book, the Lightroom Classic software, and your new digital camera sometime earlier this afternoon, I'm guessing you already have some photos on your hard drive that you'd like to import. I'll go further out on a limb and assume that you will have new photos in the future to import from your memory card. The workflow is the same in both cases, but the options you encounter will have some subtle differences, so it wouldn't hurt to go over the basic process first and then step through a couple of examples.

Employing an effective import workflow

Things you want to keep in mind before you start the import process:

>> What import method are you going to use?

>> Are you going to back up your imported copies?

>> Do you know where you want your photos to go/remain?

>> Are there things like keywords or presets you want to apply?

>> Have you created a filename template for the filenaming convention you want to use?

When you begin the import process with all your ducks in a row, it saves a great deal of time down the road. *Remember:* The import process provides the opportunity to do more than just start looking at your photos in Lightroom Classic. To see what I mean, take a Big Picture look at an import workflow that takes advantage of the import process's full potential:

1. **Initiate the import.**

   You can initiate an import in several ways, but nothing happens without your taking the first step.

2. **Select the photos you want to import.**

   No matter where your photos originate, you have to choose which ones to import.

3. **Configure the settings to meet your input needs.**

   Having answers to the questions at the start of this section allows you to quickly set up the Import dialog and click that Import button.

With the Big Picture out of the way, it's time to sweat a few of the smaller details. The next few sections help you navigate the import process.

Initiating the import

The Import dialog is the gateway that all photos have to pass through. You can open the door in several ways:

>> **Click the Import button in the Library module.** This method might be the most common way to launch an import, because the big Import button in the Library module is easy to spot (and who doesn't love to click a button?). It can be used when importing from any disk or device.

>> **Connect your camera or a memory card to your computer.** If you enable this feature in Lightroom Classic's Preferences dialog ahead of time, the Import dialog automatically launches whenever it detects the presence of a memory card — either solo or as part of a digital camera. This can be a real time-saver if the only time you connect a camera or memory card is when you want to conduct a Lightroom Classic import. For a detailed discussion of Preference settings, see Chapter 3.

>> **Choose File ⇨ Import Photos and Video from the main menu.** Use this option if you're importing files from a memory card or those already on your hard disk.

>> **Drag and drop.** You can drag and drop a folder of images from your file browser right onto the Library module to start the import process.

Selecting the photos you want to import

Although it may be true in most cases that you'll want to import every photo on the memory card, it's still worth your while to skim through the images to verify that you really want to import them all. The Don't Import Suspected Duplicates option on the File Handling panel is selected by default to ensure that you don't import the same photos twice, but when scanning the previews, you might find that you just don't need to waste time importing some of the (bad) photos.

Deselect the check box on any photos you don't want to import at that time. In some instances, you may find it easier to click the Uncheck All button at the bottom of the dialog and then just select the check boxes for photos you do want to import. You can use faster methods to sort the wheat from the chaff in the Library module, but there's no need to import photos of the inside of your lens cap.

Configuring the settings to meet your input needs

Once you know which photos you want to import, it's time to make choices regarding how they're imported and whether you're going to multitask a little and process them on their way in the door.

At the beginning of this chapter, when I first discuss the Import dialog, I mention that the dialog gives you four options along the top center. The source you're importing from largely determines which options are available in the Import dialog. Let me explain.

REMEMBER

If you're importing from a memory card, Copy as DNG and Copy are the only available options. If you're importing from a drive, all options — Copy as DNG, Copy, Move, and Add — are available. Note that newer memory card types, like Compact Flash Type B, are treated like external drives instead of memory cards, so pay extra attention that one of the Copy options is used (not Add) if importing from those types of cards.

Here's why. If you're importing from a device (say, a memory card), you don't want the Add option because memory cards are only temporary storage devices. Lightroom Classic knows this and disables the option (except in the case of some newer card types). Move also isn't an option, based on best practices for dealing with memory cards. First, you don't want to remove files from your memory card until you can visually verify that the files have been copied safely to at least one other disk (or two, if you want to be safe). The idea here is that you don't want to risk something going wrong in the moving process because you haven't yet created a backup. Second, it's better to use your camera to reformat the card when you're ready to erase the contents than it is to let your computer perform that task. When you reformat the card in-camera, the process is done in the best way for the camera, which means you experience less chance of corrupted data when the camera is writing files to the card in normal operation.

The Copy and Move file-handling options include additional settings not found when using the Add option. The reason for this is that when you're only adding, you aren't changing anything about the photos. You're simply telling Lightroom Classic where the files are located and then getting on with the business of importing their data. It would follow that if you're choosing to copy or move the photos and then import, you would need to tell Lightroom Classic where you want them to go and whether you want to change their names in the process. To that end, when you choose one of the Copy or Move file-handling options, you see the following options appear in the Import dialog:

>> **Destination:** Even though this option appears at the bottom of the Import dialog, I'm talking about it first because it's the most important. You do two things here: select the destination where the photos will go and control the folder structure that is created in the import process. You can choose three Organize methods (see the later section "Putting it all together" for how I organize):

- *By original folders:* This option is useful when you're moving or copying from a disk and you want to replicate the same folder structure on the destination disk.

- *By date:* The is the default option. Lightroom Classic provides thirteen date-based folder structures (YYYY/MM-DD, YYYY/Month/DD, and so on) to choose from. The capture dates from the photos are used to create the actual dates used, which is reflected in the space below the Organize field. The slash separating some of the date options means a folder and subfolder structure will be created.

- *Into one folder:* This option allows you to put all your photos into a single folder without regard for dates or original folder structure.

>> **File Renaming:** This option lets you change the filenames when placed in the destination folder. Choose Filename from the Template drop-down menu if you want the filenames to keep the original names. An example of how the filenames will look appears at the bottom of the File Renaming panel, using the selected template.

TIP

Lightroom Classic's file-renaming function is quite powerful and versatile. I feel it's a helpful option to have during import, but keep in mind that you can rename files later in the Library module — so don't feel pressure to do it at import. Lightroom Classic installs with a number of prebuilt filename templates for you to use, but its true power is unleashed when you use the Filename Template Editor, as shown in Figure 4-2, to create your custom templates. You access the editor by clicking the Template drop-down menu and choosing Edit.

The editor works by using what it calls *tokens* to represent various text strings that you can assemble into various configurations. There are tokens for image name data, image numbering options, date formats, metadata, and even custom text. The assembled tokens can be saved as reusable templates anytime you want to rename files. (You'll use the same editor and tokens if you rename after import as well.)

FIGURE 4-2:
The Filename
Template
Editor.

TIP

Click through the various sections to get a sense of what data is possible to include in your filenames. I'd like to call your attention to two tokens in particular:

>> **Import #:** You can use this token to include the import number in your filename. The Import Number is managed from the File Handling tab of the Catalog Settings dialog box (see Chapter 2).

>> **Image #:** You can include this token when you want to number files incrementally across multiple imports. Controlled by the Photos Imported value, Image # is managed from the General tab of the Catalog Settings dialog box (see Chapter 2).

I bring these tokens to your attention because it can be hard to draw the connection between what they represent and the Catalog Settings dialog.

To see what I'm talking about, follow along as I walk through an example where I create a custom template that combines date information and part of the original, camera-generated filename (refer to Figure 4-2 to see what the template ends up looking like):

1. **Click the Template drop-down menu, and choose Edit.**

TIP

   Doing so launches the Filename Template Editor. When the editor opens, notice that the active template appears in the Preset field at the top of the editor and that the tokens that make up that template appear in the Editing field. Take a moment to click through the other templates and see how the tokens are constructed.

2. **Delete any tokens that appear in the editing field.**

   Start with a clean slate. Just click into the field behind the tokens and press Delete (or Backspace for Windows). Notice that the example above the field changes as you add or remove tokens to preview how the filename will appear.

3. **Click the first drop-down menu in the Additional section of the editor, and choose the Date (YYYYMMDD) token.**

   Just selecting from the menu adds the token to the editing field.

4. **Click the editing field behind the date token, and type a dash.**

TIP

   You aren't limited to using just the tokens to build your filenames. You can type directly into the editing field. Just remember that, with filenames, you don't want to make them any longer than necessary, and you want to avoid all nonalphanumeric characters except for dashes and underscores, to prevent potential problems down the road.

5. **In the Image Name section of the editor, choose the Filename number suffix token from the drop-down menu.**

   This is the camera-generated file number. I use it because, when combined with the date, I know that because I typically use only one camera per shoot, it will produce a unique filename.

6. **Click the Preset drop-down menu at the top of the editor, and choose Save Current Settings as New Preset.**

   Doing so opens the New Preset dialog. In case you haven't noticed, the folks at Adobe use the words *template* and *preset* interchangeably. Don't let that confuse you.

7. **Give the preset (template) a descriptive name, and click Create.**

   I usually name my templates so that they mirror somewhat how the filename will look. In this case, I named it YYYYMMDD-suffix. After you click Create, you see this name appear on the Preset menu.

8. **Click Done.**

   You're brought to the Import dialog, with your new template selected.

Regardless of the file-handling method you use, you always have the option to apply three types of information to all imported files, via the Apply During Import panel:

>> **Develop Settings:** Although some prebuilt Develop settings are available to you out of the box, I don't recommend using any at this point. Applying a Develop setting to all photos at import can be helpful at times (such as when you're shooting in a studio and you want to apply a custom white-balance setting), but the majority of your imports can do without Develop settings — which means you should leave this one set to None.

>> **Metadata:** There's no reason not to apply a basic set of metadata to all imported photos. Create a preset (more on that later) that contains your basic copyright and contact information, and apply it every time.

>> **Keywords:** Keywords identify your photos and — when used consistently — provide a powerful means to find specific photos after your catalog grows. It isn't a sexy aspect of the import process, but do it and you'll reap the rewards. During import, you only want to be careful about getting too specific, because the keywords you enter here will be applied to every imported photo in the session.

The process for creating a Metadata preset is worth a closer look. You can create an unlimited number of Metadata presets, which can be applied during import or later in the Library module. I create a baseline *preset* (information that I want on *all* photos regardless of subject, job, or location) containing all my relevant information (copyright, name, contact info, and so on). To create a basic Metadata preset, you do the following:

1. **In the Apply During Import panel of the Import dialog, click the Metadata drop-down menu and choose New.**

   Doing so launches the New Metadata Presets dialog (see Figure 4-3).

2. **Enter a name for your new preset in the Preset Name field.**

3. **Fill out all information in the IPTC Copyright and IPTC Creator fields.**

   This is the basic information about who holds the copyright to this photo and how to contact them. Adding it here means it's written into the metadata of your exported files and can be written to the XMP metadata of your source files.

4. **Click Create.**

   This saves the preset using the name you entered in Step 1 and closes the New Metadata Preset dialog. You see the new preset in the Metadata field of the Import dialog.

The last setting to configure before clicking the Import button is Build Previews in the File Handling panel. I discuss the role of preview files in Lightroom Classic in Chapter 2, but the main thing to know here is that Lightroom Classic begins rendering the previews after the import process is complete. This setting determines the size of the previews it starts creating after import. Here are your options:

» **Minimal:** With Minimal selected, the lowest-resolution previews are grabbed from each file as quickly as possible. Lightroom Classic renders its previews as needed when you're working.

» **Embedded & Sidecar:** Some photos have a larger or full-size preview embedded within their files (or their companion metadata files). With this option, that preview is grabbed first, which may provide higher-quality viewing initially over what you see if you choose the Minimal option. This is a useful option for a fast import with the ability to check focus and separate the keepers from the deletions. I use this option almost all the time.

» **Standard:** In Chapter 2, I discuss how to configure the initial settings for controlling the quality and size of the standard preview. This setting tells Lightroom Classic to go ahead and start rendering standard-size previews based on those settings for all recently imported images.

>> **1:1:** This is a full-size, pixel-per-pixel preview of the source file that Lightroom Classic displays when you're viewing photos up close in the Library module. When this option is set, Lightroom Classic doesn't wait until 1:1 previews are needed; instead, Lightroom Classic starts rendering them after the import is complete.

Note: No matter which setting you use, Lightroom Classic still eventually renders the previews it requires when needed. The main purpose of the setting is to give you a little control over this background process that happens after the import is complete. I routinely choose the Embedded & Sidecar option.

Putting it all together

The two most common types of imports you perform are the Add (especially for new Lightroom Classic users) and Copy variants. The following sections show you how to perform each type of import.

Importing from a drive (Add)

When I started using Lightroom Classic, I had tens of thousands of photos already on my hard drive. I wanted to manage them all with Lightroom Classic, but I wanted to keep them right where they were on my hard drive. This scenario demands that you use the Add method. Here are the steps for adding existing photos to the catalog:

1. **Click the Import button in the Library module to open the Import dialog.**

   Note: To get to the Library module, press G (for Grid) from anywhere in Lightroom Classic.

2. **In the Source panel, navigate to the top-level folder that contains your photos and select it, making sure that the Include Subfolders option is selected.**

TIP

I keep all my photos on a separate drive in a folder I call Imported_Photos. Within that folder, I have a subfolder for each year, and within each year is a folder for each day I was shooting (and then I add a 1- or 2-word description after import). I like this date-based approach because it's simple, Lightroom Classic can automatically generate the structure, and every photo is assigned a single permanent home. The problem I have with any type of categorical structure is that there's always the possibility I might have a photo that could fit into more than one category. I don't want to duplicate a file, and I don't even want to waste time thinking about where to put it. Therefore, I use dates for storage, and I use keywords and collections to create and access my photos in Lightroom Classic. It works for me. So in my case, I'd select the Imported_Photos folder. In your case, it might be the Pictures folder or whatever folder you use to hold all your photos.

3. **Click Add.**

4. **Leave all photos selected for import.**

   You can use Lightroom Classic's tools later to sort out and delete any less-than-perfect photos.

5. **In the File Handling panel, set Build Previews as desired.**

   This is a personal preference. As I said, I generally set it to Embedded & Sidecar.

6. **In the Apply During Import panel, set the Develop Settings drop-down menu to None and choose a Metadata preset from the Metadata menu.**

7. **Apply any globally applicable keywords (it's doubtful that any would apply to all photos when you're first importing).**

8. **Click the Import button.**

After that final click, the Import dialog closes, and you see the progress meter advancing in the upper left corner of the interface as thumbnails start appearing in your catalog. Likewise, the Folders panel shows the imported folders. You can start working with photos as they appear, but I usually busy myself with other tasks until Lightroom Classic has completed the job.

Importing from a memory card (Copy)

TIP

After I import all my legacy photos, I tend to import all new photos directly from the memory card. I recommend using a card reader over directly connecting your camera. A card reader is cheap and portable, doesn't drain your camera batteries, and frees your camera to take more photos if you have multiple memory cards. Card readers often provide a faster data transfer rate than most cameras do. Card readers are so common these days that many laptops and monitors have them built right in!

Time to go through the steps for importing from a memory card — no matter how you connect the card to the computer. These steps are for the manual method and work only if you disable the Show import dialog when a memory card is detected preference setting:

1. **Connect your memory card to the computer, and click the Import button in the Library.**

2. **Verify that your memory card is selected in the Devices or Files section of the Source panel.**

3. Confirm that Eject After Import in the Source panel is selected.

4. Scan the previews, and deselect any photos you don't want to import.

5. Choose the Copy option at the top of the Import dialog.

6. Go directly to the Destination panel, and choose where you want the new copies to be saved.

7. Click the Organize drop-down menu in the Destination panel, and choose how you want the photos organized.

I made my case earlier for a date-based structure, but choose whatever best suits your needs.

8. Confirm that the option Don't Import Suspected Duplicates in File Handling is selected.

9. (Optional) Select the Make a Second Copy To box in the File Handling panel, and configure a backup location.

This isn't a required step, but I highly recommend you consider a workflow that involves backing up your memory card during import.

10. Set Build Previews as desired.

This is a personal preference. As I said, I generally set it to Embedded & Sidecar.

11. In the File Renaming panel, choose a filenaming template from the Template drop-down menu.

12. In the Apply During Import panel, click the Develop Settings drop-down menu, and choose None.

You're free to choose one if it suits your needs, but I prefer starting from a clean slate in Develop.

13. While you're in the Apply During Import panel, click the Metadata drop-down menu and select an existing preset or create a new one.

14. Apply any globally applicable keywords.

15. Double-check the settings in the Destination panel.

16. Click Import.

The Import process is now under way. After the progress meter is complete, it's safe to remove your memory card. Always visually verify that all the photos are where they're supposed to be before formatting that memory card!

Using Auto Import

On Lightroom Classic's File menu, you find the Auto Import option. Anytime you can automate a repetitive process, it's a good thing! Lightroom Classic's Auto Import is handy when you're shooting *tethered* (meaning your camera is connected to your computer while you're shooting) with a camera that isn't supported for tethering (more on that in a bit) or when you just want to set up a folder that will trigger Lightroom Classic to import files as soon as they appear in the folder (such as images you create while working in another application or using a scanner).

To open the Auto Import Settings dialog (shown in Figure 4-4), choose File ⇨ Auto Import ⇨ Auto Import Settings from the main menu.

FIGURE 4-4:
The Auto Import Settings dialog box.

The Auto Import Settings dialog performs the same functions as the Import dialog, with the following exceptions:

>> **Watched Folder:** The idea here is to save/place the photos you take into this folder. As soon as Lightroom Classic sees a photo hit this folder, it initiates the Auto Import process. If you're shooting tethered, this is the folder where you should save the photos from your camera.

>> **Destination:** This location is where Lightroom Classic moves your photos during the import process. This keeps the watched folder empty. The destination folder appears in your Folders panel after the import.

REMEMBER

When you use Auto Import, you don't see a preview; you must configure previews before you have photos ready to import. In fact, the watched folder needs to start empty for the process to function correctly.

Just as with a normal import, when you use Auto Import, you can configure your filename template and metadata template, add keywords, configure previews, and even apply a Develop preset, if needed.

TECHNICAL
STUFF

The next section is devoted to Lightroom Classic's built-in tethering function, but it supports only a limited number of camera models. If your camera isn't supported for tethering, you can use third-party software in conjunction with Lightroom Classic's Auto Import function to bring the photos into Lightroom Classic. Some camera manufacturers bundle this type of software (or a limited version of it) with your camera, but others make you pay for it. (Check with your camera manufacturer.) The purpose of this software is to allow your camera to save photos directly to a specified location on your hard drive (that is, the watched folder) rather than on the camera's memory card. After you have that software installed and operational, you're ready to move forward with Auto Import. If your camera is supported for tethering by Lightroom Classic, jump ahead to the "Shooting Tethered" section.

The most common way I use Auto Import these days is with my scanner (and the software to run the scanner). That said, if you want to shoot tethered with a camera that isn't supported by Lightroom Classic, here are the steps to set up Auto Import to work with your tethering software:

1. **Choose File ⇨ Auto Import ⇨ Auto Import Settings from the main menu.**

   The Auto Import Settings dialog appears.

2. **Click the Choose button next to Watched Folder, and select the empty folder you want Lightroom Classic to watch (the folder you've configured your tethering software to save photos into).**

3. **Click the Choose button in the Destination section, and select the folder you want Lightroom Classic to move the imported photos into.**

Each photo that lands in the watched folder is moved out of that folder and deposited into the destination folder you've chosen. You can use Lightroom Classic to move these photos to a more permanent location later. Check the Add to Collection box (optional), and then select (or create) a collection to have these photos added to it as they're imported.

4. **Choose a filename template from the File Naming drop-down menu.**

5. **From the Develop Settings drop-down menu, choose a Develop preset, if applicable.**

It's beyond the scope of this chapter to cover the creation of Develop presets, but check out Chapter 9 for in-depth coverage.

6. **Choose a Metadata preset from the Metadata drop-down menu.**

7. **Apply globally applicable keywords to this import session.**

8. **Configure the Initial Previews setting.**

9. **Check the Enable Auto Import box at the top of the Auto Import Settings dialog.**

10. **Click OK.**

At this point, Lightroom Classic is ready and waiting for that first photo to land in the watched folder.

11. **Connect your camera to your computer.**

12. **Launch your camera control software, and configure it to save photos into the watched folder you configured in Step 2.**

This process varies with each camera-control software, but the goal is the same. Make sure your software isn't configured for creating additional subfolders in the watched folder.

13. **Take a test shot with your camera.**

You should first see an indication from the camera software that the file is being transferred to the computer. After that, transfer is complete, and Lightroom Classic should automatically begin the import.

TIP

If your test shot was successful, you're ready to begin shooting your job. If the test was unsuccessful, double-check that you enabled Auto Import in Step 9, that the camera is saving photos to the watched folder, and that the watched folder starts out empty.

Shooting Tethered

Shooting with your camera tethered via cable to your computer is a powerfully efficient way to work. No, I'm not advocating that you set up your laptop in front of a grand landscape in the great outdoors. Shooting tethered is ideal for photographers working in a studio or just working indoors. You can use your much bigger and better computer screen for evaluating the photos and have them imported into your Lightroom Classic catalog the moment they're created. What's not to love about that?

Well, there is one rub, which is that not every camera is supported by Lightroom Classic for tethering. To see whether your camera made the cut, head over to Adobe's continually updated list: `https://helpx.adobe.com/lightroom-classic/kb/tethered-camera-support.html`

When ready, connect your camera to your computer with the correct USB cable for your camera and computer. (Wireless tethering isn't currently supported, but you can use it in conjunction with the previously mentioned Auto Import.) Once the camera is connected, follow these steps:

1. **Choose File ⇨ Tethered Capture ([Your Camera Brand]) ⇨ Start Tethered Capture from the main menu.**

   This step opens the Tethered Capture Settings dialog, as shown in Figure 4-5.

2. **Enter a name in the Session Name field, which Lightroom Classic will use to create the folder containing the photos.**

3. **Click the Template drop-down menu in the Naming section, and choose a filename template.**

4. **Click the Choose button in the Destination section, and select where you want this new folder to be created on your drive.**

5. **(Optional) Check the Add to Collection box to gain access to your collections or create a new one.**

6. **Select your metadata template, and add any globally applicable keywords in the Information section.**

FIGURE 4-5:
The Tethered
Capture Set-
tings dialog.

7. **Click OK to close the dialog and begin the tethered session.**

This step opens the floating capture bar, which displays the name of the camera and relevant settings. You can change those values from within Lightroom Classic, if needed, and you can click the Capture button to take the photo. At the bottom of the previously mentioned link showing cameras supported for tethering is a shorter list of cameras that are also supported for shooting in Live View. When using a supported camera, you also see the Live button on the capture bar (as shown in Figure 4-6), which when clicked opens a window displaying the live view from your camera.

Consider applying a Develop preset. Take a test shot, and import it. Correct the white balance in the Develop module, and save it as a Develop preset (covered in Chapter 9). You can apply that preset to the rest of the images when they're imported by clicking the Develop Settings drop-down menu on the capture bar and choosing it from the list. Alternatively, take the first photo into Develop, set the white balance for it, press E to return to Loupe view, and choose Same as previous from the Develop Settings drop-down menu in the Capture bar to have the settings you applied in Develop automatically applied to all newly captured photos.

FIGURE 4-6:
The floating
capture bar,
used when
shooting
tethered.

When the session is over, click the X on the floating capture bar to exit tethering. The Gear icon takes you into the Tethered Capture Settings dialog if you need to tweak anything. Check out my article for a more in-depth look at shooting tethered: `https://lightroomkillertips.com/a-look-at-the-latest-updates-to-shooting-tethered-part-1`

Chapter **5**

Viewing and Finding Photos in the Library

S imilar to your local library, the Library module is the place you go to find and check out your photos — except in this case, you're also the head librarian, which means you have the power to organize and manage the contents. The Library module is the hub — all your photos pass through here on their way to the other modules. Feel free to make as much noise as you want.

You can do a heck of a lot to your photos in the Library module — I hope they're good things, but you never know. This chapter focuses on the operations performed with the organizational panels. For help with sorting and applying various types of metadata to your photos, turn to Chapters 6 and 7.

Exploring the Library Module

When you first enter any building, you need to become oriented to the lay of the land. Although each of Lightroom Classic's modules contains tools and options that are task-specific, the layout of the interface is essentially the same. This common interface is designed to help you become acclimated to the modules as you move through them. More important, the common interface clues you in that you can modify many elements of the interface the same way across modules. Refer to Chapter 1 for a complete rundown of the interface controls.

Getting to know the panels and tools

The Library module, shown in Figure 5-1, is sure to become a frequent stop in your workflow.

FIGURE 5-1:
The Library
module.

The top of the interface provides the means to access menus and move between modules. The left set of panels provides the main access route to your photos, whereas the right set of panels helps you mess around with your photos. Smack-dab in the middle is the content area, which is *the* place to get a closer look at your photos. As for the other elements, the following list details the ones you should probably spend some time getting to know. (If you're following along using Figure 5-1, I'm starting in the upper left corner and moving down.)

>> **Identity Plate/Activity Center:** Also known as the *vanity plate;* a customizable component of the interface you can use to make Lightroom Classic your own (see "Creating a custom Identity Plate," later in this chapter). If you hover the cursor over it, you see a white disclosure triangle that provides access to the Activity Center, where you can enable/disable Address Lookup, enable/

disable Face Detection, and see progress bars for other activities taking place (like exports and imports).

>> **Navigator panel:** Displays a preview when you move the cursor over photos in the Filmstrip; sets the zoom level in Loupe view.

>> **Catalog panel:** Contains a small set of collections for quick access to imported photos. In Lightroom Classic terms, a *collection* is just a special grouping of photos. The ones that appear in this panel are automatically created by Lightroom Classic. You can create your own using the Collections panel (discussed shortly).

>> **Folders panel:** Provides direct access to the folders that contain your photos on your drive(s).

>> **Collections panel:** Contains all your collections and provides tools for organizing and creating additional collections.

>> **Publish Services panel:** A way to create managed exports for different connected services (like Flickr or Adobe Stock) or even local folders.

>> **Filmstrip:** Displays thumbnails of all photos in the current grouping.

>> **Library Filter bar:** Appears above thumbnails in Grid view of the Library and harnesses the power of the Lightroom Classic catalog to find and filter your photos based on a wide range of criteria.

>> **Content area:** Where your photos appear.

>> **Toolbar:** Below the content area; contains a set of tools for completing organizational tasks — stuff like applying ratings, changing the sort order, and switching between Library module views (to name a few).

>> **Module Picker:** Allows for quick movement between various modules.

>> **Histogram:** Displays a graph of the tonal values in the selected photo.

>> **Quick Develop panel:** Allows for the application of Develop settings and presets while working with photos in the Library module. I cover this panel in greater detail in Chapter 7, but the true Developing tools are covered in Chapters 8–10.

>> **Keywording panel:** Provides a display of keywords applied to selected photos as well as a means to apply additional keywords.

>> **Keyword List panel:** Displays a list of all the keywords contained in your catalog as well as tools to create, edit, and remove them.

>> **Metadata panel:** Provides a means for viewing, adding, and editing metadata. *Metadata* is data about the data about a photo, if that makes any sense. Basically, we're talking about camera-generated information that gets recorded when you press the shutter (such as f-stop and shutter speed) as well as photographer-generated information to go along with it (such as title, description, and location).

>> **Comments panel:** Used only in conjunction with certain publish service connections and synced collections through the cloud-based Lightroom. Comments made by visitors to those connected services appear here.

Becoming familiar with the menu options

There's often more than one way to perform any single task, but the menu is usually the single location that contains all the options. What's more, the menu options provide the added benefit of displaying the associated keyboard shortcut (if there is one). Therefore, it's worth becoming familiar with the menus to get a good sense of what's possible in each module. The Library and Metadata menus are unique to the Library module, the Photo menu pops up in Library, Map, and Develop, but their siblings — File, Edit, View, Window, Help — appear in all:

>> **Lightroom Classic (Mac only):** Contains the commands for opening Preferences, Catalog Settings, Identity Plate, and Watermark Setup. Windows users find these under the Edit menu.

>> **File:** Provides access to all the import and export commands, controls for the Quick Collection (one of the special collections in the Catalog panel), as well as Library Filters, the Plug-In Manager, Plug-In Extras, and more.

>> **Edit:** Where to find the Undo and Redo commands as well as all the selection commands. On Windows, this is where you go to access the Preferences, Catalog Settings, and Identity Plate setup.

>> **Library:** Home to the commands for creating new collections and folders as well as advanced filtering options and preview controls.

>> **Photo:** Where to go if you want to do stuff to your photos, like open them in your file browser or an external editor, stack them with other photos, create virtual copies of them, rotate them, apply flags, ratings, or labels to them, or remove them from Lightroom Classic and your disk.

>> **Metadata:** Where to find controls for adding and managing metadata, which also includes keywords.

>> **View:** Contains the most-often-used used keyboard shortcuts for switching between various views across modules — so commit this one to memory. Equally important are the view options for Grid and Loupe views (more on those later).

>> **Window:** A menu you use to access commands for switching between modules, changing screen modes, and selecting options for the secondary display.

>> **Help:** Where to find commands for accessing the Help file (both locally and online), checking for updates, and viewing module-specific shortcuts.

TIP

You can access many of these same menu commands by right-clicking a thumbnail, which calls up a contextual menu similar to the one shown in Figure 5-2.

Creating a custom Identity Plate

In describing the menu options on the Lightroom Classic menu (or in Windows, on the Edit menu), I mention an item called Identity Plate Setup that deserves more attention. This menu option controls the appearance of the Module Picker. Beyond the Module Picker, the Identity Plate can appear in a slideshow, in print layouts, or in web galleries.

In all cases, the Identity Plate provides you with an opportunity to personalize, or *brand*, both Lightroom Classic and the work you output from Lightroom Classic. In this section, I show you how to customize the Mod-

FIGURE 5-2:
Contextual menu options.

ule Picker, but keep in mind that the design you come up with here will show up in other places, too. Basically, you have two types of Identity Plates:

>> **Styled text:** Allows you to enter the text you want to use and then configure the font face, size, and color.

>> **Graphical:** Allows you to include your own logo — image or text — that you design as a graphic in Photoshop. Keep in mind that you have only about 40 pixels in height to work with (41 pixels high on Mac and 46 pixels high on Windows), although it can extend behind the Module Picker buttons, if that's what you want. Graphics can also contain transparency, which allows the black background to show through.

The first three steps for customizing the Identity Plate are the same for either styled text or graphical Identity Plates:

1. **Choose Lightroom Classic ⇨ Identity Plate Setup (Edit ⇨ Identity Plate Setup in Windows) from the main menu.**

   Doing so launches the Identity Plate Editor, as shown in Figure 5-3. If you don't see the same, click the Identity Plate drop-down menu and choose Personalized.

2. **Click either the Use a styled text Identity Plate radio button or the Use a graphical Identity Plate radio button, depending on your preference.**

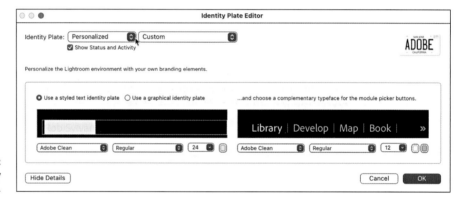

FIGURE 5-3:
The Identity Plate Editor.

What happens next depends on the type of Identity Plate you create. If you're creating a text Identity Plate, you do the following:

1. **Still in the Identity Plate Editor, select the text in the Editor window.**

   The changes you make affect only the selected text.

2. **Type the text you want to appear.**

3. **Reselect the text and then choose a font from the Font drop-down menu.**

4. **Choose the look for your font from the Font Style drop-down menu.**

   Some fonts have additional styles beyond Regular, such as Bold or Italic.

94   PART 2 Managing Your Photos with Lightroom Classic

5. **Choose the font size you want from the Font Size drop-down menu.**

   You can also highlight the number and enter a new value.

6. **Click the color swatch to launch the Color Picker and choose the color of the text.**

Because changes are applied only to the selected text, you can choose to style individual words (and even characters) with different colors and font faces. Mix, match, and experiment!

If you're creating a graphical Identity Plate, you do the following after clicking the Use a graphical Identity Plate radio button:

1. **Still in the Identity Plate Editor, click Locate File.**

2. **In the dialog that appears, navigate to the location of the graphic you want to use.**

   Graphics in PNG format are your best choice here because they offer transparency and reasonable file size, and they work equally well on Windows and Macs. Remember the height limit of 40-ish pixels!

3. **Select the file and click Choose.**

After you have the Identity Plate looking how you want (either text or graphic), you can also modify the Module Picker buttons to better suit the look of your plate. Click the Show/Hide Details button at the bottom of the Identity Plate Editor to reveal the Module Picker button options, as shown in Figure 5-3. Here are the steps to modify the buttons:

1. **Choose a button font from the Font drop-down menu.**

   When you select a font, the preview in the Editor updates to reflect the choice. Select a new font if you're unhappy with how it looks.

2. **Choose the look for your font from the Font Style drop-down menu.**

   Some fonts have additional styles beyond Regular, such as Bold or Italic.

3. **Choose a size for your font from the Font Size drop-down menu.**

4. **Click the left color swatch to open the Color Picker, and choose the color of the active button state.**

   This color indicates the active module.

5. **Click the right color swatch to open the Color Picker and choose the color of the inactive button state.**

   This color indicates the inactive modules.

After you have the Identity Plate and Module Picker buttons looking how you want, click the second drop-down menu at the top of the Editor (where it says *Custom*) and choose Save As. Give this configuration a name and click Save. Click OK to close the Editor and apply the new look.

Choosing the Right View for the Task

You have a couple of choices when it comes to seeing your photos while working in Lightroom Classic, but more likely than not, the view mode you choose is determined by the task you're performing. Expect to spend most of your time working with thumbnails in Grid view, with frequent dips into Loupe view to check focus at 1:1. That's how I use Lightroom Classic, at least.

Grid view and Loupe view work hand in hand, and a few important keyboard shortcuts make toggling between the two views rather seamless:

>> Press G to jump to Grid view from any module.

>> Press E to jump to Loupe view from any module.

>> From Grid view, select a photo and press Return (Enter on Windows) to jump to Fit Screen in Loupe. Press Enter again to jump to 1:1. Press Enter one more time to return to Grid view.

>> From Grid view, select a photo and then press and hold the Z key to jump directly to 1:1 view. Release the Z to return to Grid view.

Working with thumbnails in Grid view

Grid view could also be called Thumbnail view because thumbnails are what make up the grid. Grid view is the workhorse of view modes — the place where you spend the majority of your time when you're performing common tasks, like organizing, sorting, moving, and renaming your photos.

You do perform those tasks now and then, don't you? Whether you're watching a new import roll in, clicking into a folder or collection, or performing a keyword search of your portfolio, you'll end up seeing thumbnails. The size of the thumbnails — and, by extension, how many thumbnails fit within the content area — can be changed with the Thumbnails slider on the Toolbar or by using the + and − keys on your keyboard.

TIP

If you can't see the Toolbar, press T to toggle it on (and off if you don't want to see it). Click the drop-down arrow on the right end to enable/disable the tools that appear on it.

Changing the look of the thumbnails

You have three different grid styles to choose from, all of which offer varying amounts of additional data to appear with each thumbnail:

» Compact Cells

» Compact Cell Extras

» Expanded Cells

You can cycle through each cell style by pressing the J key and configure what information you want to appear in each cell style from the Grid View panel of the Library View Options dialog. Here's how:

1. **Choose View ⇨ Grid View Style ⇨ Compact Cells from the main menu.**

2. **Choose View ⇨ Grid View Style and deselect Show Extras on the menu.**

You're now looking at unadorned thumbnails. This view is helpful when all you want to see are photos and nothing but the photos. If this strikes you as a bit too stark, keep reading.

3. **Choose View ⇨ View Options.**

Doing so opens the Library View Options dialog, as shown in Figure 5-4, with the Grid View tab active.

The reason I want you to work through Steps 1 and 2 here is that this is a *live* dialog: While you enable options in the dialog, you see them appear on the thumbnails. By entering the dialog from the most compact state, you see that all but two options are disabled. Those are the only options for Compact Cells with no extras. I recommend leaving them selected. Now you have only Compact Cell Extras and Expanded Cell Extras to configure.

4. **In the Library View Options dialog, check the Show Grid Extras check box.**

Compact Cells should appear on the Show Grid Extras drop-down menu, and all the options are configurable. Notice that the thumbnails are now showing large index numbers behind them. You're now in Compact Cell Extras view.

5. **Using the Compact Cell Extras section of the dialog, configure Compact Cell Extras as desired.**

How you configure this style is up to you, but the only change I make is to deselect Index Number. The *index number* is a count of each photo in the grouping you're looking at. I find it to be useless and confusing because the number changes based on the filtering and sort order you're using. If you find it helpful, by all means, keep it. Otherwise, I recommend the defaults.

6. **Choose Expanded Cells from the Show Grid Extras drop-down menu.**

Note that the thumbnails change to Expanded Cells view style in the background.

7. **Using the Expanded Cell Extras section of the dialog, configure Expanded Cell Extras as desired.**

Again, Index Number appears as a default header label. Notice that the header label drop-down menus are arranged in the same way they appear within each thumbnail's header. Click each drop-down menu to choose the data you want to display. You have a wide range of metadata to choose from — you can even choose None, which is what I do in place of the index number.

8. **Click the dialog's Close button.**

   Because the settings are applied while you work, there's no need to save them. After the dialog is closed, press the J key to cycle through each style and see whether it works for you. Change as needed.

TIP

Refer to this book's Cheat Sheet for a complete diagram of a grid cell and all the icons, badges, and labels. You can find the Cheat Sheet by searching for *Adobe Lightroom Classic For Dummies Cheat Sheet* from the Search box at www.dummies.com.

Changing the sort order

How your thumbnails are arranged within the content area is the *sort order.* You can change the sort order with the controls on the Toolbar or by choosing View ⇨ Sort from the main menu. Capture Time is the most common sort order, but the others can be useful, too. The one that causes the most confusion is Custom Order, which is when you manually click-and-drag photos into a custom order — confusing because it works only under specific conditions. You can apply a custom order only when

>> **You're working within a collection.** I don't mean collection sets or smart collections, though — only when working within a single collection.

>> **You're working within a single folder.** That folder cannot have any subfolders (even empty ones).

With that in mind, here's what you do to change the sort order manually:

1. **Click into a single folder or collection containing the photos you want to sort.**

   If you want to sort photos that reside across a range of folders, you first need to put them into a single collection.

2. **Click the center of the photo you want to move, and hold the mouse button.**

   Although it's a photographer's natural tendency, don't grab the photo's frame (no need to worry about fingerprints here) because it won't work.

3. **Move the photo to the new location in the order you want, and release when the separator line at that location darkens.**

Making efficient use of space with stacks

Stacking is a function that allows you to group photos into a virtual "stack" so that only the top photo is visible. This is helpful in situations where you have multiple shots of the same subject and want to group them under a single thumbnail, like when shooting for a panorama or HDR. (But really, any reason that works for you is fine — you don't have to justify anything!)

To stack photos together, follow these steps:

1. **Select all the thumbnails you want to group together.**

   You can select multiple photos by clicking the first photo in a series, holding the Shift key, and clicking the last photo in the series to select them all or holding the ⌘ (Ctrl key in Windows) and individually clicking each photo you want to select.

2. **Choose Photo ⇨ Stacking ⇨ Group into Stack from the main menu.**

   Lightroom Classic brings the selected photos together into a collapsed stack. Note the other options under the Stacking menu command.

Stacked photos are identified by a bar on either end of the group of stacked photos, as shown in Figure 5-5 (note that the number in the upper left corner indicates how many photos are in the stack). You can expand and collapse the stack by clicking either of those bars, or by selecting the stack and pressing S.

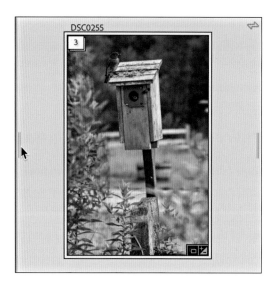

FIGURE 5-5:
Stacked photos
indicator.

Taking a closer look in Loupe view

When viewing a thumbnail isn't adequate for the job, it's time to switch to Loupe view. The easiest way to switch is to press E, which switches you to Loupe view at the Fit setting. The Navigator panel, as shown in Figure 5-6, is Loupe view's best friend, in that it displays a thumbnail of the active photo. At the top of the panel are the various zoom levels you can use in Loupe view. The default zoomed-out state is Fit, which means the entire image fits in the content area, and the default zoomed-in state is 100%, which means actual pixel view. Click each zoom level to activate, or click the drop-down menu at the end to zoom in some more. When Fill is selected (under the Fit menu), the photo is zoomed in just enough to fill the entire content area.

FIGURE 5-6:
The Navigator panel.

TIP

The choice you make at the top of the Navigator panel becomes the default zoomed-out and zoomed-in state. I find Fit and 100% to be the most useful.

When you zoom in beyond Fit, you can click-and-drag the photo to inspect different areas of the photo, or click-and-drag the white square in the Navigator panel to pan across the photo. Here's an alternative (and more efficient) method to inspect all areas of the photo when you zoom in beyond Fill:

1. **Click the photo to zoom in.**

   100% works very well for this.

2. **Press the Home key on the keyboard to jump to the upper left corner of the photo.**

   On some keyboards, there may not be a Home key (or Page Up, Page Down, or End), so the incorporation of the Function (Fn) key with your arrow keys may be required to achieve the same functionality. For example, on my Mac, holding down the Fn key and pressing the left-arrow key is the same as pressing Home on my Windows machine. Fn+up arrow equals Page Up, Fn+down arrow equals Page Down, and Fn+right arrow equals End.

3. **Repeatedly press the Page Down key on the keyboard to move over the photo.**

   Each press of the Page Down key moves you an equal amount until you reach the bottom, where one more press brings you back to the top but over to the right. You can continue to press the Page Down key until you've viewed the entire photo down to the lower right corner.

4. **Click the photo to zoom out.**

In practice, this process goes by rather quickly, and you're guaranteed not to miss a single pixel of the photo this way.

Just like in Grid view, it's possible to display some important information about the active photo. Here it's called the Loupe Info Overlay, and two versions allow for different sets of information to be displayed (but not at the same time). You can cycle through each overlay and back to the Off position by pressing the I key. To set up the Loupe Info Overlay, choose View ⇨ View Options from the main menu to launch the Library View Options dialog. It should open to the Loupe View tab, as shown in Figure 5-7.

FIGURE 5-7:
The Loupe
View tab of the
Library View
Options dialog.

Each Info Overlay can be configured by clicking its respective drop-down menus and choosing the data you want to see. The first check box in the General section toggles the display of the loading and rendering messages that appear in Loupe view. I find the messages to be a helpful reminder that something is going on behind the scenes when first viewing a low-quality preview, so I leave that box selected — and recommend you do the same. The same goes for the default positions of the Show frame number when displaying video time and Play HD video at draft quality.

Using the Panels to Access Your Photos

The Catalog, Folders, and Collections panels provide multiple ways to view, organize, and access your portfolio. Each offers a unique set of tools to help you stay in control of your portfolio. Let's examine each panel in turn.

Getting the 20,000-foot view from the Catalog panel

The Catalog panel, shown in Figure 5-8, provides quick access to a few special collections of your photos:

>> **All Photographs:** Provides quick access to all imported photos.

>> **All Synced Photographs:** Tracks the photos that are synced with the cloud-based Lightroom (see Chapter 16).

>> **Quick Collection:** A temporary holding place for photos. See the later section on the Quick Collection for more information.

FIGURE 5-8:
The Catalog panel.

>> **Previous/Current Import:** Shows the most recently imported photos. Each new import clears the last batch and adds the newest.

Using the Folders panel like a file browser

The Folders panel, shown in Figure 5-9, displays a listing of all the folders of photos you've imported as well as the disk (or volume) where the folders reside. Volumes and folders can be expanded or collapsed as needed to access the contained photos. Volumes are arranged in the order in which they're imported, whereas folders within each volume are arranged in descending alphanumeric order — an ordering that cannot be changed.

FIGURE 5-9:
The Folders panel.

The *Volume Browser* — the bar that appears above your topmost level folder — indicates the name of the volume (disk) that your folders reside on as well as a number of other functions:

>> **Shows at a glance where your photos reside.**

>> **Can be configured to display disk space, photo count, or online status.** Mine is set to Disk Space in Figure 5-9. Right-click and choose the information to be displayed.

>> **Provides a color indicator (think dashboard warning light) of how much free space is on that disk.** Green means plenty of space, but it turns to yellow then orange when it starts to get full, and then red when it is very low, and black if that disk is offline.

>> **Allows for all the folders on a given volume to be collapsed under one heading.**

If your imported folders reside on more than one disk, you see a Volume Browser for each disk. I have three disks showing in Figure 5-9.

Although the Folders panel looks a lot like your file browser (Finder on the Mac or File Explorer on Windows), it's fundamentally different. The difference is that the Folders panel shows only the folders and photos that have passed through the Import process. Your file browser, comparatively, simply browses the folder and shows its contents. That difference aside, the Folders panel reflects the reality of your actual folders in the following ways:

>> The actual folder names are shown in the Folders panel.

>> Changes made in the Folders panel are reflected on the actual folders.

WARNING

Unfortunately, changes you make to the folder structure outside of Lightroom Classic aren't updated automatically in Lightroom Classic. This is an area where you can create problems for yourself. To avoid creating problems, make changes to the imported folders (and photos) only from within Lightroom Classic.

Adding new folders and subfolders to the Folders panel

Lightroom Classic shows only the folders that have been imported; therefore, you might decide at some point that you want the parent folder of one of your imported folders to appear in the Folders panel. The quickest way to bring the parent folder into Lightroom Classic is to right-click the child folder in the Folders panel and then choose Show Parent Folder. The parent folder immediately appears in the Folders panel; however, any photos it might contain aren't visible until they're imported.

Another option is simply to create a new folder entirely. The benefit of doing this in Lightroom Classic is that the folder is not only created but is also imported at the same time. You can either create a new folder inside of one of your existing folders (also referred to as *subfolders*) or create a new folder in an entirely different location. Here's how the new subfolder thing works:

1. **Select the folder you want to use as the parent folder for the new subfolder.**

2. **Click the plus-sign (+) symbol at the top of the Folders panel and choose Add Subfolder.**

   The Create Folder dialog appears, as shown in Figure 5-10. Note that in the Folder Options section, the name of the folder you selected appears selected.

FIGURE 5-10: The Create Folder dialog.

3. **Enter a name in the Folder field.**

4. **Click Create.**

   The new folder appears in the Folders panel under the previously selected folder.

The process for creating a new folder in a new location is slightly different:

1. **Click the plus-sign (+) symbol at the top of the Folders panel and choose Add Folder.**

   Doing so launches the Browse for Folder dialog.

2. **Navigate to the disk location where you want this folder to be created.**

3. **Click the New Folder button to create a new folder, give it a name, and click Choose (or Select Folder on Windows).**

   The New Folder button appears near the top of the dialog in Windows, and near the bottom on the Mac. The newly created folder appears in the Folders panel.

TIP

The most common reason for adding a new folder to Lightroom Classic is so that you can move photos or folders into this new location. Folders can be moved by clicking-and-dragging them to the destination folder of your choice within the Folders panel. You can also move individual photos by clicking-and-dragging them from Grid view to the destination folder in the Folders panel. After you drag a file or folder to a new location, Lightroom Classic prompts you to make sure you want to complete that action, as shown in Figure 5-11. Click the Move button to proceed.

FIGURE 5-11:
The Moving a
File warning.

Along with adding new folders, you might feel the need to remove folders. If the folder you want to ditch is empty of photos and subfolders, right-click the folder and choose Remove. The folder disappears from Lightroom Classic as well as from your Mac hard drive. (On a Windows machine, that folder remains on your disk until you remove it via File Explorer.) If you remove a folder that contains photos or subfolders, the folder is removed only from Lightroom Classic. (Both Mac and Windows machines keep such folders on their hard drives.)

Keeping the catalog in sync with the folders

If you're outside of Lightroom Classic and decide to use your file browser to add new photos to a folder that has already been imported into Lightroom Classic, the photos don't appear in Lightroom Classic automatically. All photos have to pass through the import process first. Lightroom Classic's Synchronize command is helpful for making Lightroom Classic take a closer look at a given folder and, if necessary, opening the Import dialog to bring any additions into the catalog. Here's how it works:

1. **Right-click the folder you want to check.**

2. **Choose Synchronize Folder from the contextual menu that appears.**

   Doing so opens the Synchronize Folder dialog, as shown in Figure 5-12. Depending on the number of files contained in the folder, Lightroom Classic might take a couple of minutes to compare what it knows about the folder to what's actually in the folder and to determine what action needs (or what actions need) to occur to get the two in sync.

FIGURE 5-12:
The
Synchronize
Folder dialog.

3. **Select the check boxes for each operation you want Lightroom Classic to perform.**

   You can have Lightroom Classic

   - Import new photos (with or without showing the Import dialog).

   - Remove any missing photos from the catalog file — photos that were in the folder but might have been moved to another folder.

   - Check for any metadata updates that might have occurred from editing in a different application (such as adding keywords via Adobe Bridge).

4. **Click Synchronize.**

   Lightroom Classic closes the Synchronize dialog and performs the tasks you assigned.

Grouping photos into collections

The Collections panel, shown in Figure 5-13, is found just below the Folders panel. *Note:* I've created many custom collections over time, but by default you would see only a set of smart collections (more on those later in this chapter). Although, on the surface, collections appear to function just like folders, they have a critically important difference: They don't exist outside of Lightroom Classic. You can open a file browser, navigate to a folder, and see what it contains, but you can search your entire hard drive and never find a collection.

Folders are real, recognized by file browsers the world over. Collections are *virtual* folders, created out of thin air by Lightroom Classic for its purposes. In the real world, if you want to place a photo into more than one folder, you have to make copies of the source file and place one copy into each folder. With collections, all you do is create *pointers* to the source file. That way, a single photo can be placed into as many collections as you care to create, without ever needing to duplicate the source photo.

FIGURE 5-13:
The Collections
panel, showing
collection
sets, regular
collections,
and smart
collections.

Collections can contain photos from all corners of your library, which makes them a powerful organizational tool. You might have a collection containing all your best work, or all photos of a given subject, or perhaps one for each client. The purpose that collections serve and how you might name them are entirely up to you. I find that they provide a natural way to quickly access groups of photos around a specific theme.

You can create a collection a number of ways:

>> Click the plus-sign (+) symbol at the top of the Collections panel and choose Create Collection.

>> Choose Library ⇨ New Collection from the main menu.

>> Press ⌘+N (Ctrl+N for Windows).

You can organize collections within the Collections panel by putting them into a collection set. (A *collection set* is simply a grouping of collections.) For example, if you shoot weddings, you might have a collection set for each client. Within that collection set, you might have a collection for the bride, another for the groom, another for the family, and so on.

To add a collection set, click the plus sign (+) sign at the top of the Collections panel and choose Create Collection Set from the menu that appears. After you give the set a meaningful name, it appears in the Collections panel. You can then drag-and-drop existing collections into it. Collection sets cannot contain photos — only collections and other collection sets — and are denoted with a Box icon.

Quick Collection

The Quick Collection, a useful variation on the Collections idea, can come in handy when you just want to set aside some photos without putting them in a permanent collection. Quick Collection resides in the Catalog panel, and you place photos into the Quick Collection by doing one of the following:

>> Select the photos and press the B key.

>> Click the tiny Quick Collection indicator that appears in the upper right corner of each thumbnail.

   This indicator is a tiny circle that's visible only when you place the cursor over a thumbnail. (I take that back: You can also see the indicator on photos you've already included in the Quick Collection.)

>> Choose Photo ➪ Add to Quick Collection from the main menu.

Those same options also work in reverse to remove photos from the Quick Collection. You can clear all photos from a Quick Collection by choosing File ➪ Clear Quick Collection. If you decide that you want to make a Quick Collection permanent, you can save it by choosing File ➪ Save Quick Collection. After you give the collection a name, it appears where all well-behaved collections end up — in the Collections panel. Here's a cool tip for taking the Quick Collection to the next level with a Target Collection: https://lightroomers.com/target-collection

Smart collections

Smart collections are a great example of how to leverage the power of a database to do work for you. True, you already have all kinds of ways to group your photos by virtue of data they have in common — just think of the Filter bar. However, smart collections take that power to the Collections panel. A Gear icon tells you it's a smart collection.

Now, instead of having to manually select photos and put them in a collection, you can create a smart collection that automatically pulls photos into it based on the criteria you choose to include. You can think of smart collections as saved searches based on whatever criteria you choose. To get you started, Lightroom Classic comes installed with these six default smart collections:

>> **Colored Red:** All photos with a red label

>> **Five Stars:** All photos rated five stars

>> **Past Month:** All photos containing a capture date within the past month

>> **Recently Modified:** All photos with an edit date within the past two days

>> **Video files:** All imported video files

>> **Without Keywords:** All photos with an empty keyword field

TIP

If none of these starter smart collections appeals to you, you can easily delete them. Just select one (or more) and then click the minus sign (–) on the Collections header bar. Poof! — they're gone. If you want to see the rules governing a smart collection, you can right-click any smart collection and choose Edit Smart Collection. Doing so launches the Edit Smart Collection dialog, which spells out in gory detail the parameters the smart collection is using. Feel free to tweak the settings to better fit your needs and then click Save!

You can create as many smart collections as you need — and you don't need to start with one of the default sets. You can create one from scratch. One smart collection that I use as a sort of safety net is designed to collect any photo not marked as copyrighted in its metadata. Even though I include the copyright setting in my metadata template when I import photos (see Chapter 4), sometimes photos lose that setting or enter my library without it when synced from the cloud-based Lightroom; so this simple collection automatically collects any photos that would otherwise remain unnoticed. Here's how to set up that smart collection:

1. **Click the plus sign (+) on the Collections header bar and choose Create Smart Collection from the contextual menu that appears.**

Alternatively, you can choose Library⇨New Smart Collection from the main menu. This launches the Create Smart Collection dialog, shown in Figure 5-14.

FIGURE 5-14:
The Create Smart Collection dialog, showing a finished example.

2. **Enter a descriptive name in the Name field.**

3. **Choose a Collection set to put the collection in.**

4. **Select All from the Match drop-down menu.**

   A photo has to match all the provided rules to be included in the collection.

5. **Choose Copyright Status from the drop-down menu on the first rule that appears — the menu directly underneath the Match drop-down menu.**

   After clicking the rule drop-down menu, drill down to Other Metadata to find Copyright Status. Your first rule is now about *copyright status*. When you make that first choice about which criteria you want to use for your rule, the contents of the subsequent drop-down menus update automatically with relevant criteria until the rule is complete. Next, you need to define what is it about copyright status that you want to take notice of. In this example, you want all photos not marked as copyrighted, so you change that in the next step.

6. **Choose the Is Not option from the bordering drop-down menu — the next part of your first rule.**

   Great — so now you need to answer the question "Is not what?" — which you'll do next.

7. **Choose Copyrighted from the far-right drop-down menu.**

   So your smart collection is set to grab all photos whose copyright status isn't copyrighted. Perfect — that's exactly what you want to happen.

8. **Click Create.**

   The new collection appears in the Collections panel.

This is just one example of the many ways you can make smart collections work for your needs. Click through each of the criteria options to see what's possible. Many of my smart collections involve a single criterion, but feel free to use as many criteria as you need to get the job done. Because smart collections are basically saved searches, they operate automatically and instantaneously. The only way a photo appears in a smart collection is if it meets the rules, and the only way it can be removed is if it no longer meets the rules.

Creating Virtual Copies

Virtual copies are based on all Lightroom Classic adjustments being recorded as a set of instructions waiting to be applied at output. A *virtual copy* is essentially an alternative set of instructions that references the same source file as the original.

Here's a simple example: You have a color photo and wonder how it might look in black-and-white, so you create a virtual copy and convert the copy to B&W. In Lightroom Classic, you see two versions of that source file: one color and one B&W. If you look in the folder where the source file is saved, you see only the original. The grayscale copy is simply an alternative set of instructions stored in Lightroom Classic's catalog waiting to be applied during output.

TIP

You can recognize a virtual copy in Grid view by the page-curl effect in the lower left corner, as shown in Figure 5-15.

FIGURE 5-15:
The page-curl effect represents a virtual copy.

You can create a virtual copy in three separate ways:

» Choose Photo ⇨ Create Virtual Copy.

» Right-click an image and choose Create Virtual Copy from the contextual menu that appears.

» Press ⌘+' (Ctrl+' for Windows).

If you decide that you prefer the virtual copy to the original, you can make it the new master version of the file and make the old master into a virtual copy. With the virtual copy selected, choose Photo ⇨ Set Copy as Original. You see the page-curl effect "jump" from one thumbnail to the other.

Chapter **6**

Getting Organized with the Library

O ne of the first tasks I perform when working with a batch of newly imported photos is to weed out the worst of the bunch. I keep anything that has at least some redeeming quality, but any poor exposures or photos with improper focus are sent straight to the trash. I do want to note that, even though photos I flag as rejected are deleted from disk, I do retain an archived copy of my original import as a fallback. This provides me with enough peace of mind to be a tougher critic of my own work, which I feel is integral to my own growth. That's one of the things I really like about Lightroom Classic: It gives me the tools I need to evaluate my work in an efficient manner.

An additional result of this tough-love editing process is that I don't have to spend time organizing, sorting, or applying additional metadata and keywords to photos I don't plan to keep. But this is just *my* approach to this process. I've structured this chapter to reflect a common workflow scenario and illustrate how certain functions work, and I encourage you to develop and refine a workflow that best suits your style and needs.

Evaluating Photos

The Library module has five view modes: Grid, Loupe, Compare, Survey, and People. I cover Grid and Loupe — the workhorse view modes — in Chapter 5 — you'll still be using them as you move between Compare and Survey (which I tackle in just a bit). People view is its own special case; I cover it in Chapter 7. Each view can serve a variety of purposes, but I find that when it comes to evaluating photos, the Survey and Compare views are the ones I reach for most often. They still work hand in hand with Grid view and Loupe view, but they offer different ways to interact with — and see — your photos.

Survey view

Survey view, as shown in Figure 6-1, is helpful when you want to move from Grid view to look only at a small group of photos by themselves, and possibly reduce that selection further. To enter Survey view, just select the thumbnails you want to look at together while in Grid view and then press N. Don't ask me why N is the shortcut, and don't ask me why it's called Survey view, for that matter. I'm just here to tell you what's what. As an alternative (there's always an alternative), you can enter Survey view by selecting photos and clicking the Survey view button on the Toolbar, choosing View ⇨ Survey from the main menu, or right-clicking a selected photo and choosing Open in Survey from the contextual menu that appears.

FIGURE 6-1:
Three photos shown in Survey view.

Lightroom Classic automatically arranges the selected photos to fit within the available content area. The more photos you select, the smaller each photo appears; whereas the more screen real estate you provide to the content area, the larger the photos appear. For this reason, you might find it helpful to maximize the content area (if you're not already in full screen) by

>> Pressing Shift+F to jump to Full Screen with Menu Bar mode (and keep pressing to cycle back to normal)

>> Pressing Shift+Tab to collapse all panels (and pressing again to expand the panels)

The photo with the border is the *active* photo (the one that any flags, ratings, metadata, or adjustments will be applied to). You can use the arrow keys on your keyboard to change the active photo or just click a different photo to make it the active one.

TIP

If you want to zoom in to take a closer look at any photo, click it to make it the active photo and then press and hold the Z key to zoom to 1:1. As long as you hold the Z key, you can pan around the photo (by clicking and dragging) for closer inspection. When you're done, just release the Z key to return to Survey view. If you don't want to keep holding down the Z key, you can just press it once to jump to 1:1 Loupe view, examine the photo at your leisure, and then press the Z key to return to Survey view. Either way, Lightroom Classic provides you with a free round-trip ticket to Loupe view and back.

You can also remove photos from this view by clicking the X icon that appears in the lower right corner when you move the cursor over the photo or by ⌘+clicking (Ctrl-clicking in Windows) the photo itself. As photos are removed from view, Lightroom Classic adjusts the remaining photos to fill the newly available space. Removing from this view simply deselects that photo, so this can be a way to pare down a selection of photos to just the ones you want.

Compare view

The most useful view mode for side-by-side comparison of one photo to another is the aptly named Compare view. This view is best for situations where you have multiple shots of the same subject and you want to determine — after careful consideration — which one you like best. To get Compare view up and running, start out from Grid view, select the thumbnails you want to compare, and then press C. (You can also enable Compare view from the button on the Library Toolbar or the main menu or via the contextual menu.)

TIP

You can see an example of Compare view in action in Figure 6-2. Similar to Survey view, Compare view fills the available content area. The trick here is that Compare view limits itself to showing two photos at a time. Collapsing panels to maximize the content area allows the photos to be larger.

FIGURE 6-2:
Two photos in
Compare view.

The first photo you select before entering Compare view is labeled the Select. The *Select* is the photo you're comparing against all the others. When the other photos appear in the content area, they're referred to as the Candidate. The Select is always on the left, and the Candidate is on the right. You can see the Select and Candidate labels appear as an overlay on the photos themselves (refer to Figure 6-2). Additionally, the Select has a white Diamond icon display on its thumbnail in the Filmstrip, whereas the Candidate displays a black Diamond icon in the Filmstrip. The Diamond icons are helpful visual cues when you have a large selection of photos to compare. You can use the arrow keys on the keyboard to swap other photos into the Candidate position.

TIP

The active photo has a white border around it in the content area. (The Select is active in Figure 6-2.) Click either the Select or the Candidate in the content area to set it as the active photo. When the Select is active, clicking another photo in the Filmstrip sets it as the new Select. Likewise, when the Candidate is active, clicking another photo in the Filmstrip sets it as the new Candidate. The active photo is also the one that can have flags, ratings, labels, Quick Develop settings, and metadata applied to it.

TIP

To aid in the evaluation process, you can also zoom into each photo by either clicking into the active photo or using the Zoom slider on the Toolbar. If the Lock icon on the Toolbar is closed, both the Select and Candidate zoom by the same amount. When the Select and Candidate are zoomed and locked, both photos pan in sync when you click the active photo and pan around. If the Lock icon is open, you can zoom and pan each photo independently. If you click the Sync button next to the Zoom slider, both photos zoom to the same section of each photo. The Z key shortcut I describe in the earlier "Survey view" section works here, too.

You can have the Candidate become the Select, and the Select become the Candidate, by clicking the Swap button on the Toolbar, as shown in Figure 6-3. You can also promote the Candidate to become the Select by clicking the Make Select button on the Toolbar. (It's the button just to the right of the Swap button.) You can exit Compare view by either switching to a different view mode or clicking the Done button on the Toolbar.

FIGURE 6-3:
The Compare view Toolbar buttons.

Flags, Ratings, and Color Labels

Having all the various view modes and their associated tools at your disposal won't do you a lick of good if you can't integrate them into your workflow in a way that makes the process of evaluating your photos more efficient. I've come up with my workflow model, but don't think of it as carved in stone. Perhaps you already have a system of, say, color labels or ratings that works for you. By all means, do what works. In these next few sections, I cover the available organizational tools and how they work in a typical workflow. Feel free to pick and choose the pieces that fit your needs.

Using flags to pick the winners and losers

Flags are a fantastic tool for quickly making a first-pass edit of your photos so that you can separate the shots you want to keep from the ones that no one else needs to see. You have three flag states to choose from, represented by the Flag icons, shown in Figure 6-4:

>> **Pick:** These are your keepers and are marked with a white Flag icon.

>> **Rejected:** These are your rejects and are marked with a black Flag icon.

>> **Unflagged:** These haven't been evaluated and do not show an icon (unless the cursor is over the photo).

FIGURE 6-4:
Three photos,
showing
picked,
rejected, and
unflagged pho-
tos from left to
right.

Flags (of each type) can be applied to one or more selected photos at a time. Unflagged photos don't show a flag, but if you position the cursor over an unflagged photo, you can see the outline of the Flag icon. This clickable target can be used to set a flag. Click the icon once to set it as picked, and click again to unflag. You can also apply flags by

>> Clicking either the Pick or Rejected Flag icon on the Toolbar

>> Right-clicking a photo and choosing Set Flag and then choosing one of the three flag states from the contextual menu that appears

>> Using keyboard shortcuts: P for Pick, X for Rejected, and U for Unflagged

>> Choosing Photo ➪ Set Flag from the main menu

TIP

The easiest and most efficient method to apply flags is to use the keyboard short-cuts. This process is expedited by choosing Photo ➪ Auto Advance from the main menu (it should be enabled by default). When enabled, the focus automatically advances to the next photo after applying the flag.

Here's a quick workflow using the Library Filter bar above the thumbnails in Grid view (which I cover in more detail later, in the section "Finding Photos with the Library Filter Bar") for making your first-round selections:

1. **Press G to jump to Grid view.**

2. **Press Shift+Tab to hide all panels and maximize the content area.**

3. **Adjust the Thumbnails slider on the Toolbar as needed to get a good size for evaluating each photo.**

TIP

When you need to quickly see a 1:1 view of your photo while working in Grid view, press and hold the Z key to zoom. While holding the Z key, you can even click-and-drag the photo to inspect other areas. When you release the Z key, you return directly to Grid view.

4. **On the Library Filter bar, click the Attribute label to display the Attribute filters; then right-click anywhere on the Flag icons in the Attribute filter, and choose Flagged and Unflagged Photos from the contextual menu that appears (see Figure 6-5).**

This step sets a view filter that tells Lightroom Classic to display only photos that are flagged as either Pick or Unflagged, which results in Lightroom Classic hiding (not deleting) any photos flagged as Rejected. This way, when you flag a photo as Rejected, it immediately hides from view and advances you to the next photo.

5. **Make sure Photo ⇨ Auto Advance is selected.**

6. **With the first image selected, evaluate and flag as a Pick or Reject.**

TIP

Press P for Pick and X for Rejected. Lightroom Classic automatically advances to the next thumbnail. If you just can't decide, press U (Unflagged) to advance to the next photo. I deal with unflagged photos in Step 8.

7. **Continue applying flags until you reach the last image.**

At this point, you should only see photos that are flagged as Pick or Unflagged. Skip to Step 10 if you didn't leave any photos unflagged.

8. **On the Library Filter, right-click anywhere on the Flag icons and choose Unflagged Photos Only.**

Now all picks and rejected photos are hidden from view, and you're left with only unflagged photos.

9. **Flag the remaining photos as either Pick or Rejected.**

When photos are flagged, they're hidden from view because of the Unflagged Photos Only filter. You know you're finished when you have no photos left.

10. **On the Library Filter, right-click anywhere on the Flag icons and choose Rejected Photos Only.**

Photos flagged as rejected appear faded; this is normal and helps them stand out when you see a mix of flag states.

11. **Verify that you're satisfied with your rejected photos, and change any to Pick if needed.**

12. **Press ⌘+Delete (Ctrl+Backspace in Windows), and choose Delete from Disk.**

    This is the keyboard shortcut to delete rejected photos — you find the same command on the Photo menu.

13. **Press ⌘+L (Ctrl+L in Windows) to turn off all filters.**

    You should now be left with all the photos you flagged as Pick!

Deleting photos from Lightroom Classic

Lightroom Classic is careful (as it should be) in its approach to deleting photos from disk. You're always prompted with a confirmation dialog, as shown in Figure 6-6, before a deletion is allowed to take place. When prompted, click the Delete from Disk button to complete the deletion process and have Lightroom Classic move selected photos to the Trash (Recycle Bin in Windows). Clicking Remove from Lightroom removes the photo only from the Lightroom Classic catalog (and leaves the photo, or photos, on your drive).

You can delete a photo from disk with the Delete key only when you're working in a Folder view. If you're working in a Collection view and press Delete, selected photos are removed only from that collection. (For more on Folder views and Collection views, check out Chapter 5.)

FIGURE 6-6:
The Confirm dialog appears when attempting to delete photos.

Using ratings to rank images

Ratings provide another means to sort your photos by subjective criteria. There's no hard-and-fast rule on what criteria correlate to any number of star ratings. It's entirely up to you to develop your system! Because I use a flag system to cull all the bloopers first, I don't use ratings to mark which photos stay or go. I find ratings helpful for quickly identifying the best of the best while ignoring the photos that aren't so bad to warrant deletion, but at the same time, just aren't good enough to do much with.

To prevent a lot of hemming and hawing over the difference between a 4-star photo and a 5-star photo, I typically use a scale of 0–2 stars. If I think it's a use-able shot, I assign one star; if I think a photo is excellent, I assign 2 stars; and if I can't decide, I leave it at 0. I find that this system helps me refine and focus my energy on processing rather than on ranking.

As with most Lightroom Classic tasks, there's more than one approach to accomplishing the same result. After selecting the photo, you can apply ratings in the following ways:

>> **Press the number keys, 0–5, depending on the number of stars you want to apply.** Each number key corresponds to the number of stars.

>> **Click the appropriate star under each photo cell in Grid view.** Press J to cycle through Grid cell styles if you don't see rating stars.

>> **Right-click, select Set Rating from the contextual menu that appears, and then choose a rating from the menu.**

>> **Choose Photo ⇨ Set Rating from the main menu and then choose a rating from the menu.**

Applying color labels to photos

Color labels provide a visual you can use to further sort and organize your photos. How these are used is entirely subjective, and perhaps you might not use them at all. They do offer some unique benefits:

>> **Labels are very flexible.**

>> **Labels can be used as criteria in the creation of smart collections.**

>> **Labels can be used as a filter on the Library Filter.**

I've seen people use labels to assign a different color to each photographer for easier sorting after an event with multiple shooters. I've seen others assign different colors to different states in the editing process (such as a color for Needs Keywords, another for Ready to Deliver, and so on). Maybe you'd find labels use-ful for labeling groups of photos that you intend to send to other applications for additional processing. However you use them, consider setting up a smart collec-tion for each color label to provide quick access to those special groupings.

Rather than try to remember what each color means in your system, you can create a custom label set with names that make sense to you. Here's how to create your custom label set:

1. **Choose Metadata ⇨ Color Label Set ⇨ Edit from the menu.**

   Doing so launches the Edit Color Label Set dialog.

2. **Enter a name for each color in the set you want to use.**

3. **Choose Save Current Settings as New Preset from the Preset drop-down menu.**

   The New Preset dialog appears.

4. **Enter a name and click Create.**

   The preset name appears on the Preset drop-down menu of the Edit Color Label Set dialog.

5. **Click Change to close the editor and begin using that set.**

REMEMBER

You can use only one color label set at a time, so when you change to this new set, you won't see any color labels applied with a previous color set. A *color label* is simply a tag in the file's metadata. When that label matches the color label set in use, Lightroom Classic displays the corresponding color. Changing the set doesn't change the label that's applied; you just won't see Lightroom Classic display a color. You can change color label sets by selecting them from the Metadata ⇨ Color Label Set menu.

Applying color labels to folders and collections

In addition to photos, you can also apply color labels to folders and all types of collections and collection sets. The colors you apply to folders and collections aren't linked to the color label set you choose, and applying a color label to a folder or collection doesn't apply that color label to the photos within it. These color labels can be used to give you another visual cue for locating groups of photos based on the color label you assign. It's up to you to think of how this can be useful in your workflow, but suppose that you assign a yellow color label to all folders and collections you're currently processing to make those stand out from the rest. Or perhaps within a given shoot, you assign one color to the folder or collection containing the originals and a different color to finished files for delivery. I do a lot of High Dynamic Range (HDR), panoramas, and focus stacking, so I've assigned a different color to represent folders and collections containing those types of photos. There's no wrong answer — only what helps you find and organize your library.

To apply a color label to a folder or collection, simply right-click the folder or collection in question and then use the Add Color Label contextual menu to select a color. You can change or remove color labels the same way as your needs and workflow dictate.

Filtering folders and collections

Here's the real benefit to applying color labels to folders and collections, though: You can filter the view of the contents of each panel based on the color label! At the top of both the Folders and Collections panels is an easy-to-miss field with a tiny Magnifying Glass icon that you can click to access a menu of items to choose from for filtering the view of that panel. Additionally, you can type into the field itself and refine the filter further to show only folders or collections that match what you type. For example, if I want to see only folders with the yellow color label applied whose names include the word *falls,* I can use the filter to show precisely that and nothing else (refer to Figure 6-7).

FIGURE 6-7:
Filter the contents of the Folders panel to show only what you want.

My example and the corresponding figure show the Folders panel, but the filter in the Collections panel works in the same exact way. One way I've seen other people use these filters is when visiting with a client: They filter each panel to show only work that's relevant to that client while temporarily hiding everything else. To clear each filter, click the Magnifying Glass icon again, choose All from the menu, and then delete any text you typed into the field to restore all content back into view.

Filenames and Metadata

With every shutter click, your digital camera creates a file, assigns it a name, and embeds all the settings used to make the capture into the file's metadata space. When you begin to work with your photos, you want to add additional custom metadata (such as your contact information) to your files. When doing so, you might discover that the camera-generated filenames don't particularly fit your needs. Lightroom Classic has an excellent set of tools to aid you in managing this aspect of your portfolio.

As described in Chapter 4, you can both rename and apply custom metadata during the Import process. However, that doesn't fit everyone's workflow. For some, the Import process is just getting photos off the memory card as quickly as possible, and everything else can come later. For others, it only makes sense to apply a minimal amount of custom metadata at import and then complete the job after the first round of edits — so that time isn't wasted working on files destined for the trash heap. Similarly, you might want to wait to rename all photos until after you remove the duds so that you don't end up with any gaps in the filenames. Lightroom Classic allows for a flexible approach.

Batch renaming with filename templates

After you import your photos into Lightroom Classic, it's in your best interest to perform all your renaming tasks from within Lightroom Classic because Lightroom Classic stores each file's name in its catalog. If you were to rename files outside of Lightroom Classic, the data in the catalog wouldn't match the new names, and Lightroom Classic then would consider those files missing or offline. Though it *is* possible to reconnect Lightroom Classic to the newly named files, doing so is an onerous task that I wouldn't wish on anyone. I can't tell you how many times I've seen people do this. Please don't fall into that trap!

Thankfully, the renaming function within Lightroom Classic is powerful, extremely configurable, and easy to use. Lightroom Classic comes installed with a number of filenaming templates that you can use as is, or you can create custom templates to fit your needs (as explained in Chapter 4). Each filenaming template is composed of *tokens* — little widgets that represent a chunk of data used to build the filename. These tokens include things like custom text, date/time values, sequence numbers, metadata elements, and parts of the original filename. As shown in Chapter 4, these tokens are assembled and arranged with Lightroom Classic's Filename Template Editor. Here's how to rename a batch of photos with a template you choose:

1. **Select the photos you want to rename from Grid view.**

2. **Choose Library ⇨ Rename Photos from the menu (or press F2).**

   The Rename Photos dialog appears.

3. **Choose a template (or create one) from the File Naming drop-down menu.**

Note that if your template includes custom text, you must enter that text before proceeding to the next step.

4. **Click OK to apply that template to the selected photos.**

REMEMBER

Keep in mind that renaming photos in Lightroom Classic renames the actual photos on your drive.

Creating metadata templates to embed information into each image

The Metadata panel, located on the right side of the Library module, (see Figure 6-8) is useful for displaying any metadata embedded in an image, but you can also use it to add new metadata, edit some existing metadata, or access other photos that share common data points. Because so much data about each photo can be displayed, the Metadata panel has a number of different view options accessible via the drop-down menu in the panel's header. This enables you to pick a view that shows only the type of metadata you're interested in, which makes work much easier.

FIGURE 6-8:
The Metadata panel, set to Default view.

Within the Default view of the Metadata panel, you have the ability to configure which metadata fields are visible, as well as their order within the panel. Click the Customize button to open the Customize Metadata Default Panel dialog, as shown in Figure 6-9. Here you can select the check box next to any field you want included in the Default view or deselect the box next to fields you don't want to see. There are a lot of potential fields to include, so be sure to scroll down to see the entire list. Note that including a large number of fields can impact performance, so go easy.

If you want to customize the display order of your selections after you have made them, click the Arrange button to open the Arrange Metadata Default Panel dialog (see Figure 6-10). Simply click the field's label and drag-and-drop it into the order you want to see the fields appear within the Metadata panel, and then click Save to accept your changes and close all dialogs. If you don't want to customize the display order, you can click the Done button on the Customize Metadata Default Panel to accept your changes and close the dialog.

The Preset drop-down menu at the top of the panel gives you access to your custom metadata templates — as well as the controls to create *new* templates. Any templates you've created via the Import dialog are also accessible here. To create a new metadata template, follow these steps:

1. **Choose Edit Presets from the Preset drop-down menu.**

   The Edit Metadata Presets dialog appears, and looks the same as the New Metadata Preset dialog you see in Chapter 4 during import. You can also access this dialog by choosing Metadata ⇨ Edit Metadata Presets from the main menu.

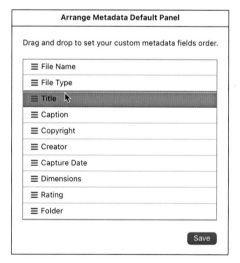

FIGURE 6-10:
The Arrange Metadata Default Panel.

2. **Complete all applicable fields.**

Depending on your needs, you can complete as much or as little of the dialog before saving it as a template.

3. **Choose Save Current Settings as New Preset from the Preset drop-down menu.**

Doing so launches the New Preset dialog.

4. **Enter a name in the Preset Name field and click Create.**

The name of the preset appears on the editor's Preset drop-down menu.

5. **Click Done to close the editor.**

You can apply a preset by selecting your photos in Grid view and then selecting a preset from the Metadata panel's Preset drop-down menu. Lightroom Classic prompts you with the Apply Metadata Preset dialog, where you can choose to apply the preset to just the active photo (meaning the selected photo with the brightest highlighted thumbnail) or to all selected photos. Select the Don't show again check box if you don't want to be prompted in the future. (The choice you make becomes the default behavior when the prompt is turned off.)

If you have multiple photos selected, you may notice the words *Target Photo* become highlighted within the Metadata panel (below the Preset drop-down menu, in Figure 6-8). This means that any metadata you enter into the panel will be applied to only the active photo selected. However, if you want to add the same metadata to all selected photos, click the Selected Photos label to enable that capability. Just be aware of which label is highlighted when applying metadata so that you don't accidentally apply things to only the most selected photo.

Additionally, you can click the Eyeball icon at the top of the Metadata panel to enter Edit Only mode, which hides fields that aren't editable (and the icon changes to a page with a pencil). Click the icon again to reveal all fields.

Keywording

I don't know anyone who loves the task of adding keywords to their photos, but I also don't know anyone who isn't glad to have well-keyworded photos when it comes time to find them. *Keywording* is your chance to describe the contents of your photos with words that aid you in finding them. By doing so, the words you use form a structure of their own inside your catalog. If you're thorough and consistent in the application of keywords, you'll reach a point where you can find all photos of a given subject with just a click (or two).

Although it's possible (and often helpful) to start keywording at import, you'll find the Library module is where you do most of your keywording activities. Both the Keywording panel and the Keyword List panel have supporting roles in this process.

The Keywording panel, shown in Figure 6-11, is made up of these three sections:

>> **Keyword Tags:** The top section of the panel, Keyword Tags, provides a means to enter new keywords and to display the applied keywords of a selected photo. Use the Keyword Tags drop-down menu to access other options for displaying keywords.

>> **Keyword Suggestions:** While you add keywords to your photos, Lightroom Classic begins generating a list of suggested keywords based on other photos that have similar keywords applied to them. Click any suggested keyword to add it to the selected photo.

>> **Keyword Set:** This section is another keyword-entry aid. You can create an unlimited number of keyword sets of up to nine keywords in each. Lightroom Classic comes installed with three common sets that you can use or modify to fit your needs. Holding the Option key (Alt key on Windows) reveals the keyboard shortcuts for each word in the set. This makes for speedy keywording by selecting photos and pressing Option+number. Use the Keyword Set drop-down menu to access an existing set, or choose Edit Set to create a new one.

The Keyword List panel, shown in Figure 6-12, consists of the following elements:

>> **Add/Remove keywords buttons:** Click the + or – buttons in the Keyword List header to add or remove keywords.

FIGURE 6-11:
The Keywording panel.

FIGURE 6-12:
The Keyword List panel.

>> **Filter Keywords:** Your keyword list can grow quite large. Enter a word (or part of a word) in the Filter Keywords field to display the keywords containing only that word (or part of that word). The disclosure triangle at the end hides/shows additional filter options by keyword type. (You can find more on People keywords in Chapter 7.)

>> **The master list of keywords:** The master list of keywords holds all the keywords you've created in Lightroom Classic or that were imported along with photos that had been keyworded in another application before being imported into Lightroom Classic. Additionally, if you've enabled the automatic addition of keywords to Enhanced images on the File Handling tab of the preferences (described in Chapter 3), you see an Enhanced parent keyword appear in the list after using the Enhance feature, which is covered in Chapter 7.

Adding and organizing keywords

You can add keywords to selected photos in the Library module in a number of ways:

>> **Drag selected photos onto a keyword in the Keyword List panel.**

>> **Drag selected keywords onto selected photos.**

>> **Select photo(s) and enter keywords via the Keywording panel.**

>> **Use the Painter tool (see the section "Using the Painter Tool," later in this chapter).**

You can't say Lightroom Classic doesn't give you choices! Just to narrow down the realm of possibilities, though, I walk you through *one* way — creating and applying a keyword in the same step:

1. **Select a photo to keyword from Grid view.**

In this example, I use a photo of my dog, Niko (see Figure 6-13).

2. **Expand the Keywording panel, and then click into the smaller field at the top.**

Always use this field to add new keywords so that you don't accidentally delete keywords that appear in the larger field as you go.

3. **Enter a keyword and press Enter.**

In this example, I simply type **dog** and press Enter.

FIGURE 6-13:
Applying
keywords to
a photo using
the Keyword-
ing panel.

At its most basic level, that's all there is to it (of course, you can repeat that process and add as many keywords as you feel are needed). The keyword *dog* has been applied to the photo, and the keyword will appear in the Keyword List panel (or the photo will be applied to the existing keyword, if applicable). If I have another dog photo, I can drag the photo onto the keyword (or vice versa) to apply the keyword to the photo. Alternatively, if I prefer to type the keyword, I can repeat the previous steps; however, as soon as I type **d,** Lightroom Classic kicks into Autocomplete mode and displays possibilities from my keyword list that I can then choose from, as shown in Figure 6-14.

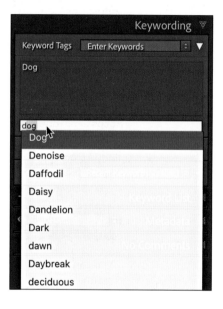

FIGURE 6-14:
Keyword autocomplete example.

You can assign multiple keywords to selected photos by entering them into the active field in the Keywording panel, separating each word with a comma. For example, I could also type **pets, autumn, Niko** and then press Enter. As more keywords are added to each photo, they appear in the Keyword List panel.

TIP

As you can imagine, the Keyword List panel keeps growing as each new word is added, so much so that, pretty soon, it becomes rather unwieldy. To maximize the effectiveness of your keywords, you might want to consider arranging them into a hierarchical structure that adds both additional meaning and organization to your keyword list.

To put your existing keywords into some kind of order, you can drag-and-drop keywords onto each other, which puts them into a parent/child relationship. For example, I originally added *autumn, dog, pets,* and *Niko* to the photo shown in Figure 6-13. If I want to start building a structure with those words, I'd probably select *dog* in the Keyword List panel and drag it to *pets.* (I'm such a logical guy.) After releasing *dog,* it's nested under *pets,* and so on. Years ago, I purchased a premade keyword list of thousands of words (from `https://` `controlledvocabulary.com`), as shown in Figure 6-15, that has helped me with my work, but may be overkill for some people. You can import a plain-text keyword list like that one by choosing the Metadata ⇨ Import Keywords command. You can find free keyword lists at `https://lightroom-keyword-list-project.blogspot.com`.

FIGURE 6-15:
Nested keyword structure.

Rather than create your structure after you add words to your photos, you can reverse the process and create the structure first. This gives you the benefit of thinking about how you want to arrange your keywords beforehand and generally leads to a much more thorough keywording process. The Keyword List panel provides the tools to aid you in the creation of new keywords. For example, to continue building on the *pets* structure, I might want to add the keyword *cat* and nest it underneath *pets* in anticipation of future cat photos. Here's how:

1. **Select the parent keyword.**

   In this case, I selected *pets* because I want to add *cat* as a child keyword.

2. **Click the + symbol at the top of the Keyword panel to open the Create Keyword Tag dialog, shown in Figure 6-16.**

3. **Enter the keyword in the Keyword Name field.**

4. **Enter any synonyms.**

   Separate each synonym with a comma. Synonyms aren't searchable inside Lightroom Classic, but they can be included as a keyword in exported copies.

5. **Note that the Put Inside check box is selected because I selected "pets" first.**

FIGURE 6-16:
The Create
Keyword Tag
dialog.

6. **Make sure the Add to Selected Photos box is deselected.**

In this case, I'm adding a keyword in anticipation of a future photo, not adding a keyword to any photos I have selected, so I deselect this option. Of course, you can select it if you want to apply it as part of the process.

7. **Select the Include on Export check box.**

If you want this keyword included in the exported copies, you need to select this box. If you just want the keyword to exist as an organizational aid in your catalog (such as a high-level category heading), leave this box deselected.

8. **Check the Export Containing Keywords box.**

The parent keyword will also export. In this case, I want to ensure that *pets* exports as a keyword along with *cat.*

9. **Select the Export Synonyms check box.**

10. **Click Create.**

My new keyword, *cat,* is now added to the Keyword List panel under *pets.* The process is the same for adding other new keywords while you flesh out a keyword structure.

Using the Keyword List to find photos

Now that you've added a few keywords and begun creating an organizational structure, you can use the Keyword List panel to jump directly to a group of photos that share the same keyword. Figure 6-17 shows the Keyword List panel with my dog photo selected. Notice that the keywords *pets* and *dog* have a check mark next to them in the Keyword List. Those check marks identify all keywords applied to the selected photo. Also, notice that the cursor is hovering over the *dog* keyword in the list.

I want you to know about two important options:

» **The check mark inside a box:** When you move the cursor over any keyword, you see a check box appear. Deselecting a keyword removes it from the selected photo. Adding a check mark applies that keyword to the selected photo.

FIGURE 6-17:
The Keyword List panel, showing explicitly and implicitly applied keywords.

» **The right-facing arrow next to the counter:** Clicking that arrow applies a Library filter that displays only the photos in the catalog that have that same keyword. Click None in the Library Filter to turn off the filter.

In my case, I have a large hierarchical keyword list, and you can see an em dash (—) next to *mammal*, *animals*, and *Keywords* in the list. That mark means those keywords are implied by virtue of their children keywords *pets* and *dog* being explicitly applied. That means, because I explicitly applied the keyword *dog,* my photo also gained *mammal* and *animals*, which is a real time-saver.

Before we move on to the often-mentioned Library Filter bar, there's one more cool tool I want to introduce you to that will make adding all these various types of flags, metadata, and keywords a lot more fun.

Using the Painter Tool

The Painter tool is the little Spray Can icon on the Grid view Toolbar. You can use the icon to apply keywords, labels, flags, ratings, metadata, Develop settings (the same Develop presets you saw in the Quick Develop panel), or photo rotations. You can even use it to assign a photo to a specific collection. It's quite simple to use if you prefer a more hands-on approach to adding the same piece of information to a large group of photos.

As a way to introduce you to a growing world of Lightroom Classic content I write besides this book, I invite you to learn more about the Painter tool by heading to the Lightroom blog I contribute to at `https://lightroomkillertips.com/ painting-photos-information`.

Finding Photos with the Library Filter Bar

Okay, you've invested a lot of time in managing your portfolio, so you may as well take a look at one of the ways you can start to get a return on that investment. Let me officially introduce you to the Library Filter bar, shown in Figure 6-18. The Library Filter is visible above the thumbnails only in Grid view. The Library Filter bar display can be toggled on and off by pressing the backslash (\) key. This doesn't turn off any active filter; it just hides the bar to maximize the content area. Filtering is turned on and off by pressing ⌘+L (Ctrl+L in Windows) or by clicking None on the Filter bar.

FIGURE 6-18:
The Library
Filter bar.

The Library Filter bar allows you to drill down into your portfolio as follows:

>> **Searching text fields:** It isn't limited to searching by keyword; you can search on filenames and metadata fields as well.

>> **By status indicators:** Clicking Attribute reveals the options for refining your view using flags, export status, edit status, ratings, labels, and virtual copy status.

>> **Leveraging metadata:** Enabling the Metadata filter opens worlds of possibilities for gathering photos based on information about, or embedded in, each file, such as capture date, file type, aspect ratio, shutter speed, location, camera used, and more!

Filters can be used singly or in multiple mix-and-match combinations. I could have a hankering, say, for all TIF files with the keyword *flower* that were taken with my (very) old D200 and that have a rating of two stars or greater.

TIP

For a deep dive into filtering what you can see, check out my article on that topic: `https://lightroomkillertips.com/a-look-at-filtering`.

Chapter **7**

Exploring the Library Module's Advanced Features

Although the Library module is packed with tasks primarily focused on managing your photo library over time, it does have a few additional superpowers you'll want to know about so that you can leverage them when the time comes. This chapter covers those, and wraps up with a look at the Map module, because its functions can help you organize and find your photos by location.

People View

If you're like me, you have photos of people in your Lightroom Classic catalog. Wouldn't it be great to finally get names assigned to all the people in your photos so that you can find them easier down the road? Fortunately, Lightroom Classic has a facial recognition function that can churn through all your photos to look for faces and then group similar faces together for you to name. Let's look at how it works.

Finding faces

You can jump into People view, as shown in Figure 7-1, by clicking its icon on the Toolbar or pressing the O key while in the Library module.

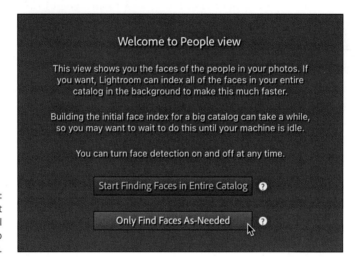

FIGURE 7-1:
You must enable facial recognition to begin.

As you can imagine, the process of examining all your photos is resource-intensive. The more photos you ask it to process, the longer it takes, and you may not want it to run while you're trying to do other work in Lightroom Classic. I suggest starting small by working on one folder at a time until you get a feel for what's happening. When you first enter People view, you see the welcome message, and I recommend clicking Only Find Faces As-Needed so that it only churns through the folder or collection you're currently viewing when switching to People view. If you ever decide you want Lightroom Classic to examine your entire catalog, open the Catalog Settings dialog, choose the Metadata tab, and then select Automatically detect faces in all photos. You can pause/resume face detection via the Activity Monitor, hidden in the ID plate.

Once enabled, Lightroom Classic starts to find what it thinks are faces and then groups similar faces together. These appear in the Unnamed People section, as shown in Figure 7-2, with question marks underneath them.

As cool as this technology is, it isn't always perfect and needs our help to finish the job.

FIGURE 7-2:
Faces are
being found.

Tagging faces with names

Once you have some faces showing, you can start to tag the faces with their names. You can also remove any mistakes the facial recognition process makes and even manually assign face tags to photos that got missed by the automated process. The tags you apply to faces are similar to the keywords I discuss in Chapter 6, except that they're called *Person Keywords* (to make it easier to strip them out during export). Over time, as Lightroom Classic learns who is who, it pulls from the Person Keywords you create to suggest names for faces.

I walk you through a basic workflow to get you started, but feel free to improve on my suggestions to tailor the process to your needs (note that all names used here are fictional for privacy reasons):

1. **Select a folder you want to process, and press O to enter People view.**

2. **Create a parent tag to contain all your people tags.**

   While Lightroom is churning away, you can keep your Keyword List panel tidy by nesting your people tags under one parent. I created a new keyword tag, named People, and disabled all export options in the Create Keyword Tag dialog (refer to Chapter 6 for a refresher on creating keywords). Then right-click that tag and choose Put New Person Keywords Inside This Keyword from the contextual menu (you'll see an asterisk on that tag).

3. **Add Person Keywords to unnamed photos by clicking the question mark (?) under photos.**

I decided to use a [*Last Name*] [*First Name*] convention for my person keywords to keep people with the same last name grouped together in my list, but use what works for you. The name you add appears under the parent Person Keyword you created in the previous step, and it begins suggesting that name on faces it thinks are that person.

4. **Approve names for correctly identified people.**

As soon as you've added a few names, Lightroom Classic starts suggesting names for faces it thinks you've identified. It isn't 100 percent accurate, so you need to manually approve each suggestion, as shown in Figure 7-3. Enter the correct name for any mismatches to keep Lightroom Classic learning.

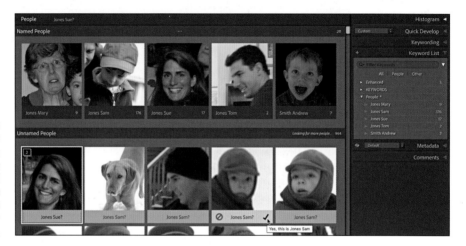

FIGURE 7-3: Sometimes Lightroom Classic gets it right, and sometimes it confuses someone for the dog.

5. **Speed things up by dragging a selection of unnamed faces onto the correctly named face.**

Hold down ⌘ (Ctrl on Windows) and click all faces of the same person in the Unnamed People section to select them; then drag-and-drop them on the correctly named person in the Named People section to apply that name in one go.

6. **Verify that all faces were found, and manually add face regions if needed.**

Once you've successfully tagged all the people in the current view, you should verify that no one got missed. Double-click the first thumbnail in the Filmstrip to see the entire photo along with the face regions Lightroom Classic assigned, as shown in Figure 7-4. Use the arrow keys to advance through the photos.

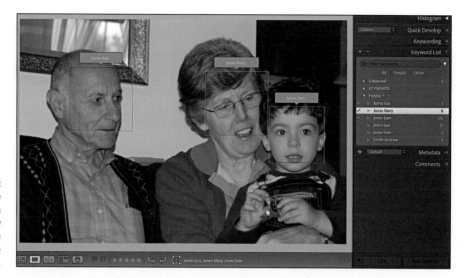

FIGURE 7-4:
Viewing the full photo in People view shows you the assigned face region.

7. **Draw face regions for any faces that were missed.**

If you find a photo where a face was missed, or if you just want to manually assign a Person Keyword to a nonperson photo (such as one of your dog), you can draw out a region anywhere on the photo and then assign a Person Keyword to it, as shown in Figure 7-5. The Draw Face Region tool is active when entering this view, so just click-and-drag to draw a region. You can also select an existing face region and delete it if it's a misfire. **Note:** Manually drawn face regions aren't factored into the algorithm Lightroom Classic uses to learn faces.

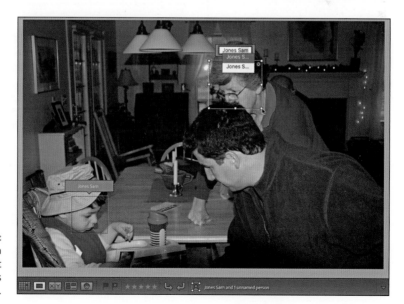

FIGURE 7-5:
You can draw out face regions manually.

This process gets easier and easier the more you use it, but you definitely want to start small.

Adjusting Your Photos in the Library

Although not intended to take the place of the Develop module, the combination of the Histogram and the Quick Develop panels in the Library module can provide valuable information about your photos and allow for tweaks that can further inform your selection process. Quick Develop panel adjustments can be applied while in Grid, Loupe, Survey, or Compare view.

Considering the Histogram

A *histogram,* in the digital photo world, is a graph representing all the tones in a selected photo. The left side of the graph represents the darker tones, and the right side represents the lighter. In the Lightroom Classic interface, the Histogram panel has a place of honor — first position — on the right.

The bottom of the Histogram panel displays the ISO, focal length, aperture, and shutter speed of the active photo to aid in that photo's evaluation. With all this information, you can use the tools on the Quick Develop panel to make adjustments without leaving the Library module. You see more about it when I cover the Develop module in Chapter 8.

Making adjustments with Quick Develop

The default rendering of your raw photos may not always be enough to judge the potential of a given photo. Perhaps a photo was slightly underexposed, or perhaps the wrong white balance was selected in-camera. Those issues (among others) can be corrected relatively quickly and should not be the cause for tossing out an otherwise good photo. The Quick Develop panel, shown in Figure 7-6, gives you the tools to do some quick rehab work, and contains three subsections that can be collapsed or expanded by clicking the (difficult to see) arrow at the top of each subsection:

>> **Saved Preset:** This one provides quick access to all Develop presets while also letting you crop to any aspect ratio and switch between color and B&W.

>> **White Balance:** White balance is the setting that compensates for the color of the light used to capture the scene so that subjects appear in the photo the

way our eyes see them (our brains do this for us automatically). **Note:** The White Balance preset options are different for raw photos and rendered photos (JPG, PNG, TIFF, and PSD files). When working with raw data, an absolute white balance hasn't been "cooked" into the pixels, so it's possible to switch the absolute white balance value as needed. However, all rendered photos have a white-balance value applied to the pixels when the file is created, so all future white-balance adjustments are relative. When working with a rendered file, your White Balance preset choices are As Shot, Auto, and Custom.

» **Tone Control:** This final subsection contains all the adjustments affecting the tonal range of the photo.

FIGURE 7-6:
The Quick Develop panel, with all subsections expanded.

TIP

The Reset All button at the bottom of the panel removes *all* adjustment settings, including any adjustments made in the Develop module. However, you can reset any single Quick Develop adjustment by double-clicking the label of that adjustment.

You can apply adjustments to the active photo while in Loupe, Survey, or Compare view. When in Grid view, any adjustments you make are applied to all selected photos (not just the active photo). This "one fell swoop" approach is not only handy during the evaluation process but also a real timesaver when you want to apply the same adjustment to a lot of photos.

TIP

A good example of a bulk application of the Quick Develop panel is applying a new aspect ratio to a group of selected photos in Grid view. Here's how:

1. **Press G to jump to Grid view.**

2. **Select all the photos you want to crop to the new aspect ratio.**

3. **Expand the Saved Preset section of the Quick Develop panel.**

4. **Select an aspect ratio from the Crop Ratio drop-down menu.**

You see the thumbnails of the selected photos change to reflect the new crop ratio. When you apply the crop in this manner, you center the crop in each photo. Press R to jump to the Crop tool to tweak each crop for best composition. (I cover the Develop module's Crop tool in detail in Chapter 9.) The benefit of starting from the Quick Develop panel is that the aspect ratio is already set when you enter the Crop tool, which greatly speeds the process.

Along the same lines, if you adjust a single photo (whether using Quick Develop or the Develop module) and want to apply the same settings to multiple photos, you can use the Sync Settings button, located at the bottom of the right panel group. Here's how:

1. **Press G to jump to Grid view.**

2. **Select the adjusted photo first.**

3. **Select the other photos you want to sync with the same settings.**

4. **Click the Sync Settings button.**

   Doing so launches the Synchronize Settings dialog, shown in Figure 7-7.

FIGURE 7-7:
The Synchronize Settings dialog.

5. **Select only the check boxes that correspond to the settings you want to apply to the other photos.**

6. **Click Synchronize.**

You see all the thumbnails of the selected photos update to reflect the newly applied settings from the first photo.

Merging Photos into HDR and Panos

One of my favorite features in Lightroom Classic is the ability to merge multiple raw photos into High Dynamic Range (HDR) images, panoramic (pano) images, or even HDR panos. The resulting merged file contains the cumulative data from the individual captures saved in the DNG format. What's DNG, you ask? Well, we'll dive into it later on, but it's essentially Adobe's version of a raw file format. This means if your original photos captured for the merge operation are all raw files, the resulting merged photo contains all that raw goodness when it comes to editing (such as changing the camera profile or white balance).

The key step in each situation is that you captured the set of photos with the intention of merging them later in your software. Discussing the capture of each type of these photos is beyond the scope of this book, but a simple Google search will yield a dizzying array of tutorials on the topic (check your camera manual, too). So go out and create a few of each type; then come on back and we'll delve into how the merge function works.

Photo Merge to HDR

HDR photos often get a bad reputation due to how surreal they have looked in the past. I think the editing pendulum has swung in the other direction, because it's now possible to make extremely natural-looking HDR photos using the Merge to HDR function in Lightroom Classic. By *natural,* I just mean photographs that contain a lot more shadow and highlight detail than a single exposure can contain, just as our own human eyes are able to see.

This function can work with exposure-bracketed JPG photos, but you ideally want to shoot in raw mode to capture more data, which in turn provides more data for the final HDR image. You need at least two photos with different exposures to combine into the single HDR image. You can use more than two, but one benefit of using only two photos is that there is likely to be less movement of objects (like blowing branches) between fewer photos. You can use more exposures if that is what's needed to contain all the shadow to highlight information. With at least two photos selected, do the following:

1. Starting in either the Library or Develop module, choose Photo ⇨ Photo Merge ⇨ HDR.

I prefer to start in Library because it's easier to select the correct photos. You can also access the Photo Merge menu from the right-click contextual menu.

This step opens the HDR Merge Preview window (see Figure 7-8).

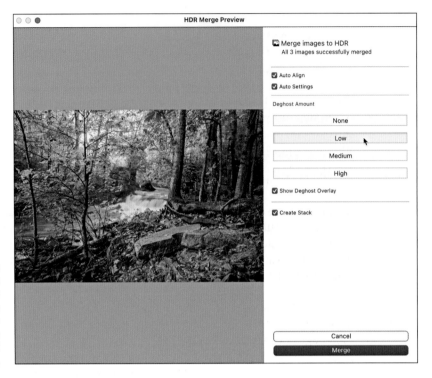

FIGURE 7-8:
The HDR Merge Preview dialog. The red overlay shows where deghosting will happen.

2. **(Optional) Select the Auto Align, Auto Settings, and Create Stack check boxes.**

These are optional but useful settings to consider. Auto Align automatically aligns all the photos and crops out uneven edges, which is critical for the HDR merge to work. Auto Settings is a *nondestructive* way (meaning you can change it later) to automatically adjust exposure settings (more on this in Chapter 8). Create Stack stacks the source photos with the final HDR image to declutter the view of the folder.

3. **Select one of the Deghost Amount options if the source photos include an object that moved from one photo to the next (such as moving clouds or swaying branches).**

Deghosting works by filling in the area of movement with the information from just one photo rather than a merged composite from all frames. If the movement is slight, try the Low setting; use a higher setting if that doesn't resolve the problem. Select the Show Deghost Overlay check box to see the affected areas in the image in a red overlay.

4. **Click the Merge button to begin the process of merging the photos into one DNG file.**

Once this button is clicked, you see the progress meter in the upper left corner. The merged result has -HDR appended to the end of the filename. If you chose the stacking option, it appears at the top of the stack.

That's all there is to it. You can select the HDR image and press the D key to head to Develop to edit the photo, just like you would any other raw photo. Because it's raw, you can apply a camera profile, change white balance, and apply lens corrections, and you'll notice the Exposure slider now has a range of +/− 10 stops (compared to the +/− 5 stops of a non-HDR image). I talk more about the Develop module in Chapters 8 through 10.

Recently, Adobe added the ability to edit and export in HDR to Lightroom Classic. Though you could previously edit HDR photos, you could only do so using Standard Dynamic Range (SDR) tools (and you can still do this the same way if your hardware doesn't support this new tech). This new functionality is for customers who are using new HDR-compatible displays, which are not yet widespread.

For example, my new MacBook Pro laptop is HDR compatible, but my desktop display is not. If you do not yet have a compatible HDR display, you cannot take advantage of this new capability. It's still pretty early in the adoption of HDR displays (though most new mobile devices are likely to be HDR compatible). I appreciate Adobe's effort to stay ahead of the curve on this technology, but because my main computer display isn't compatible, I'm not using it. I will continue to edit my HDR photos the same way I edit my non-HDR photos, but will definitely keep HDR compatibility in mind the next time I update my desktop display.

TIP

To learn more about this new technology, the minimum system requirements, and recommended HDR displays, check out Adobe's Help page on HDR editing and output: https://helpx.adobe.com/lightroom-classic/help/hdr-output.html.

After you get a handle on the settings, you may find that you don't need to see that dialog each time you want to merge. To start the merging process without opening the HDR Merge Preview dialog, select the photos for the merge and press Shift+Control+H (the same keys on both operating systems). This applies the last settings used. The progress meter indicates when the process has started. You can queue up multiple Merge to HDR processes this way.

Photo Merge to Panorama

As with Merge to HDR, the coolest part of the Merge to Panorama function in Lightroom Classic is that it can merge raw photos into a final pano that is also raw. This feature has opened whole new worlds of capturing very high-resolution raw photos composed of multiple individual frames. Yes, you can create the conventional very long horizontal panoramic views, but you can also create vertical panoramas, or even a very high-resolution wide field of view. For example, I once created a 137-megapixel raw photo by merging 60 individual frames using this function. Search using your favorite Internet search engine for tutorials on how best to capture images for a panorama merge. When you're ready, select the photos you captured for the panorama merge and follow these steps:

1. **Starting in either the Library or Develop module, choose Photo ⇨ Photo Merge ⇨ Panorama.**

   I prefer to start in Library because it's easier to select the correct photos. You can also access the Photo Merge menu from the right-click contextual menu. Note for future use the keyboard shortcut that appears on the menu.

   This opens the Panorama Merge Preview window (see Figure 7-9).

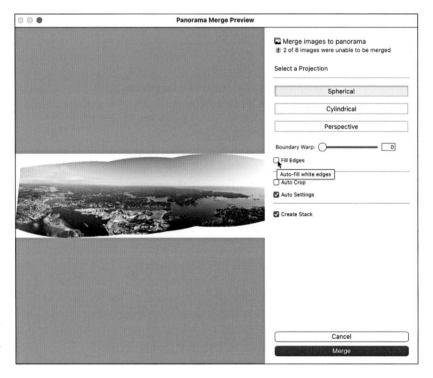

FIGURE 7-9:
The Panorama Merge Preview dialog.

2. **(Optional) Select the Auto Crop, Auto Settings, and Create Stack check boxes.**

   These settings are optional, but they're useful settings to consider. Auto Crop crops out empty areas around the edges of the final image. Auto Settings is a *nondestructive* way (meaning you can change it later) to automatically adjust exposure settings (more on this in Chapter 8). Create Stack stacks the source photos with the final Panorama image to declutter the view of the folder.

3. **Choose a projection method.**

   Lightroom Classic creates the final image by mapping the frames using one of the three projection options. Using Spherical (a good choice for most merges), the individual frames are mapped onto the inside of a sphere, where they are then aligned and blended together. The Perspective option maps to a flat surface, which is good for keeping straight lines straight (such as in buildings). The Cylindrical option maps to the inside of a cylinder and does a good job of keeping vertical lines straight (try for really wide panoramas). You can click each one to see a live preview and then choose the one that looks best. I usually stick to Spherical.

4. **(Optional) Use Boundary Warp and/or Fill Edges.**

   Instead of using Auto Crop (or in conjunction with using it), try using the Boundary Warp function to warp the image to fill the empty areas around the edges. The higher the value, the more the image is warped to fill the space, so there's no single correct answer. Alternatively, or in addition, select the Fill Edges check box to have Lightroom Classic create new pixels based on the surrounding pixels to fill in remaining white areas around the edges. Refer to Figure 7-9, before I used Boundary Warp a little and will use Fill Edges to finish the job.

5. **Click the Merge button to begin the process of merging the photos into one DNG file.**

   Once this button is clicked, you see the progress meter in the upper left corner. The merged result has –Pano appended to the end of the filename. If you chose the stacking option, it appears at the top of the stack.

Once the merged result appears, you can head off to the Develop module to edit just as you would any other raw photo. You don't need to edit the individual images before merging into the panorama.

As with the Merge to HDR process, once you get a handle on the settings, you might find that you don't need to see that dialog each time you want to merge. To start the merging process without opening the Panorama Merge Preview dialog, just select the photos for the merge and press Shift+Control+M (the same keys on both operating systems). Lightroom Classic applies the last settings used, and you see the progress meter when the process has started. You can queue up multiple merge-to-panorama processes this way.

Photo Merge to HDR Panorama

Now, you might be thinking, "What if I shot the individual frames of the panorama as a bracketed exposure so that I could use all the images to create an HDR pano?" You'd be in luck! The Merge to HDR Panorama option takes all the goodness of the previous two options and gives you the ability to select an entire set of photos captured with the intention of creating a panoramic HDR final raw photo.

You do need to capture this set of photos with this intention, though: This means that each bracketed set of photos must contain the same number of photos (three exposures is usually enough), each bracket should have the same +/− exposure offset (+/− 1 stop is often enough), and the entire set needs to be captured one after the other. So, before you press the shutter for the first photo of your panorama, dial in your autoexposure bracketing amount, capture the first frame of the pano as an HDR bracket before rotating the camera to capture the second frame of the pano, and so on, until all frames of the panorama are captured.

Back in Lightroom Classic, select all the individual frames of the HDR panorama and choose Photo ⇨ Photo Merge ⇨ HDR Panorama to open the HDR Panorama Merge Preview window. It looks the same as the Panorama Merge Preview window shown earlier, in Figure 7-9.

It should be no surprise that this dialog looks just like the Merge to Panorama window, because it does require the same options. On the HDR side, deghosting is set to Off, so if your HDR brackets do require deghosting, you should merge the HDR brackets separately, and then you can funnel the merged HDR results into the regular merge-to-panorama function. Otherwise, follow the same steps as I outline previously for the Merge to Panorama option. The final merged result is a single DNG file, ready to be edited in Develop.

Enhance with machine learning

Wouldn't it be cool if Lightroom Classic had a way to leverage the power of software magic to improve image quality, remove noise, and even increase the pixel dimensions of your photos? Good news: It does! Adobe utilized machine learning, a branch of artificial intelligence, which is a technology Adobe used to train algorithms (using millions of photos) to give us these tools. You can access this cool technology from the Photo menu, or by right-clicking a photo and choosing Enhance. (You can also access the Denoise function from the Detail panel of the Develop module.) This opens the Enhance Preview window, shown in Figure 7-10.

FIGURE 7-10:
The Enhance
Preview dialog.

Three options are available, depending on the file type of the selected photo, to choose from within Enhance, as shown in Figure 7-10. The first, called Denoise, does an amazing job of reducing/removing noise from a photo (only raw photos for now). I use this feature frequently on high ISO photos where the preexisting noise reduction tools are unable to remove enough noise without damaging detail. This is my favorite aspect of Enhance, and the default settings are a good start.

Raw Details, is, as the name suggests, for raw photos only. If you have a non-raw photo selected (like JPG, PSD, TIF, or PNG), that option is unavailable. Raw Details was originally called Enhance Details when first released, and as that name implies, its singular function was to create a copy (with the same pixel dimensions) of the selected raw photo with improved detail edge contrast, improved color, and fewer artifacts than the original. In my own testing, the improved results were minor, and it isn't a feature I have found useful in my own workflow. However, your results will depend on the camera used to capture the photo, and I encourage you to explore how it works with your own photos, especially any that you plan to print at a large size. It's automatically included with Denoise and Super Resolution.

REMEMBER

You cannot run Denoise and Super Resolution at the same time.

The third option, called Super Resolution, creates a copy of the selected photo, raw and nonraw alike, that has pixel dimensions twice as long in both height and width of the original photo. In other words, the pixel dimensions of the copy created by Super Resolution is four times larger than the original. This can be useful for instances where you need to severely crop into a photo when you can't physically get closer to your subject or zoom in closer with your lens, or for simply enlarging the original photo to be printed at a larger size. The better the quality of the original, the better your final results will be, but I've been pretty impressed with the results so far. If you start with a raw photo, the Raw Details function is also applied when using Super Resolution, for even better results.

The copy created using either Denoise, Raw Details, or Super Resolution will have the word *Enhanced* appended to the copy's filename (along with two letters signifying which of the three functions was used), and it will have the DNG file extension. If any of the options is unavailable, the selected photo likely isn't supported for that function. Refer to Adobe's Help page for additional information, system requirements, and supported file types: `https://helpx.adobe.com/lightroom-classic/help/enhance-details.html`.

What Is DNG?

As I mention earlier in this chapter, DNG is Adobe's file format for raw image data. In case you're unsure, DNG is an openly documented file format for holding raw data. Because the format is openly documented (unlike the proprietary raw file formats), third-party software developers can support the format (some do, some don't). This openly documented aspect is also valuable for those looking for an archival solution that lasts decades into the future. DNG creates an internal `checksum` value that can be used to validate the integrity of the image data, which is another key benefit. I've mentioned some advantages, so let's get the main disadvantages to converting to DNG out of the way. If you convert to DNG:

>> You may not be able to open DNG files in some non-Adobe image editing software.

>> You may have problems with certain photo competitions if your camera has no native DNG creation (always read the contest fine print).

>> You may not feel it's worth the time to convert to DNG.

Trade-offs are involved in every decision you make in photography, and this is just one more of those decisions you must evaluate against your own needs and circumstances. There is no single correct answer.

Types of DNG

You can create two basic types of DNG files in Lightroom Classic. One uses a lossless compression algorithm (best-quality option), and the other uses a lossy compression algorithm (similar to JPG compression). The key difference between these options is that, with the lossy compression option, you can create a DNG file that's smaller in file size than with the lossless compression. In addition, with the lossy compression option, you gain the option of resizing the pixel dimensions smaller as part of the process.

The lossless compression type of DNG is the one that has been around since the start. This is intended to be an archival format for raw photos, so you wouldn't want to lose any image data as part of the conversion process. This lossless type of DNG is the only option available if you choose the Copy as DNG method in the Import window.

The lossy compression type of DNG is a relative newcomer, and it tries to find a middle ground between the reduced file size benefits of the JPG format and the editability of the original raw photo. In some ways, you can think of it as a super-powered JPG that still allows you to edit things like camera profile, white balance, and lens profiles with the same options as a raw photo. You can find this as an option when exporting from Lightroom Classic, or choose Library ➪ Convert Photo to DNG to convert original raw files to DNG after import.

TECHNICAL STUFF

To learn more about all the ways the DNG format appears in a Lightroom Classic workflow, download this free PDF I wrote for *Lightroom Magazine*: www.light roomers.com/L4D/DNGinWorkflow.pdf.

Converting to DNG

One of the DNG benefits that has been of the greatest value to me over the years is its ability to compress raw data without any loss. This was the original flavor of DNG that was rolled out more than a decade ago. I've leveraged the lossless DNG conversion to convert older raw photos simply to reduce file size (in bytes) and gain more space on my drives without losing any raw data. Yes, storage is (relatively) cheap, but I have a long list of other things I'd rather spend money on, and I can't tell you how many Help Desk problems I see every year related to managing multiple drive issues. Here's what I would do:

1. **Select the source of the photos you want to convert to DNG in Grid view of the Library module.**

2. **Click the Metadata tab of the Library Filter and configure a column to display the file type.**

    Click Raw to filter by only the raw photos in your source. You can skip this step if you know you have only raw photos in your source. Select all the raw photos. Refer to Chapter 6 for information on the Library Filter.

3. **Choose Library⇨Convert Photos to DNG to open the Convert Photos to DNG dialog, shown in Figure 7-11.**

4. **Select the check box to Only convert Raw files.**

   Why bother with the Library filter if the dialog has this check box? Because you want to be in the driver's seat for what happens, and you want to know how many files will be affected.

5. **Decide whether you want to select the check box labeled Delete originals after successful conversion.**

   I understand that this step can be scary. Make sure you have a good backup in place first. My reason for conversion in this instance is to reduce overall file size, so I opt for deletion of originals after successful conversion so that I am left with only the DNG versions. You need to make the best decision for your workflow.

6. **(Optional) Select the check box labeled Embed Fast Load Data.**

   This step embeds a small preview in the DNG file that Lightroom Classic reads first to speed up slider activation in the Develop module.

7. **Choose a file extension and preview size (Medium is a good compromise).**

For this purpose, I leave Use Lossy Compression deselected because I want to use only lossless compression and retain all my image data. I also opt to leave Embed Original Raw File deselected because I want to end up with a smaller file size.

8. **Double-check your settings and click OK.**

As that DNG conversion runs, you see your proprietary raw files replaced with a DNG version. I usually set this to run and walk away to do other things until it's finished.

If you're interested in converting to DNG from the moment of import, you can choose the Copy as DNG option on the Import screen. This works just like the neighboring Copy option, except that once the photos have been copied to the destination (and imported into the catalog), the conversion to DNG begins automatically. The options to control what happens during that DNG conversion can be found at Lightroom Classic ⇨ Preferences ⇨ File Handling (Edit ⇨ Preferences ⇨ File Handling on Windows). This screen has fewer options because it applies to raw files only. You wouldn't want to choose the lossy DNG option at this stage, so it isn't an option.

Putting Photos on the Map

Having a GPS-enabled camera has become much more common in recent years (look no further than your mobile phone). Visualizing on a map where photos were taken can be both useful and interesting. The Library module has several options to help find and organize photos; location is just one more aspect of that. For that reason, I think of the Map module as basically an extension of the Library module, which is why I've included it in this chapter.

The Map module has two functions: It can show you where photos with geolocation data are located on the map, or it can be used to put photos without geolocation data on the map. Let's take a look around.

Getting oriented to the Map module

The Map module, shown in Figure 7-12, has relatively few panels compared to the other modules, so I just want to highlight what's different here:

>> **Navigator panel:** You can pan the map to move around by clicking-and-dragging.

>> **Saved Locations panel:** Allows you to quickly and easily apply saved location information to photos via drag-and-drop.

>> **Content area:** This is an interactive map of the world that requires an Internet connection to view. At the top is the Location Filter, which can be used to control which photos are visible in the Filmstrip and allow searching the map for specific locations.

>> **Toolbar:** Provides controls for switching between map views, locking markers on the map, and working with a tracklog.

The Collections panel and Metadata panel are just the same as in the Library module and serve the same purposes. The Filmstrip contains photos from the selected source.

FIGURE 7-12:
The Map
module.

Map module basics

You have a couple of ways to access the Map module, and some start in the Library module. When looking at thumbnails of your photos in Grid view with thumbnail badges showing (see Figure 7-13), the badge showing a pin is a clickable button that takes you to that photo on the map in the Map module.

FIGURE 7-13:
The thumbnail badge for photos with embedded geolocation data looks like a pin.

Alternatively, if you expand the Metadata panel and select a photo containing geolocation information, you see the coordinates appear in the GPS field. To the right of that field is a clickable arrow button that takes you to that photo on the map.

You can of course simply click the Map button in the Module Picker to switch to the Map module. When you do so, any photos containing geolocation information appear on the map. After you're in the Map module, you can drag-and-drop photos without geolocation information from the Filmstrip onto the map to apply location information to their metadata.

The Map module is pretty straightforward to use, and the best way to learn it is to see all these features (and more) in action. Download this free PDF I wrote for *Lightroom Magazine*: www.lightroomers.com/L4D/MapModule.pdf. I even demonstrate how to use a tracklog to put your photos on the map if your camera has no GPS functionality.

Working in Lightroom Classic's Digital Darkroom

IN THIS PART . . .

Using the Develop module tools to edit photos

Troubleshooting and saving time

Using Lightroom Classic's advanced editing features

IN THIS CHAPTER

» Getting familiar with the Develop module

» Switching between view modes

» Choosing a starting profile

» Performing basic tonal adjustments

» Correcting color casts

» Making photos pop

Chapter **8**

Editing Photos in the Develop Module

Welcome to the Develop module! This is where Lightroom Classic's real magic happens. Since its release, Adobe has dedicated a lot of resources toward continually adding new tools and updating the existing features for editing photos — so much so that the need to send photos to an external editor has been decreased significantly. Because this module has so much to offer, I split the coverage of the Develop module across Part 3 (this chapter through Chapter 10).

In case you're puzzling over the use of the word *develop* here, you need to keep in mind that Lightroom Classic was primarily designed to work with *raw* photos, which have not yet been processed for final output. So Lightroom Classic approaches photos with the mindset that photos first need to be *developed* before they're ready to leave Lightroom Classic and face whatever comes next. That's not to say it can't work with nonraw photos, because it absolutely can do that as well. Aside from getting you oriented to where everything is located in the Develop interface, this chapter focuses on the most common, or essential, Develop tasks before digging deeper in Chapters 9 and 10.

Exploring the Develop Module

At first glance, it's easy to be a little overwhelmed by all the panels, sliders, and buttons in this module. Don't be! The layout is essentially the same as all the other modules. You find the Module Picker across the top; the left side holds the panels that pertain to saved settings (called *presets*) and various states of your photos; the right side contains all the adjustment controls. In the center, you find the content area and the Toolbar, and the ever-present Filmstrip runs along the bottom. Refer to Chapter 1 for ways to modify the interface to suit your needs.

Getting to know the panels and tools

To know the Develop module is to love it, so go ahead and get acquainted with the interface, shown in Figure 8-1. Here's an overview of what you can find lying about (I omitted elements covered in earlier chapters):

FIGURE 8-1:
The Develop module interface.

» **Navigator:** This element displays a preview of your presets as you hover the cursor over the contents of the Presets panel.

» **Presets:** On the left side, the Presets panel contains all the preinstalled and (soon to be created) custom Develop presets.

» **Snapshots:** A snapshot is a means to preserve a specific state in your editing process. Snapshots are useful for creating multiple versions of a single file and storing them for easy access later.

» **History:** Still on the left, the History panel records a running history of every tweak and adjustment you make to each photo. This allows for an unlimited undo operation because you can always step back through the Develop history to any earlier point.

» **Copy and Paste:** These buttons allow you to copy and paste Develop settings from one photo to another.

» **Content area:** This is your workspace, which provides a live preview of the photo you're working on.

» **Toolbar:** Just below the content area, the Toolbar contains the buttons for switching between view modes, along with additional tools available via the Toolbar drop-down menu for navigating between photos; playing an impromptu slideshow; controlling zoom level; and applying flags, ratings, and labels.

» **Histogram:** This element provides a way to visualize your image data on an interactive graph of the all the tones contained in the active photo.

» **Tool Strip:** This is the collection of adjustment-tool icons nested under the Histogram, which includes the buttons Jump to Edit, Crop Overlay, Remove, Red Eye Correction, and Masking (all covered in Chapter 9).

» **Basic:** Why basic? Well, you touch these adjustments almost every time you bring a photo into the Develop module. You need to get these settings straight (such as White Balance and Exposure) before you can move on to other tasks.

» **Tone Curve:** This is the best tool for putting the finishing touches on adjusting brightness and contrast.

» **Color Mixer/B&W:** This element allows for the tweaking of individual colors as well as adjusting the conversion to black-and-white (note that the panel displays B&W only when you click the B&W button at the top of the Basic panel).

» **Color Grading:** This feature provides the ability to shift the color in the shadows, midtones, and highlights of your photos. It can be used for creative color modifications (on color or black-and-white photos) or neutralizing color casts.

» **Detail:** These tools are for increasing sharpening and reducing noise.

» **Lens Corrections:** This one contains the options for enabling lens profile corrections and manual controls for removing that annoying purple fringe (that is, *chromatic aberration*).

» **Transform:** This is the perspective distortion correction suite of tools.

» **Lens Blur:** This new feature lets you add simulated lens blur to photos.

>> **Effects:** Effects are used for applying creative darkening (and brightening) to a photo's edges, as well as for the creative addition of simulated film grain.

>> **Calibration:** Calibration provides the ability to switch process versions (the secret sauce for rendering raw photo data) as well as the legacy controls for tweaking the default rendering settings.

Becoming familiar with the menu options

The Lightroom Classic (Mac only) File, Edit, View, Window, and Help menus remain consistent across all modules, but the Develop module also has a dedicated set of menu options. Menus are certainly useful for accessing specific functions, but they also serve to remind you about all the options and their respective keyboard shortcuts. I cover all the functions in their context over the course of the three Develop module chapters in Part 4, but here's an overview of what you find on the Develop module menus:

>> **Develop:** Contains the commands for creating new snapshots and presets, erasing the contents of the History panel, and navigating between photos.

>> **Photo:** A group of commands that pertains to stuff you can do to the active photo, such as adding it to the Target Collection; showing its location; sending it to an external editor; creating virtual copies; rotating and flipping; applying flags, ratings, or labels; writing and reading the metadata stored in the photo; deleting; and more.

>> **Settings:** Provides access to all the commands for copying, pasting, syncing, and applying Develop settings as well as converting to black-and-white and certain cropping-related settings.

>> **Tools:** Where you'll find commands for accessing various Develop tools and any related tool *overlays* (helpful visual guides).

TIP

You might find it more efficient in many cases to use the contextual menus that appear when you right-click various panels, settings, and photos. Don't be shy — click around and see what you find!

Understanding the view options

Working in the Develop module is obviously a visual process. You can scrutinize every nudge of every slider to get your photos looking how you want. Lightroom Classic offers the following three view modes (with multiple options) to help you see what you're doing and how far you've come:

- » **Loupe view:** The default working view (pronounced "loop") when you enter the Develop module — and where you do almost all your work. You can zoom in or out by clicking the photo or by using the controls in the Navigator panel or the Zoom slider on the Toolbar. You can jump to Loupe view in the Develop module by pressing D no matter where you are in Lightroom Classic.

- » **Reference view:** A special working view where you can compare two photos side by side while processing one (the active photo) to look more like the reference photo.

- » **Before and After view:** Allows you to switch out of Loupe view for a comparison between the work you've done and the photo you started with. There are several variations on how you can arrange views for comparison to offer some choice over which might work best for a given photo. See the section "The Before and After views," later in this chapter.

TIP

No matter which view you're working in, to cycle through the Info Overlay displays — that little summary of information about the active photo that appears in the content area — press the I key or choose View⇨Loupe Info. To customize the information shown on the overlay, press ⌘+J (Ctrl+J on Windows).

Loupe view

Just like in the Library module, the Navigator panel, shown in Figure 8-2, controls the zoom level. The default is Fit (the entire photo fits in the content area), with a zoomed-out level of 100% (as in actual pixel view). You can change the zoom level by clicking the labels in the Navigator panel. When you zoom beyond Fit view, you can pan around the photo by clicking-and-dragging in the content area or by clicking-and-dragging inside the Navigator.

FIGURE 8-2:
The Navigator panel.

Reference view

You may not use this view as often as the others, but file it away for a situation where you want to see two photos side by side, as shown in Figure 8-3, while you edit one (the active photo) to look more like the static reference photo. This can be useful if you shoot JPG + raw and want to compare the JPG as the reference photo while you edit the raw photo to look similar; or perhaps you have a photo with a certain "look" and want to try to emulate that look on a different photo to give it a similar feel. This makes it easier to match white balance across a set of photos or perhaps create a preset that helps you achieve a certain look.

FIGURE 8-3:
The reference photo is on the left, and the active photo is to its right.

Here's how to get started with Reference view from within Develop:

1. **Click the R A button on the Toolbar (or press Shift+R).**

   This sets the selected photo as the active photo. You can choose between Left/Right and Top/Bottom reference views by clicking the drop-down menu on the R A button.

2. **Drag and drop a photo from the Filmstrip to the Reference pane to set the reference photo.**

   You can also right-click a photo and choose Set as Reference Photo from the contextual menu.

3. **Make any desired adjustments to the active photo.**

   Use any of the adjustments possible to bring the look of the active photo in line with the reference photo. Select any other photo in the Filmstrip to make it the active photo and adjust.

4. **Exit Reference view when finished by pressing the D key.**

Although it isn't something you're likely to use every day, Reference view is a handy feature to have if you need it.

Before and After views

Although much of your work happens in Loupe view, sometimes it's hard to appreciate how far you've come until you look at where you started. You can compare Before and After views in several ways:

>> **Left/Right:** Choose either a side-by-side view of the whole photo showing each state or a split view (shown in Figure 8-4) that shows the Before image on the left and the After image on the right.

>> **Top/Bottom:** Choose to have the Before image on top and the After image on the bottom, or a single photo split between the two views.

>> **Before Only:** This option is useful for toggling between Before and After views for a quick peek by pressing the backslash (\) key.

FIGURE 8-4:
Before/After Left/Right Split view.

REMEMBER

These views aren't just for looking, though! All the adjustment sliders are still active and can be applied while looking at the Before and After views.

You can access all these view options from the button on the Toolbar (or the View menu). *Note:* When you're in Before / After view, three additional icons appear on the Toolbar (refer to Figure 8-4). Here's what they do (from left to right):

>> **Copy Before's Settings to After:** If you want to start over, you can quickly revert your After state's settings to the way they were before.

>> **Copy After's Settings to Before:** If you're satisfied with the After state, you can save it as the new Before state so that you can press on with additional edits and have this state to compare against (and revert to).

>> **Swap Before and After Settings:** This is handy if you want to create a new version that goes in a different direction from the original Before state and preserves the current After state for later comparison.

These commands are also accessible from the Settings menu and can be applied from Loupe view, if needed.

Applying settings to other photos

Okay, I'm sure you're itching to dive into the Editing tools (and you will!), but first I want you to have the big picture in mind before you start pushing sliders around. I promise you'll be knee-deep in adjustments soon enough.

I want to call your attention to the two buttons at the bottom of the left panel group and the two buttons at the bottom of the right panel group (refer to Figure 8-1). Here's what they do:

>> **Copy:** Allows you to copy settings from the active photo so that they can be pasted onto other photos (one at a time). When clicked, the Copy Settings dialog opens (same options as the Synchronize Settings dialog, shown in Figure 8-5), allowing you to choose which settings to copy.

FIGURE 8-5:
The Synchronize Settings dialog.

>> **Paste:** Applies the copied settings to only to the active photo when clicked. For multiple photos, use Sync/Auto Sync, which I cover in a bit.

>> **Previous:** Applies all the settings from the last photo you worked on to the active photo. This button is visible only when you have a single photo selected in the Filmstrip.

>> **Reset:** Returns all adjustments to the default settings.

The Copy/Paste function is useful when you want to keep a collection of settings ready to be pasted to any single photo when needed. However, when you want to apply a collection of settings across a selection of photos, you need to use either the Sync button or its alter ego, the Auto Sync button.

If you have more than one photo selected, either in the Filmstrip or if you're using the secondary window in Grid view, you notice that the Previous button has changed to Sync. When you click the Sync button, the Synchronize Settings dialog appears, as shown in Figure 8-5. This dialog functions just like the Copy button in that it allows you to choose which settings in the active photo you want to apply, but in this case, the settings are applied to the other photos you select. After selecting the check boxes next to the settings you want to sync, click the Synchronize button.

TIP

You can synchronize settings across any number of selected photos, which is most effective when you want to selectively synchronize a subset of settings across multiple photos. If you're in a situation where you have a grouping of photos that you want to process exactly the same way and in real time (almost), you should change the Sync button to Auto Sync, by holding ⌘ (the Ctrl key on Windows) and clicking Sync, or click the little button to the left of Sync to flip it to Auto Sync. As soon as you press that key, you see Sync change to Auto Sync — clicking the button completes the transformation. After you turn on Auto Sync, every adjustment you make to the active photo is automatically applied to the rest of the selected photos. This is a huge time-saver!

REMEMBER

Here's the catch: Once Auto Sync is on, it's on until you turn it off (just click it again without holding down any key). I must tell you that I've accidentally auto-synced a bunch of files more than once. Fortunately, you have that faithful Undo shortcut, ⌘+Z (Ctrl+Z on Windows)!

Development Essentials

Lightroom Classic's Develop module is both an image processor and an image editor. I'll tell you where I draw the line, but I'll be the first to admit that the distinction has blurred, thanks to Lightroom Classic.

Raw versus JPG: Why it matters

When your camera is set to capture in JPG mode, it takes the raw capture data and processes it by using the in-camera settings (such as contrast, saturation, and sharpening) to produce a rendered JPG version of the captured image data.

The benefit of shooting JPG is that you're using the camera for both capture and processing, which can certainly be a time-saver. The downside is that the original *raw* capture data is lost after the JPG version is created. If you bring that JPG into Lightroom Classic's Develop module, you're not processing the capture data, but instead editing the rendered image data. Of course, with Lightroom Classic, the actual pixels in the source file are never changed, so, technically speaking, only the pixels in exported copies are edited — though I hope you can see the distinction.

Here's why it matters. In contrast to JPG, when you shoot raw, you take the camera out of the processing business. The result is that the camera is primarily a capture device that saves the raw capture data to your memory card. That raw capture data needs to be processed by some type of raw-processing software. I'll assume you're using Lightroom Classic for that task.

REMEMBER

When you bring a raw photo into Lightroom Classic, you take over the image processing tasks formerly performed by the camera in the JPG example. You decide how much contrast, saturation, and sharpening (to name just a few settings) will be applied to create a rendered version of the photo (during output). The benefit is that you can customize those settings to maximum effect on a photo-by-photo basis, and you never lose the original capture data! You can reprocess the raw data in any number of ways. The downside is that you need to add that processing step into your workflow, which takes time.

The reason the line between processing and editing has blurred is that Lightroom Classic can perform a much wider range of adjustments on your photos than any camera could dream of performing. Red-eye removal, cropping, and spot removal used to be tasks that could be done only in a pixel editor (like Photoshop). With the introduction of the Linear Gradient, Radial Gradient, and Brush in earlier versions of Lightroom Classic (now all part of Masking), the line between processing and editing is almost erased.

That said, the place where the rubber meets the road (as far as each Lightroom Classic user is concerned) is that, whenever you bring a rendered file (JPG, TIF, or PSD) into Lightroom Classic, you're working with processed data. Therefore, all adjustments you make in Lightroom Classic are made relative to whatever processing decisions have previously been made. When you bring a raw file into Lightroom Classic, the adjustments are absolute settings — no processing has already been done — giving you much more leeway in how you process each photo.

Using the Histogram panel

The Histogram panel, shown in Figure 8-6, is another way to look at your photo, by displaying it as a graph of all the tones it contains. When this information is used in conjunction with the Live view of the photo in the content area, it greatly informs the adjustment decisions you make.

Although the actual graph is the same as the one shown in the Library module, the Develop module's Histogram panel has a few additional features:

FIGURE 8-6:
The Histogram panel.

>> **It's interactive.** When you hover the cursor over the Histogram, you see how each area of the Histogram relates to the tonal adjustment sliders in the Basic panel:

- *Blacks:* The far-left end of the graph, showing the darkest shadows
- *Shadows:* The tonal range between the darkest shadows and the midtones
- *Exposure:* The midtones, from the shadows to the highlights
- *Highlights:* The tonal range between the brightest tones and the midtones
- *Whites:* The far-right end of the graph, showing the brightest tones

Similarly, if you place the cursor over each of the tonal adjustment sliders in the Basic panel (except Contrast), you see the respective sections of the Histogram panel brighten. You can click-and-drag within the Histogram to make tonal adjustments, and when you do so, the respective sliders adjust in tandem. (This isn't the best way to edit, but it makes the connection between the graph and sliders.)

>> **It has clipping indicators.** The arrows at either end of the Histogram are white when data in all three channels has been clipped, or take on a color when only one or two channels are clipped. (*Clipping* means that pixels in the image have exceeded the tonal range on an end of the Histogram — blacks or whites — and no longer contain any image data.) In some instances, this is okay, such as shadow areas you want to be all black, or bright highlights — reflections of the sun on chrome, for example. At other times, however, clipping isn't nice at all — such as when all the detail in a white wedding dress is lost to overexposure.

In addition to the Histogram indicators, you can enable a visual clipping indicator that appears in your photo. Press the J key to enable the indicator (or just click the clipping-indicator arrows). When enabled, areas that are clipped on the shadow end are shown in blue, and areas clipped on the highlights end are shown in red. Figure 8-7 shows an image with both shadow and highlight clipping.

» **It's helpful for RGB readouts.** The photo you see in the content area is made from the image data contained in the Red, Green, and Blue channels of the photo. Lightroom Classic uses a scale that ranges from 0 percent (black) to 100 percent (white). As you move your cursor over the photo, the RGB values of the pixels under the cursor appear under the histogram.

FIGURE 8-7:
An example of shadow and highlight clipping indicators.

The relationships between the Histogram, the basic tonal adjustments, the clipping indicators, and the RGB readouts make the Histogram an important tool for evaluating what's happening in your photos, which is why the Histogram panel remains visible at the top of the rightmost panel group, no matter how far down you scroll to the other adjustment panels.

Making basic adjustments

It's almost a given that you'll make certain kinds of adjustments to almost all your photos. These adjustments are grouped into five sections in the Basic panel, as shown in Figure 8-8:

» **Top (formerly Treatment):** At the top you'll find the Auto, B&W, and HDR buttons. I talk about Auto a little later, when discussing tonal range; I cover black-and-white conversions in Chapter 10; and you can learn more about HDR in chapter 7.

» **Profile:** Choosing the profile is similar to choosing an in-camera picture style (such as portrait, landscape, vivid, or neutral) that can have a major impact on color and contrast rendering at a foundational level.

» **White Balance:** This section provides tools you can use to neutralize color casts or to creatively interpret the lighting conditions that existed at the moment of capture. White balance is subjective. Have fun with it.

» **Tone:** This one contains the controls for adjusting the range of tones in the photo. You can set highlight and shadow-clipping levels and adjust midtone brightness levels as well.

» **Presence:** These controls have a big effect on how people respond to your photo. Texture is designed to enhance (in positive amounts) or smooth (in negative amounts) the contrast of medium-size areas of detail (think of it as a specialized form of sharpening). The Clarity slider is essentially a midtone contrast adjustment (which can improve apparent depth and sharpness); Dehaze is another type of contrast adjustment (useful for correcting atmospheric haze); and Vibrance and Saturation adjust the colors. I go over each one in more detail a little later in this chapter.

Click to open Profile browser

FIGURE 8-8:
The Basic panel.

With that overview in mind, you can make your way through the next few sections, where I delve deeper into the Basic panel.

Choosing a starting profile

If you've used previous versions of Lightroom, you might never have known that a camera profile was being applied to all your raw photos, because the setting was buried in the Calibration panel. One of the first new features added when Lightroom was renamed to Lightroom Classic was the relocation of profiles to the Basic panel (refer to Figure 8-8) and the expansion of how many profiles you had to choose from. Adobe added so many new profiles that a Profile Browser, shown in Figure 8-9 had to be added in order to organize them.

You can open the Profile Browser by clicking the button to the right of the Profile drop-down menu (refer to Figure 8-8) or choose Browse from the bottom of that same Profile drop-down menu list.

The contents of the Profile Browser are dictated by what type of file (raw or nonraw) is selected, and if it's a raw

FIGURE 8-9:
The Profile Browser, displaying in List view.

photo, by which camera it came from. In Figure 8-9, you see the profiles for a raw photo from a Canon R1. The Profile Browser is divided into at least three sections, but if you've installed third-party profiles, you also see a fourth section (with the names reflecting the third-party creators of the profiles). Those main three sections are

>> **Favorites:** You can customize which profiles are shown here, which also determines which profiles are shown on the Profile drop-down menu. Clicking the star on any profile marks it (or removes it) as a favorite.

>> **Raw / Basic:** When you have a raw photo selected, the next section down contains various raw profiles organized into subgroups with headings for

Adobe Raw and Camera Matching. You may see more or fewer profiles in this area, depending on the camera used to create the raw photo. If you have a nonraw photo selected (PSD, TIF, JPG, or PNG), you see just a group named Basic that has one profile for color and one for monochrome.

>> **Creative:** The section at the bottom containing groupings for Artistic, B&W, Modern, and Vintage appears for both raw and nonraw photos. These profiles provide for some *creative* looks to try.

If you're new to this part of Lightroom Classic, I strongly suggest that you check out all these profiles to get a feel for how they look on your photos. Try some with people photos, try some with landscapes, and try some with whatever other types of photos you have. You can always go back to the default Adobe Color at any time by selecting it or just clicking the Reset button to go all the way back to your default settings. Here's how to explore the Profile Browser:

1. **Select the photo you want to edit.**

   Although you can change a profile at any time, you get the best results by applying the profile as one of the first things you do.

2. **Expand the Basic panel and click the Profile Browser button to see its contents.**

   The file type of the selected photo determines what profile groups and profiles appear in the browser.

REMEMBER

3. **Simply hover the cursor over profiles to see a live preview in the content area without having to click a profile.**

   Expand each profile group to explore all the options.

4. **Click any profile in the Creative group at the bottom to apply the profile, and note the Amount slider that appears in the Profile Browser (refer to Figure 8-9).**

   Each of the profiles in the Creative section comes with an Amount slider that allows you to tone down (or even turn up) the effect of the profile.

5. **Click the Star icon on any profile you want added to the Favorites group.**

6. **Once you've explored all the options, click the profile you want to apply to the selected photo and close the Profile Browser.**

That's all there is to applying a profile. Eventually, you'll find that you use just a few most often, but it's nice to have options. You can also include profiles in presets you create, which I cover in Chapter 9.

Controlling color casts

White-balance adjustments — where you attempt to make objects that appeared white when you saw them in person appear white in the finished photo — are subjective. How you process your photos is how you express your vision of the scene you captured. The color of the light has an impact on how others react to the image. The choice you make depends, of course, on your vision.

Lightroom Classic offers three methods for adjusting the white balance:

>> **White Balance Selector tool:** This neutralizing tool is in the White Balance section of the Basic panel. You can activate this tool by pressing W or clicking the eyedropper-shaped icon (press W or Esc or the re-dock eyedropper to exit). Your goal is to find and select a highlight that's close to being *neutral;* that is, all three RGB values should be pretty close to each other. The Selector tool has a special loupe — the gridlike object behind the cursor, shown in Figure 8-10 — that shows you the pixels and their RGB values under the tool while you move the eyedropper to find the right spot to click. RGB values in the 80s and 90s work best, but lower values can work, too. Lightroom Classic attempts to neutralize the color cast by adjusting the R, G, and B channels at that location to equal values.

White Balance Selector

FIGURE 8-10:
The White Balance Selector tool.

When the White Balance Selector tool is active, the Toolbar (under the photo) contains the following options:

● *Auto Dismiss:* By default, the White Balance Selector tool disappears after you click a spot. However, at times, you might want to try sampling multiple locations before manually dismissing the tool. Deselect this check box to stop Auto Dismiss.

- *Show Loupe:* The Loupe is a helpful tool, but you can also see the RGB values appear under the Histogram. Deselect it to turn it off.

- *Scale:* This setting adjusts the size of the grid in the Loupe.

» **White-balance preset:** When working with raw images, you can set the white balance based on the lighting at the time of capture by using the appropriate preset, or choose Auto to let Lightroom Classic work its magic. The absolute white-balance value has already been set in rendered files (JPG, TIF, or PSD), so your preset options in Lightroom Classic are limited to leaving it as is (As Shot) or letting Lightroom Classic try to adjust automatically (Auto). *Custom* is displayed if the Selector tool or the Temp and Tint sliders are used to make a manual adjustment.

» **Temperature and Tint sliders:** Make manual adjustments to the color temperature and its tint. As the colors on the sliders indicate, dragging the Temp slider to the left introduces more blue (cooling the image), and dragging the Temp slider to the right introduces more yellow (warming the image). Similarly, as indicated on the Tint slider, dragging the slider to the left introduces a greenish tint, and dragging it to the right introduces a magenta tint.

Your starting point will always be the As Shot setting. If your starting point using the As Shot setting looks good to you, don't feel compelled to continue adjusting. When it doesn't feel right, you need to make some decisions. My preference is to reach for the White Balance Selector tool and attempt to achieve a neutral result, and then, based on the scene, adjust the Temp and Tint sliders until it looks the way I think it should. When I'm working on one photo that's part of a series shot under the same lighting conditions, I use the Sync button to apply the same setting to those photos as well. After you settle on a white-balance setting you like, you can move on to making tonal adjustments.

Adjusting tonal range to bring out the best

The tone adjustments in the Basic panel provide you with the creative freedom to make the most of the settings you used in the camera to capture the image data. I talk about the relationship between the tonal adjustments and the Histogram earlier in this chapter, and now you're going to use all the tools at your disposal. The Tone section of the Basic panel (refer to Figure 8-8) contains the following adjustments:

» **Auto:** The Auto setting got a complete overhaul recently and works quite well for many photos (note the button at the top of the panel). Adobe uses artificial intelligence and machine learning to do a better job of optimizing the tonal settings based on the photo itself. It can make for a great starting point.

» **Exposure:** The slider's scale is based on f-stops. Adjustments will affect the entire tonal range, but the biggest impact is on the brightest tones. Adjust as needed to improve overall image brightness. If some highlight clipping occurs, it might be possible to correct it with the Highlights slider.

» **Contrast:** Increasing contrast makes bright areas brighter and dark areas darker, and decreasing contrast does the reverse.

» **Highlights:** Use this adjustment to recover detail in extreme highlights by reducing highlight values until they're no longer clipped.

» **Shadows:** This one helps to open detail in the light shadow areas with minimal impact on the darkest values (to help keep blacks black).

» **Whites:** Use this slider to determine what areas of the image clip to all white (no detail), which sets the white point.

» **Blacks:** Use this slider to determine what areas of the image (if any) to clip to all black (no detail), which sets the black point.

How you approach these adjustments largely depends on how well the image was exposed in-camera. Are you compensating for over- or underexposure or just optimizing a proper exposure? Does the scene contain bright highlights as well as dark shadows? This is where you need to make an evaluation based on what you see in the content area (in conjunction with the Histogram) to decide how to get from where you are to where you want to be. Here's a basic workflow you can use:

1. **Evaluate the image.**

   Note problem areas, such as clipped highlights, clipped shadows, and muddy midtones. Think about how you intended the photo to look.

2. **Click Auto in the top section.**

   Notice that all the sliders in the Tone section may have changed, as well as Vibrance and Saturation. Reevaluate the photo and consider tweaking the sliders (as needed) to fine-tune the result.

3. **(Optional) Press J to turn on the clipping indicators.**

   This is an easy way to see exactly whether any area of the photo is being clipped.

4. **Adjust the Exposure slider.**

   Your goal is to fine-tune the overall image brightness. You can also hold the Option key (Alt on Windows) while you drag the slider to get a view of any image areas that might be clipping.

5. **Adjust the Blacks slider.**

You always have much less detail in the shadow areas than in the highlights. In many cases, you can create a more pleasing image by clipping the darkest shadow areas to black. As you can do with the Exposure slider, you can hold the Option key (Alt on Windows) while dragging the slider to see just the areas that are clipping to black.

6. **Adjust the Whites slider.**

Tweak if needed to set the white point. The Option key (or Alt key on Windows) works to show clipping here, too.

7. **Adjust the Highlights slider.**

Not every image needs to have the highlights pulled back, but for those that do, the Highlights slider is a fantastic tool. Adjust as needed.

8. **Adjust the Shadows slider to brighten the darker areas of the photo.**

Many images can benefit from a little bump to open up the shadows.

TIP

A quick way to return any slider to its original state is to double-click its label. Likewise, you can double-click the Tone label above the sliders to reset all sliders in that section. This works for all sliders and sections in Lightroom Classic.

I left out the Contrast slider from that process because I tend to leave it as a finishing touch at the end of my developing process, and I prefer the control offered by the Tone Curve panel. There's no single correct way to approach this, so if you prefer using the Contrast slider, do so.

Making images pop

Not every image needs the adjustments in the Presence section, but they make an impact on the ones that do. However, precisely *because* they can have an impact, you need to be careful not to overdo it. With that warning out of the way, take another look at Figure 8-8, casting your eyes to the five sliders in the Presence section of the Basic panel:

>> **Texture:** As you can tell by its name, this adjustment targets the medium-size texture (detail) in a photo. When moved in a positive direction, this adjustment enhances the texture in a photo (useful for landscapes). If moved in a negative direction, this adjustment can be used to smooth out texture (think skin) for a softening effect. Be sure to zoom to 1:1 to better gauge the effect of using this adjustment.

» **Clarity:** This contrast adjustment is designed to give the image a little oomph. When it was in development, Adobe considered naming it Punch because that seemed an apt description of its effect. This adjustment is also best applied while zoomed to 1:1, to better gauge its effect on the detail in the image. Use in moderation.

» **Dehaze:** This is another form of contrast adjustment that has been formulated to reduce the impact of atmospheric haze and bring out detail in landscape photographs. Alternatively, you can move it in a negative direction to add haze to your photo.

» **Vibrance:** This sophisticated saturation adjustment mostly affects the less-saturated colors while protecting skin tones and preventing clipping in the most-saturated colors. It's a great all-around color booster.

» **Saturation:** Use this slider to adjust the saturation of all colors equally in both directions. Decrease saturation by dragging to the left, and increase saturation by dragging to the right (although increased saturation isn't helpful for skin tones).

TIP

A useful starting point for Presence on some photos is contained in the preinstalled Develop preset called Punch (now hidden). Click the plus icon in the Presets header and select Manage Presets, then check the box next to Classic - General to restore this original group of presets. (Refer to Chapter 9 for more info about presets.) Just click it one time to apply it to the selected photo and then adjust to taste. All it does is set Clarity to +30 and Vibrance to +25.

Customizing the panel order

Before moving on to other panels in Develop, I want to point out a little customization trick that's hidden under the hood. Adobe gives you the ability to customize the order of the panels on the right side of the Develop module (currently the only place this works). Simply right-click any of the panel headers below the Histogram panel and choose Customize Develop Panel to open an interactive dialog where you can reorder those panels to suit your workflow.

Within the Customize Develop Panel dialog, you simply drag-and-drop the panels into the order you prefer. You can even deselect the check box next to a panel and hide that panel. I'm so used to the way things are that I'm sticking with the default order, but feel free to check it out and see whether you find it useful. If you change the order, click the Save button, which prompts you to restart the program to see your changes take effect. You can always return things to normal by invoking the Customize Develop Panel dialog and clicking the Default Order button (and restarting the program).

TIP

While you're looking at the contextual menu that appears when right-clicking a panel header, select Solo Mode to force Lightroom Classic to close any open panel whenever you expand a different panel. This keeps only one adjustment panel open at a time and saves you from having to scroll up and down all the time to find a given slider.

IN THIS CHAPTER

» **Cropping to an aspect ratio**

» **Removing distractions**

» **Applying linear and radial gradients**

» **Painting adjustments with a brush**

» **Automatically selecting subjects and the sky**

» **Creating presets, using snapshots, and reviewing history**

Chapter **9**

Solving Problems and Saving Time

Sometimes the road to making your photos look amazing involves fixing a few problems along the way. Lightroom Classic has a specialized set of tools designed to help you correct a range of issues you might encounter. This chapter covers them and wraps up with a look at a few panels on the left side of the Develop module that can help you save the adjustments you make as presets, preserve editing states as snapshots, and even go back in time to undo changes.

Fixing Common Problems

Just below the Histogram panel is a collection of editing tools referred to as the Tool Strip, as shown in Figure 9-1. These are often referred to as local-correction tools because they give you the ability to work on isolated areas of the photo rather than just the entire photo (global edits).

Edit   Remove   Masking

FIGURE 9-1:
The Tool Strip.

Crop Overlay   Red Eye Correction

The Tool Strip contains these commands:

>> **Edit:** The button you use to exit the other tools in this strip and return to global editing.

>> **Crop Overlay:** Allows for cropping to a specific aspect ratio; also functions as a straightening tool.

>> **Remove:** Functions similarly to the Clone and Heal tools in Photoshop, which allow for the removal of distractions (like sensor spots and skin blemishes) by borrowing pixels from another part of the image or creating new pixels and blending them with the photo.

>> **Red Eye Correction:** Handy for those times when you just had to use on-camera flash for people or pets.

>> **Masking:** Formerly known as the Graduated Filter, Radial Filter, and Adjustment Brush, tools that have been revamped into what is now known as Masking. All the original tools are still there (though their names have changed a little), but they've gained new functionality, a new interface, and companion tools for making selections based on object, subject, background, the sky, color, luminance, and depth.

Need some practical tips on how to use all these tools? Read on.

Creating stronger compositions through cropping

Cropping in-camera might be the goal, but it isn't always the reality. However, even if you do get it "right" in-camera, on some occasions, you might still need to produce an image with an aspect ratio different from the aspect ratio of the original photo. The only way to change the aspect ratio is to crop. The Crop Overlay tool provides both a means for practical corrections and creative composition adjustments.

REMEMBER

It's worth mentioning that the histogram always reflects the area of the photo inside the crop rectangle. In some cases, you might want to make cropping your first adjustment. This way, the histogram reflects just the data you're keeping and, therefore, is more accurate when making tonal adjustments.

TIP

You can jump into the Crop Overlay tool by clicking its icon in the Tool Strip, but I prefer using the keyboard shortcut R because it works in any module. This strategy is especially handy after applying a crop to a batch of photos via the Quick Develop panel in the Library module — press R to jump into Crop Overlay to finesse each photo.

As soon as you press R, the Crop Overlay appears over the photo, and the following cropping options appear on the Tool Strip, as shown in Figure 9-2:

>> **Crop Frame Tool:** Click the icon next to *Aspect* to draw a cropping rectangle as an alternative to readjusting the resizing handles.

>> **Aspect drop-down menu:** Access a list of preinstalled aspect ratios or create a custom aspect ratio.

>> **Aspect Ratio Lock:** When closed, the crop rectangle can be resized, but the aspect ratio doesn't change. When it's open, you can resize and change the aspect ratio as needed. Press A to toggle between open and closed.

>> **Straighten Tool:** This option allows for quick straightening. Select the tool (the icon next to *Angle*), and then click and drag along any straight line in the photo that should be either vertical or horizontal. When you release the mouse, the photo rotates accordingly.

>> **Auto button:** If your photo has a crooked horizon, give the Auto button a click to see whether Lightroom Classic can straighten it automatically for you.

FIGURE 9-2:
The Crop tool, being used to improve composition.

>> **Angle slider:** Click-and-drag to rotate a photo. Place the cursor over the slider handle and use the up- and down-arrow keys to nudge the rotation, or place the cursor over the number field to see the scrubby slider and drag slowly left or right for finer control.

>> **Constrain to Image:** If you've performed a perspective distortion correction in the Transform panel that left empty pixels along the edges of your photo, you can select this check box to automatically remove them.

>> **Reset:** This option returns the image to its uncropped state.

>> **Close:** Click to exit the Crop Overlay. (I prefer to simply press D.)

REMEMBER

Notice the crop rectangle, its resize handles, and a guide overlay (Triangle) inside the content area. You can resize and reshape the crop rectangle as desired, but you have to move the actual photo to reposition it behind the overlay. In other words, you can grab any resize handle to change the crop rectangle, but you need to click-and-drag the photo to move it to a new position. If you click-and-drag outside the crop rectangle, you can rotate the photo.

TIP

The Toolbar contains a Tool Overlay drop-down menu that controls the visibility of the crop guide overlay. By default, visibility is set to Always, but when set to Auto, the crop guide overlay appears only when you resize or reposition the crop rectangle. If you choose Tools ⇨ Crop Guide Overlay, you can then choose from any of the overlay options to assist you in making the strongest composition. Pay special attention to the keyboard shortcut for cycling through the various overlays (O) for ease of use. The Edit button on the Toolbar is another option for committing the crop and exiting the tool.

Removing spots and healing blemishes

Undoubtedly, you will encounter photos that contain something you want to remove; the most common objects are spots caused by dust on the sensor, background distractions, or blemishes in a subject's skin. Lightroom Classic comes to your aid in this regard with a powerful set of Remove tools, as shown in Figure 9-3.

You can access the new AI-powered Remove tool, along with the original Heal and Clone tools, by clicking its icon in the Tool Strip or by pressing Q. When it's activated, you see the following options:

>> **Remove:** A new addition to the panel, the eraser-shaped icon provides access to the new generative-AI-powered tool for removing unwanted distractions. When selected, the Use generative AI and Detect objects check boxes appear (I tell you more about these later). This is the tool to use for removing large and complicated items from a photo.

FIGURE 9-3:
The Remove
tool panel, with
the Remove
options
showing.

» **Heal:** The Band-Aid–shaped icon provides access to the original healing brush behavior, which borrows pixels from a different area but goes a step further by sampling the color and texture of the area you're "healing" and attempting to blend the two. Heal usually works best for items like sensor spots and minor blemishes.

» **Clone:** The Clone Brush simply takes pixels from one area and pastes them into another.

» **Size:** This option adjusts the size of the brush. Use the left-bracket ([) key to decrease the size and the right-bracket (]) key to increase the size.

» **Feather:** When using Heal or Clone, you can use this slider to soften the edge of your brush to better blend the repair with the background. The higher the number, the softer the edge.

» **Opacity:** This slider appears after applying a brush stroke and controls the strength of the brush. The lower the number, the more the original spot shows through the adjustment — helpful when you only want to deemphasize an area rather than remove it.

» **Eyeball button:** That little eyeball-like button in the lower left corner of the panel can be used to toggle the results of the tool on and off for comparison purposes by clicking and holding to turn off, then release.

» **Reset:** This option clears all removal points.

» **Close:** Click to exit the tool.

The Heal and Clone tools have existed in this panel for over a decade and work the same now as then. However, the newly added Remove option has elevated this tool to be almost as good as using Photoshop for removing complex objects from your photos. To see how this new tool works, follow along as I clean up unwanted distractions from a photo, as shown earlier, in Figure 9-3:

1. **Select the photo in Grid view and press Q to jump to the Remove tool in Develop — if you're not there already.**

2. **Click the Remove icon.**

   In this example, I want to remove the player and the dark line sticking up in the lower right corner of the photo, which is too big of a job for Heal or Clone. This is a job for Remove using Generative AI.

3. **Size the brush as needed with the [and] keys.**

4. **Select the check boxes for Use Generative AI and Detect Objects.**

   When the Use generative AI option is selected, you're leveraging the power of Adobe's Firefly engine to analyze the selected area and create new pixels to replace the pixels you want to remove (an Internet connection is required in order to use this feature). Click the Question Mark icon next to the check box to view the terms for using generative AI. If you leave this option deselected, Adobe's Content-Aware engine is used to create the new pixels, which may not work as well but doesn't rely on AI and doesn't require an Internet connection.

5. **I'll use the brush to loosely paint around the player in the lower right corner (refer to Figure 9-4).**

   With an obvious object, like the player, enabling Detect Objects makes it easier to select him by simply painting around him with the brush. Lightroom Classic detects him as an object and fills the area with a buffer around the edge for better blending.

FIGURE 9-4: Lightroom Classic detected and completed the selection of the player shown in red.

6. **In the Selected panel, choose Add or Subtract to refine the area being selected.**

   The moment you release the brush, the Selected panel opens, displaying Add and Subtract buttons and a brush-size slider. You can choose Add to select more areas or choose Subtract to deselect areas and refine your selection. I clicked Add and brushed over the dark line sticking up from the bottom.

7. **Click the Remove button in the Selected panel to generate three versions of new pixels.**

   After generating new pixels, you can click through the first three versions using the arrow buttons in the Selected panel (refer to Figure 9-5). Click the Generate button to have Lightroom Classic create three new variations.

FIGURE 9-5: Viewing the different versions of new pixels generated to replace the selected area.

8. **Press Q to accept the change and exit the tool, or click the Close button.**

You can go back later and readjust if needed because this is a completely non-destructive adjustment. You can delete the generated pixels by selecting the pin representing the replaced pixels and pressing the Delete key (or Backspace on Windows).

If all you have are a few sensor spots in the sky or something similarly easy to remove, choose the Heal icon and simply click on the unwanted spot to have Lightroom Classic replace it with pixels from another part of the photo. The Visualize Spots check box and associated slider can help you see smaller spots in the sky.

Correcting red-eye problems

Although the dreaded red-eye is always best avoided at the moment of capture, it's still helpful to remove it with minimum hassle when it's encountered. There isn't much to see with this tool until you apply it to an eye. When it's first expanded, you see a button for Red Eye (people) and Pet Eye, so you choose based on your subject. Once applied, it's in Edit mode and you have the following options:

» **Pupil Size:** Adjusts the size of the affected area inside the pupil.

» **Darken:** Darkens or lightens the affected pupil.

» **Eyeball button:** A little button in the lower left corner of the panel that can be used to toggle the results of the tool on and off (click and hold).

» **Reset:** Clears all red-eye correction spots.

» **Close:** Exits from the Red Eye Correction tool.

Applying the correction is straightforward. Here's what you do to fix the red-eyed cutie in Figure 9-6:

FIGURE 9-6: The Red Eye Correction tool.

1. **Select the photo in Grid view and press D to jump to Develop.**

2. **Click the Red-Eye Correction tool icon in the Tool Strip.**

3. **Click the first eye, and then adjust the size of the tool to exceed the size of the eye.**

   You can control the tool's size with the [and] keys or by simply clicking-and-dragging until you reach the desired size. Press and hold the spacebar to zoom in for a closer look, if needed.

After you release the mouse button, Lightroom Classic moves to Edit mode, analyzing the area and finding the "red" that needs to be removed. You're just telling Lightroom Classic where to look.

4. **In Edit mode, adjust the Pupil Size and Darken sliders as needed for best results.**

   You just have to eyeball this one (sorry!).

5. **Repeat for the other eye (or as many eyes as there may be).**

6. Click the Close button to exit.

Pets have eyes, too! Sometimes Fido moves into the shot and the flash from your camera reflects off the back of his eyes in a way that makes it appear as though he has lasers blasting from his pupils. That's known as *pet eye,* and the Red Eye Correction tool has Pet Eye mode for just that occasion.

After you click the Pet Eye button (within the Red Eye Correction tool), the operation is essentially the same as I outline for people. The exceptions are that you can't control the Darken amount, and you have an option to add a fake *catchlight* (that little highlight reflecting the light in someone's eyes). You'll know right away whether the fake catchlight helps, so give it a shot. If you do add one, you can click-and-drag it to reposition it within the darkened area.

REMEMBER

In a typical workflow, you should always perform all your *global* (entire photo) adjustments first, which, aside from the adjustments in the Basic panel, may also include some or all of the other adjustment panels below it, before you start using the Masking tools. However, because I'm already describing at the contents of the Tool Strip, I cover these tools now.

Getting oriented to masking

The revamped Masking tool represents one of the biggest and most powerful changes to Lightroom Classic in years. If you've used an older version of Lightroom Classic, you may find this new interface disorienting, but once you get acquainted with what it has to offer, I think you'll be amazed at what you can accomplish.

If you've ever shot with a graduated neutral density filter to properly expose a photo containing a bright sky and darker land, you'll appreciate what Lightroom Classic's Masking is trying to do. However, unlike the actual filter that is placed in front of your lens, Masking allows you to adjust exposure, contrast, saturation, clarity, sharpness, and more, after the photo has been taken! You might find yourself using the real filter less and less often. However, Masking goes way beyond just the Linear Gradient tool by providing ten other ways to select a specific area of the photo that you want to adjust without affecting other areas.

The key to understanding Masking is that the first step involves choosing the type of mask you want to add. From there, you apply the mask to the photo, refine the mask to cover the area you want to adjust, and then dial in the settings needed to achieve the desired result. It may sound complicated, but it makes more sense when you start to put it to work. To open the Masking panel, click the Masking icon in the Tool Strip or use one of the keyboard shortcuts shown to open the panel and activate a specific Masking tool (refer to Figure 9-7).

The Mask types are described in this list:

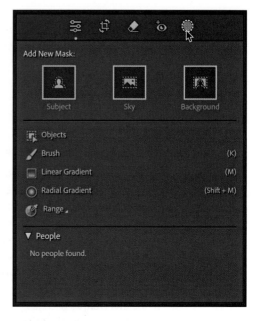

FIGURE 9-7:
The Masking panel.

>> **Subject:** Using the power of Adobe Sensei (Adobe's AI and machine learning technology), you can select the subject of your photo with a single click.

>> **Sky:** This one is like Select Subject, except that this tool can detect and select the sky in a photo.

>> **Background:** This one is like Select Subject, except that this tool can detect and select the area around the subject.

>> **Objects:** Loosely brush over a clear object in a photo to have Lightroom Classic attempt to detect its edges and complete the selection.

>> **Brush:** This option provides the ability to "paint" with multiple adjustment settings. Think of it as a Dodge and Burn tool on steroids! A good example is the application of additional sharpening to the eyes in a portrait without sharpening the surrounding skin, but that just scratches the surface of what this tool can do.

>> **Linear Gradient:** This option enables the application of multiple adjustment settings in a user-controlled gradual fade across any area of the photo. For example, you can correct an overcast sky by applying a gradual exposure compensation and saturation boost to just the sky and having it fade naturally at the horizon.

>> **Radial Gradient:** This option enables the application of multiple adjustments in a user-controlled, oval-shaped fade in any area of the photo. For example,

you can brighten a person's face by drawing an oval Radial gradient around it and then increasing exposure within the inner area of the oval.

>> **Color Range:** Create a selection based on a range of colors within the photo.

>> **Luminance Range:** Create a selection based on a range of brightness values within the photo.

>> **Depth Range:** Use the depth map embedded in photos taken by some mobile devices to create a selection based on distance from the camera.

>> **People:** Another AI-powered tool, Lightroom Classic can detect people in a photo and create specialized masks for each person (and even aspects like hair, eyes, and teeth).

Each of these types of masks can be used alone or in any combination of other types of masks. For example, to edit a landscape, you might start with Select Sky to select the sky and then use the Brush to subtract or add to that original mask to include just the areas of the photo you want to adjust. Additionally, each of these mask types can be inverted, so perhaps you would start with Select Sky to leverage the power of Adobe Sensei to make the initial selection and then invert that mask to select the foreground instead to make an adjustment. Let me walk you through the process of applying a Linear Gradient mask to start, to see how these work in practice and get familiar with other parts of the interface that will appear when any mask type is applied.

Applying a mask

Once you activate the type of mask you want to use, the interface changes to reveal a panel containing all the masks you can apply, a panel containing all the settings you can use to adjust the masked area, and a panel specific to the type of mask being used. Refer to Figure 9-8 to see these panels in the context of applying a Linear Gradient to a 50% gray background (to better see the affected area). For this example, I'm using the Linear Gradient to show the interface changes common to all mask types. To apply the initial mask, with the Masking panel open, click the Linear Gradient tool to activate it (or press M as shown in the panel).

Once enabled, the interface changes as follows:

>> **Masks:** The floating Masks panel contains all masks applied to the photo, as well as the tools for controlling the color overlay, a button for creating new masks, and functionality for renaming masks (click the three-dot menu next to Mask) and controlling their visibility. You can reposition the Masks panel anywhere within the content area or dock it below the Tool Strip by dragging-and-dropping it into position. Click the Question Mark icon in the upper right corner of the panel (highly recommended) to access additional Masking help and a list of all Masking shortcuts.

FIGURE 9-8:
Note the panels that appear after a mask type is applied to a photo.

» **Tool-specific panel:** The contents of this area (at the top of the panel) depend on the type of mask that's active. In this case, it provides a check box to invert the Linear Gradient.

» **Adjustments:** Contains all the settings you can use, alone or in tandem, to achieve your desired results. The Preset drop-down menu contains existing and custom Masking presets, which allow you to save specific settings for reuse (these are shared among all Masking tools). The adjustment panels are grouped in a similar fashion as the respective global adjustment panels (still visible if you scroll down). Each adjustment panel group can be collapsed or expanded as needed. The key to understand here is that you now have the power of those same adjustments to be applied selectively based on what is being masked at the time. Note that you can quickly reset all sliders within a panel group by holding down the Option key (or the Alt key on Windows) and clicking the word *Reset* that appears at the top of each panel group. Additionally, the Reset Sliders Automatically check box resets all sliders each time a new mask is applied (selected by default).

» **Eyeball:** Click and hold the eyeball-toggle button at the bottom to disable the results of the adjustment, which is good for a quick comparison to how things looked before. Click the Delete All Masks button to clear all masks at one time.

The actual Linear Gradient is represented by the three lines shown earlier, in Figure 9-8. The space between the lines is where the gradual adjustment takes place. The way to apply it is to click into the photo where you want the fading of the effect to begin and drag toward the area you don't want affected by the settings. In the 50% gray test image, I initially clicked where the bottom line appears and dragged upward (with +2 Exposure dialed in). The result is that the area below where I clicked got the maximum effect of the settings, the space between the guide lines was gradually faded, and the area above the mask was unchanged.

TIP

When placing a Linear Gradient, you can click and drag in any direction. I encourage you to grab a photo and play with this tool until you get a good feel for how it works. After you apply the mask, you can increase and decrease the fade area by clicking-and-dragging either outside guideline or move the entire mask by clicking-and-dragging the Edit pin — the icon with the black center. You can even rotate the filter by clicking-and-dragging the center line. Hold the Shift key when you first apply the filter to prevent any rotation and to achieve a perfectly horizontal or vertical line. You can apply multiple masks (of any type) and readjust at any time by simply selecting the desired mask in the Masks panel or its corresponding pin on the photo. Press Delete (or Backspace on Windows) to delete a selected pin and the associated mask.

TIP

If you place the cursor over a pin, a color overlay appears to show you where your adjustment will be applied. This is especially helpful with subtle adjustments. The color overlay vanishes when you move away from the pin. Press Shift+O while the overlay is on to cycle through white, black, red, and green highlight colors (which may help you see it better, based on the colors in the photo you're adjusting). This process works the same with the other mask types. You can also press O to show (or hide) the overlay.

Putting the tool to use

The best way to explain this tool is with an example. Looking at the photo in Figure 9-9 shows the Linear Gradient and the settings used. My goal was to make adjustments to the sky without affecting the foreground.

Here's how:

1. **Select a photo in Grid view and press D to jump to Develop.**

2. **Press M or click Linear Gradient in the Masking panel.**

   You can even press M from Grid view to jump right to the Masking interface.

3. **Set the Show Edit Pins options to Auto and set Overlay Mode to Color Overlay on the Toolbar.**

FIGURE 9-9:
The Linear Gradient is affecting only the area above the horizon in a gradual transition.

4. **Click-and-drag toward the area you don't want affected by the mask.**

   This is a crucial step. In this example, I don't want to affect the foreground with my adjustments, so holding the Shift key, I click directly below the horizon line and drag downward. Everything above the point I click gets the maximum effect of the adjustment. The effect is gradually faded in the space between where I start dragging and where I stop. The area below where I stop is completely unaffected.

5. **Adjust mask position and size as needed.**

   Don't worry if you didn't click-and-drag in just the right spot the first time. You can resize, rotate, and reposition the mask as needed (and it's always needed).

6. **Adjust settings as needed.**

   As soon as you start moving an adjustment slider, the color overlay vanishes automatically. In this example, I used Exposure, Contrast, Shadows, Whites, Texture, Dehaze, and Clarity to make the sky and mountains more dramatic. Using a combination of settings in Masking is part of what makes it so powerful.

Adding to or subtracting from a mask

But that's not all! Sometimes you can apply a mask and have it affect only the desired region, but at other times you may find that you want to fine-tune your mask to avoid affecting certain items (like the trees and moose antlers in Figure 9-9 that protrude above the horizon), and that's where the ability to add or subtract comes into play.

Note that you can use any of the other mask types to add or subtract from a mask, which is essentially enabling one type of mask to edit another. For this photo, I use a Color Range mask to subtract from my Linear Gradient to exclude the moose antlers and trees from being affected by the adjustment. The basic process of adding or subtracting from a mask is the same regardless of the mask type.

Follow these steps:

1. **Select the mask you want to add or subtract in the Masks panel.**

2. **Click the Add button to add to the mask, or click the Subtract button to subtract from the mask, and then choose the mask type you want to use to perform that task from the pop-up menu that appears.**

   For my photo, I chose Subtract from Mask with Color Range to subtract a specific range of color from within the existing mask. This adds the new mask type to the Masks panel, with a plus or minus sign (+ or –) to indicate addition or subtraction (refer to Figure 9-10).

FIGURE 9-10: Subtracting from a Linear Gradient with a Color Range mask. The red overlay shows the area affected by the mask.

3. **Configure the parameters of the new mask type to refine the existing mask as desired.**

How you configure the parameters of the new mask depends on the type of mask you select. Let's take a closer look at the panels specific to Color Range, Luminance Range, and Depth Range together because they each have unique controls in a similar interface. Before diving into these mask types, I want to stress that they can each be used completely on their own as well as in combination with another mask.

Selecting Color Range changes the cursor to the Color Range Selector tool and displays the associated Refine slider in the Color Range panel that appears, as shown at the top of Figure 9-11. Click the Color Range Selector on the color in your photo you want to use to limit the range of the mask. Hold the Shift key while clicking to add up to five sample points, or click–drag at first to include a wider range of hues. Adjust the Refine slider to the left to limit the range or to the right to increase the range. Press O to enable the mask overlay to see how the mask is constrained.

FIGURE 9-11:
From top
to bottom:
Color Range,
Luminance
Range, and
Depth Range
options.

Color Range Selector

Refine slider

Luminance Range Selector
Luminance Range slider

Falloff slider

Depth Range Selector
Depth Range slider

Falloff slider

Selecting Luminance Range changes the cursor to the Luminance Range Selector tool and displays the associated Range and Falloff sliders, as shown in the center of Figure 9-11. Click the Luminance Range Selector tool on the area in your photo that represents the brightness values you want to use to limit the range of the mask. Once clicked, the Range slider changes to reflect the range of tones selected. Adjust the range to include or exclude tonal values; then adjust the Falloff sliders on either end of the range to further refine the smoothness of the area affected by the mask. Select the Show Luminance Map check box to see a grayscale representation of the brightness values in the photo as a visual aid for selecting the desired tones.

The Depth Range mask is available only when a photo with a compatible depth map is selected. If this option is grayed-out, Lightroom Classic doesn't support the depth map embedded in the selected photo, or there isn't one. (At the time of this writing, this feature works only with photos from iPhones using Portrait mode in HEIC format.) Once selected, it changes the cursor to the Depth Range Selector tool and displays the associated Range and Falloff sliders, as shown at the bottom of Figure 9-11. Click the Depth Range Selector tool on the area in your photo you want to use to limit the range of the mask based on how far that is from the camera. Once clicked, the Range slider changes to reflect the depth selected. Adjust the range to include or exclude regions closer or further from the camera; then adjust the Falloff sliders on either end of the range to further refine the area affected by the mask. Select the Show Depth Map check box to see a grayscale representation of the depth map embedded in the photo as a visual aid for selecting the desired regions. I've made an HEIC photo with a depth map available for exploring the Depth Range option if you'd like to try it out: www.lightroomers. com/L4D/Depth.zip.

You may be wondering about Select Sky and why I didn't use it to create the initial mask in the photo of the Alaskan lake. The sole reason was that I wanted that gradual fade toward the horizon that only the Linear Gradient can provide. However, you will undoubtedly encounter photos where having a circular filter works better than the Linear Gradient. That's where the Linear Gradient's close relative, the Radial Gradient, comes in handy. The only real difference between the two filters is its shape, so I'll skip a rehash of the sliders and options in the panel and just highlight where it's different.

Applying a Radial Gradient

As I mention at the end of the previous section, the Radial Gradient shares the same panel and options as the Linear Gradient with exceptions related to controlling the fade from the edge and whether you're applying the settings to the inside or outside of the oval. Figure 9-12 shows all the same sliders as before, but at the top is a section with a Feather slider and the Invert check box.

You can access the Radial Gradient by clicking it in the Masking panel or by pressing Shift+M from the Library or Develop. After you enable the Radial Gradient, click the photo and drag outward to create the oval that defines the area you're adjusting. You can use the O key shortcut to see the mask overlaying the affected area (if it isn't already showing). If the mask is on the inside of the circle and you want to adjust the outside of the circle, select the Invert check box to swap regions (or vice versa). You can click the center pin and move the Radial Filter as needed to the desired position, and you can click-and-drag the outside edge to resize or even rotate the filter. If needed, hold the Shift key while dragging out a filter to constrain to a circle.

FIGURE 9-12:
The Radial
Gradient.

I use this type of mask for tasks like adding a custom off-center vignette, adding small "pools of light" to draw the viewer's eye around a photo, adding sharpening to a subject's eyes (very subtle), and so on. Right-click a pin to see a contextual menu of other useful options. It's incredibly versatile, and it can be used in conjunction with any of the other mask types, or on its own.

Painting edits with a Brush

If you thought the Linear and Radial Gradients were cool, your jaw will hit the floor when you get to know the Brush. It works in essentially the same way, except that you use a brush to paint on the effects with a great deal of control, as opposed to drawing out an oval or a linear gradient. Just like the other two local adjustment tools, the Brush allows you to paint with any combination of exposure, contrast, saturation, clarity, sharpness, and so on. This allows for an amazing level of local adjustment possibilities!

To activate the Brush, you click it in the Masking panel or select your photo and press K from the Library or Develop. When the Brush is active, you see its settings appear below the Tool Strip. The settings are the same as with the gradient masks with the following exceptions, due to its being a brush:

>> **Brush:** Controls the brush settings. You can't adjust any of these settings after the effect is applied, so get this right before you start. Here are the options:

- *A/B:* You can configure two different brush settings to make switching between favored settings easier.

- *Erase:* You can "paint" with an eraser to clean up stray strokes. You can click the Erase button to activate, or you can hold down Option (or Alt on Windows) while painting. ***Note:*** The Brush cursor switches from a plus sign (+) to a minus sign (–) when Erase is enabled.

- *Size:* Brush size can also be adjusted by pressing the [and] keys.

- *Feather:* This option adjusts the softness of the edge of the brush; it can also be adjusted by holding down Shift in conjunction with the [and] keys.

- *Flow:* A low flow amount allows you to build up the effect slowly with each stroke. A high flow amount applies more of the effect with each stroke.

- *Density:* Limit the strength of the effect.

- *Auto Mask:* When this box is selected, Lightroom Classic attempts to detect the edges of the object you're painting to prevent the effect from spilling over the edge and affecting other areas. The clearer the edge, the better Auto Mask works.

When you first apply a brush stroke to your photo, Lightroom Classic marks the first spot of contact with an Edit "pin," as shown in Figure 9-13. You can click and release as often as needed to continue brushing the effect to other areas of your photo. All your painting continues to be associated with that original Edit pin until you deactivate the Brush or decide to create a new mask. At any point, you can activate an Edit pin by clicking it once to adjust the settings applied by the associated strokes. The adjustment panel highlights when you're in Edit mode to show you which settings can still be adjusted. Click the Edit button in the Tool Strip to exit Masking, or press K to commit the edit and be able to create a new Brush mask.

FIGURE 9-13:
Brush and
Edit pin.

Selecting subject, sky, background, and objects

More and more, I am seeing Adobe Sensei–powered technologies make their way into various Adobe software, and why not? Subject detection and selection is a perfect job for a machine learning algorithm to be used to do the heavy lifting and allow you to finesse the final results. Unlike the other Masking tools, there are no special controls within these options. If you have a photo with a prominent subject and you want to select that subject, simply click the Subject button and let Lightroom Classic do all the work. The more clearly defined the main subject, the better the results. The same is true for Select Sky: If your photo contains a recognizable sky, click the Sky button to select it in one move. Think of Select Background as the opposite of Select Subject, which, until this button was added, you'd use and then invert the selection to select the background.

The ability to select objects is also powered by AI, but it isn't a single-click solution, like the others. Instead, once you click the Objects button, you need to use either the Brush Select tool or Rectangle Select tool to define the area in the photo where you want Lightroom Classic to detect the object within. I've written an in-depth tutorial on this tool, which you can find at https://lightroomkillertips.com/select-objects.

I've been consistently impressed with the results of each of these options, and thanks to the ability to improve masks by adding or subtracting with other mask types, we users have gained an incredible amount of control for selectively editing areas of photos that we'd previously be able to do only in Photoshop.

TIP

Head over to https://lightroomkillertips.com/intersect-mask to learn how to use the powerful Intersect Mask feature, and then search the tutorials to see more examples of all these local adjustment and Masking tools in action.

Selecting people

If you photograph people, you'll love using this AI-powered selection tool. The People mask has a unique set of options and deserves a closer look. First, it works only when a person appears in the photo, so select such a photo and click the Masking icon in the Tool Strip to see this feature in action. With the People section of Masking expanded, you'll first see it going through the motions of detecting the people in the photo (there can be more than one). Once they're detected, an icon representing each person is shown. Click a person's icon to see the available masking options for that person, as shown in Figure 9-14.

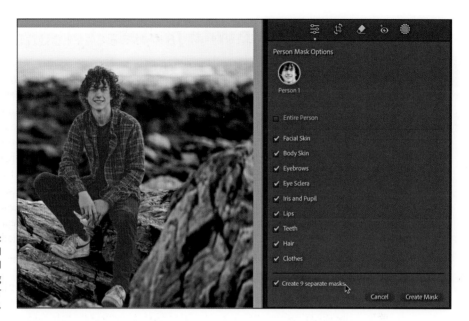

Each check box represents an aspect of the person that can get its own dedicated mask. Most of those are self-explanatory, but in case you didn't know, the whites of your eyes are called the *sclera.* If you want to create a single mask that encompasses the entire person, select the Entire Person check box at the top. However, if you want to apply different settings to each aspect of the person, select the check box next to each aspect (facial skin, body skin, eyebrows, and so on) and then select the Create [N] Separate Masks check box at the bottom. Finally, click the Create Mask button to have Lightroom Classic create each separate mask, where they will appear in the Masks panel. Then select each mask in turn and make any adjustments you want. You can, of course, use People masks in conjunction with any of the other masking tools for ultimate control.

Working with Presets, Snapshots, and History

Understanding how the Presets, Snapshots, and History panels function greatly improves your understanding of how all the Develop module settings are applied. The next few sections fill you in on the details.

Saving time with presets

The Presets panel, located on the left side of the Develop module, is where you can save a combination of settings to be reused on other photos. Various groupings of presets come preinstalled and populate the panel at first. Any new presets you create (see the next section) are stored under the User Presets section by default, or you can create new folders to store them.

Creating your own presets

Because a *preset* is simply a combination of settings pulled from the active photo, the first thing you need to do is apply some adjustments to said photo. After you take care of that business, here's how you save those adjustments as a new preset:

1. **Click the plus-sign (+) icon at the top of the Presets panel and choose Create Preset.**

   Doing so launches the New Develop Preset dialog, shown in Figure 9-15.

FIGURE 9-15:
The New
Develop Preset
dialog.

2. **Enter a name for your new preset in the Preset Name field.**

3. **(Optional) Click the Group drop-down menu to choose where to place the preset.**

This step is optional because all presets are placed in the User Presets folder by default. You only need to change the location if you want them somewhere else. That said, at the time of this writing, this is the *easiest* way to create a new preset group.

4. **Select the check box next to each setting you want to include in the preset.**

Note the Check All and Check None buttons at the bottom of the dialog.

5. **Click Create.**

The new preset appears in the Presets panel within the group you select.

Move the cursor over any preset to see a preview of its effect in the Navigator panel and the main content area. If you find the live preview in the content area distracting, you can go to the Performance tab of the Preferences and deselect the Enable hover preview of presets, history, and snapshots in Loupe option to disable it. Additionally, if you find that some presets are missing from the panel, go to the Presets tab in Preferences and select Show Partially Compatible Develop Presets to keep them from being hidden.

TIP

If you realize that you forgot to add a particular setting or you made a new adjustment and want to add it to the preset, just right-click the preset and choose Update with Current Settings from the contextual menu that appears. This launches the Update Develop Preset dialog (which is the spitting image of the New Develop Preset dialog). Select and deselect your desired settings and click Update.

TIP

Although the preinstalled presets are useful learning tools, you may find that they can clutter up the panel after you start creating your own custom preset groups. You can hide any preset group you no longer want to see by clicking the plus-sign (+) icon at the top of the Presets panel and choosing Manage Presets. When the Manage Presets dialog appears, simply deselect any group you no longer want to see in the panel (you can always come back and show them again).

Freezing time with snapshots

The Snapshots panel is a way to collect different states (or versions) of a photo and store them so that you can revisit a state later. Whatever state a photo is in can be saved as a snapshot. Just click the + icon at the top of the Snapshots panel and give the new snapshot a name. Create as many snapshots as you need. Moving the cursor over the snapshots shows a live preview in the Navigator panel.

If you make additional tweaks after saving a snapshot and like that version better, right-click the snapshot and choose Update with Current Settings from the contextual menu that appears. You can even set a snapshot as the Before state for comparison purposes from that same contextual menu. To remove a snapshot, just select it and click the minus sign (−) icon at the top of the panel.

Going back in time with the History panel

It's never too late for a do-over in Lightroom Classic. The History panel, below Snapshots, records every adjustment and tweak you make in the Develop module. You can open a photo any time and step to any earlier point in its Develop history by clicking an earlier History step. You can even save a History state as a snapshot by right-clicking and choosing Create Snapshot from the contextual menu that appears. You can use that same menu to set a specific history step to the Before state for comparison purposes as you work. (You may not always want to compare against the import state after you've been working for a while.)

If you click an earlier history step, the photo reverts to that moment in time. If you make any adjustment to the photo from that point, all the previous history steps above where you clicked are wiped away (because you're now taking the photo in a different direction from that point in time). This is where saving a snapshot can be helpful if you want to preserve an editing state and then take the editing in a new direction.

IN THIS CHAPTER

» Using the Tone Curve

» Enhancing color or converting to black-and-white

» Adding color to highlights, midtones, and shadows

» Adding capture sharpening and reducing noise

» Correcting distortions

» Removing purple fringe and working with vignettes

» Using creative effects and grain

Chapter **10**

Taking Your Photos to the Next Level

I address the most common adjustments you make to most of your images in Chapters 8 and 9. In this chapter, I explore the rest of what the Develop module has to offer (that is, all the adjustments below the Basic panel). These are the settings you can use to truly set your photos apart. Often, the difference between an okay photo and a fantastic one is subtle — so subtle that the untrained eye may not even perceive what that difference is, but you know it when you see it. Typically, this difference is related to the attention to detail and finishing touches applied by a person skilled at their craft. The tools in this chapter focus on the techniques you can use to give each photo that "something special" that elevates it above a well-exposed capture.

Working with Contrast and Color

Being able to manipulate contrast and color digitally is powerful and fun. Like anything else, the more you do it, the better you get at it. More important, the more you do it, the more you refine your eye and your own style. The adjustments you make in this area have a dramatic effect on how people react to your work. You can easily lose a little perspective on your own work after you've looked at it, tweaked it, and changed it. To help with that problem, take advantage of the tools Lightroom Classic offers — from creating snapshots of your progress to preserving certain settings as presets, from creating virtual copies to creating multiple versions — to bring some objectivity back into the creative process. Never forget that everything you do in Lightroom Classic can be undone! Take some time to step back and look at the history to see how far you've come, and possibly change course if things aren't going the way you'd envisioned.

REMEMBER

Keep in mind, though, that the basic tonal adjustments you've made already aren't set in stone. If you decide to work with the Tone Curve, convert to black-and-white, or apply a preset, for example, go back and tweak your earlier settings for better results. All these adjustments are performed on the same set of image data, which is why the Histogram panel is attached to the top of the rightmost panel. Refer to it often, and toggle the clipping indicators on and off from time to time (by pressing J) to make sure that contrast boost didn't blow out a highlight or that a creative vignette didn't clip some important detail to black.

Mastering the Tone Curve

The Tone Curve panel, shown in Figure 10-1, provides a set of tools for adjusting the amount of contrast in your photos, as well as providing another means for fine-tuning brightness values. Heck, by using the individual R, G, and B curves, you can even affect color! A lot of power is packed into this little panel. *Contrast* gives photos a depth and a richness that most people find pleasing. Images lacking contrast are often referred to as *flat*. Contrast is increased or decreased by adjusting the brightness of the tones within your photo. A typical contrast adjustment might involve decreasing the brightness

Targeted Adjustment Tool

Tone Curve

Adjust:

Parametric Curve

Region

Highlights ... 0
Lights ... 0
Darks ... 0
Shadows ... 0

FIGURE 10-1:
The Tone Curve panel.

of the darkest tones (making them darker) while simultaneously increasing the brightness of the lighter tones (making them brighter), which increases contrast between these bright and dark regions and results in a subtle *S* shape in the curve. The more exaggerated you make the bends (or curves) in that *S* appear, the greater amount of contrast you see in your photo.

In the top half of the Tone Curve panel, you see a square window that contains the histogram of the active photo in the background and a diagonal line running from the lower left corner to the upper right corner. That diagonal line is the *curve.* By bending that line, you're in effect increasing or decreasing the brightness of all the pixels at a given point in the histogram. In Figure 10-1, the curve represents Lightroom Classic's default *linear* curve (even though the line is flat, the default profile does include a slight contrast boost).

Along the top are a series of circular icons, which control the type of tone curve being displayed. By default, it's set to the parametric curve, represented by the first icon. The second icon switches to the point curve, and the three colored icons allow you to apply a curve to the red, green, and blue channels, respectively. More on those later.

REMEMBER

Any curve adjustments you make are reflected in the *real* histogram — the one perched in the Histogram panel, sitting there on top of the Tone Curve panel. The histogram inside the Tone Curve panel, however, remains unchanged no matter how many adjustments you perform — as a reminder of the Before curve state. The greater the curve adjustment you make, the more difference you see between these two histograms.

Enough of the preliminaries — it's time to look at how you make things happen and bend that line. As is consistent with every other part of Lightroom Classic, you can achieve the same result in a few ways. Here are the ways you can make contrast adjustments with the Tone Curve panel:

>> Click-and-drag points on the curve itself using any or all of the five different curves.

>> Adjust the sliders below the curve.

>> Click-and-drag the photo with the Targeted Adjustment tool.

>> Apply a Point Curve preset.

Some of these methods may sound a bit techy — especially the Targeted Adjustment tool — but don't let that worry you. I go over each method in detail in the next few sections.

Interacting with the curve

Starting with the *parametric curve* (because we're changing a set of parameters), you make adjustments by manually manipulating the curve. That line represents all the tones, from black to white, that could exist in your photo. The Tone Curve histogram is a graph showing you the number of pixels in your photo at each tonal level. By clicking a point on that line, you can move that point up or down to increase or decrease the brightness of all the pixels at that tonal level. As an alternative, you can hover the cursor over a point in the window and use the up- and down-arrow keys to make the adjustment in + or − 5 increments (hold the Shift key for + or − 20 increments).

When you make adjustments, you may notice that there are hard stops in place, represented by the highlighted region, that limit how far you can go at any given point on the curve, as shown in Figure 10-2. This limit exists only in the parametric curve. In the upcoming section "Manipulating the point curve," I explore how to gain access to the *point curve* that doesn't have these built-in limits.

FIGURE 10-2:
The built-in limits of the parametric curve.

TIP

Because being able to go back is always good, you can access a helpful Reset contextual menu by right-clicking anywhere inside the window. Double-clicking the word *Region* resets all sliders, and double-clicking the label of any single slider resets just that one.

Sliding the sliders

Not too much to this one: The Highlights, Lights, Darks, and Shadows sliders correspond to the four regions that make up the complete tonal range of your image. Click-and-drag a slider to increase or decrease the brightness of the pixels in the corresponding region. Alternatively, you can place the cursor over the number field to the right of the sliders, and a small scrubby slider appears that you can click-and-drag to make an adjustment.

Using the Targeted Adjustment tool

Pronounced "tat" for short, this is the tool for people who'd rather just work directly in the photo instead of looking at sliders, numbers, or curves. After a little practice, you may just find that it feels more natural and intuitive.

Click the TAT icon (shown earlier, in Figure 10-1) to activate it and then move the cursor over the photo. Notice that the cursor changes to a *crosshair* (this is the working end of the TAT tool) with the TAT icon trailing behind it (this is just a reminder that the tool is active). To make an adjustment, click a spot in the photo that represents the tonal region you want to adjust and then drag upward to make that tonal range brighter or downward to make it darker. As you click-and-drag, you see the adjustments reflected in the Tone Curve panel. The TAT is associated with the type of curve selected from the buttons across the top of the panel, and it works the same way for each curve.

Manipulating the point curve

The parametric curve is useful if you're new to using curves, but for the most control, you'll want to click that icon to the right of the Parametric Curve icon to switch to Point Curve mode, as shown in Figure 10-3. Notice that the Region sliders go away and a Point Curve drop-down menu appears.

When using the point curve, the adjustment you create affects all three (RGB) channels equally. It works the same way as the curve in Parametric mode, but you no longer have any limitations on how severe your curve can become. This is awesome for people who want total control or to apply creative effects not otherwise possible. These are some additional things to keep in mind with the point curve:

FIGURE 10-3:
Switching to Point Curve mode.

>> Clicking the curve adds a point (up to a maximum of 16 total).

>> You can delete a point by right-clicking it and choosing Delete from the contextual menu.

>> You can right-click the area around the curve and choose Reset Channel from the contextual menu to reset back to Linear mode.

>> Hold the Option key (or Alt on Windows) while dragging a point for finer control.

>> Hold the Shift key while dragging a point to constrain movement to only up or down.

>> You can save a custom point curve by clicking the Point Curve drop-down menu and choosing Save from the menu.

>> Using the individual red, green, and blue channel icons, you can adjust each channel independently.

When using the individual color channel curves, you see a color gradient appear in the background of the panel corresponding to the color you've chosen. Dragging upward shifts the affected tones toward the corresponding color, whereas dragging down shifts the tones toward its opposing color displayed in the panel. The individual color channel curves are for advanced color correction and creative effects due to how significantly they can shift colors in a photo. Experiment with each one to get a feel for how it works, and then right-click within the area around the curve to reset as needed.

Applying a preset

If you're working with raw images, some amount of contrast is likely built into the profile being applied (see Chapter 8 for more on profiles). A quick way to modify contrast is to choose one of the contrast presets found on the Point Curve drop-down menu, and if you like it, you're done! Keep in mind that you aren't required by law to change the contrast if you're already happy with the default state, but here are the preset options you can select from the Point Curve drop-down menu:

>> **Linear:** Takes the curve out of the curve, which means no additional contrast adjustment has been made beyond what is in the applied profile; applied by default

>> **Medium Contrast:** Adds a slight *S* curve, which means slightly darker shadows and slightly brighter highlights

>> **Strong Contrast:** A larger *S* curve than medium contrast, which means darker shadows and brighter highlights

As I mention in the previous section, if you save a custom point curve, it's also available via this drop-down menu and can be applied as desired.

Enhancing and changing colors

Who doesn't like the Color Mixer panel (formerly named HSL/Color)? In fact, this is one of those panels where you might find yourself getting a little carried away simply because it *is* so much fun. My advice: Gather some practice images and get all that wild colorizing out of your system. That way, when you really need to use this panel, you can be a little more subtle.

Unless you've selected a true *monochrome* image (a photo that has only one channel), the photos you work with in Lightroom Classic are RGB (red, *green*, *blue*) images, which means you always have the information contained in each of the three RGB channels to work with, even when you look at a photo you've converted to black-and-white in Lightroom Classic.

REMEMBER

By default, when working with a color photo, this panel is named Color Mixer, and when you click the B&W button in the Basic panel or choose a black-and-white profile, this panel changes to B&W. Because black-and-white conversion is a topic unto itself, I cover it in detail in the next section.

The Color Mixer panel is two panels in one. At first, you see it set to Mixer along with its respective controls. At the top is a button for Mixer and another for Point Color, which I come back to after describing the options for Mixer. In Mixer, the Adjust drop-down menu allows you to switch between HSL and Color, which are essentially variations on the same set of controls that allow you to adjust the hue, saturation, and luminance values in your photo.

FIGURE 10-4:
The Color Mixer panel, set to Color.

Figure 10-4 shows the Mixer face of the Color Mixer panel with Adjust set to Color — the Red section, to be more precise.

Along the top of the panel is a row of color circles that represent each of the colors you can adjust. Click any circle to activate the controls for that color, or click the multicolored button (on the far right) to see all the controls at one time. Each color has three possible adjustments:

>> **Hue:** This adjustment shifts the color between all its possible hues.

>> **Saturation:** Use this slider to change the intensity of the hue.

>> **Luminance:** This slider changes the brightness level of the hue.

FIGURE 10-5:
The HSL section of the panel, set to Luminance.

The HSL options, shown in Figure 10-5, group the adjustments by hue, saturation, and luminance rather than by color. You can see the labels for each grouping across the top of the panel. Click each label to activate the controls for that group, or click All to see the controls for all three groups at one time.

I think you'll find that using the HSL face of the panel is a more intuitive way to work, mainly because of the way the Targeted Adjustment tool (TAT) has been integrated for each group of adjustments. The Targeted Adjustment tool functions just like it did in the Tone Curve panel, except that it controls the adjustment of sliders in your chosen group: Hue, Saturation, or Luminance. I most commonly use this tool to adjust luminance and/or saturation of individual colors using the TAT. It's too easy to stray into odd colors when you start tweaking the hue.

Point Color is a relatively new addition for providing a high degree of control over a customizable range of color. To help you learn more, I invite you to read an in-depth article I wrote on Point Color: `https://lightroomkillertips.com/get-to-know-point-color-in-lightroom-classic`.

Creating black-and-white images

In the absence of color, an image becomes a study in light and shadow, texture, and detail in a very different way than would be the case with color photos. Because of this, black-and-white (B&W) photos can often achieve a visual impact that color photos can't. When you're converting a color photo to black-and-white, the process starts with a conversion to black-and-white, but the process doesn't end there. To see all that's involved, start by looking at the B&W panel and then follow along as I address how you can call on a few other Lightroom Classic panels to enhance the final result. To initiate a black-and-white conversion and transform the Color Mixer panel to B&W, try one of the following methods:

> » Press V.

> » Click the B&W button in the top section of the Basic panel.

> » Click a preset that converts to black-and-white.

> » Choose a B&W profile from the Profile Browser.

TIP

Several black-and-white presets and profiles come preinstalled with Lightroom Classic — I highly recommend exploring those to see what is possible, and potentially use one as a starting point.

To see how this whole black-and-white conversion process works, follow along as I recount the steps I take to move a photo from its color state to a B&W state:

1. **Select the photo in the Filmstrip, and open the Profile Browser in the Basic panel.**

   Click the B&W button in the Profile Browser to show only black-and-white profiles in the Browser.

2. **Move the cursor over each profile to find one you like as a starting point, and click it to apply.**

   I ended up with B&W 10 as the starting point for the photo in Figure 10-6. Remember, depending on the profile you select, you might be able to further modify the look using the associated Amount slider (near the top of the Browser) for that profile. Close the Profile Browser when you're done.

FIGURE 10-6:
The black-and-white profiles are a useful starting point.

3. **Adjust white-balance settings in the Basic panel as needed.**

REMEMBER

   Keep in mind that even though you see a black-and-white image, all the color data in the original image is still at your disposal. Adjusting the Temp and Tint sliders can bring out additional detail and texture.

4. **Readjust basic tonal settings in the Basic panel as needed.**

As with white balance, now that you're working with a range of black-and-white values, you may find that an adjustment to exposure or to the black clipping level is required to achieve your desired result.

5. **Expand the B&W panel, as shown in Figure 10-7.**

FIGURE 10-7:
The Black &
White Mix
controls.

TIP

This is your opportunity to pick up where Lightroom Classic left off and adjust the mix of color data to bring out the tonal qualities of the image you're after. Try clicking the Auto button to see how that looks. Double-click the Black & White Mix label to reset all sliders back to 0 if needed.

6. **(Optional) Click the Targeted Adjustment tool (TAT) inside the B&W Mix panel.**

Although you can certainly adjust individual color sliders in the panel, you'll find that working directly inside the photo with the TAT is a much more intuitive and satisfying process.

7. **If you decide to use the TAT, click a tone in the photo and drag downward to darken or drag upward to brighten.**

TIP

This is where your creativity and vision come together! While you click-and-drag the TAT, the corresponding Black & White Mix sliders move within the panel. You can always undo an adjustment by pressing ⌘+Z (or Ctrl+Z on Windows) or by stepping back to an earlier history state. This exploration process is also a good time to make use of the Snapshots panel if you want to preserve a particular state. (For more on the Snapshots panel, see Chapter 9.)

8. **If you chose the TAT route, dock the TAT back in the B&W panel after you complete your mix adjustments.**

   Figure 10-7 shows you the kinds of transformations you can achieve with the B&W panel.

Just because you've completed the B&W mix doesn't mean the photo is finished. Depending on the photo and the result in your mind's eye, you may go on to do any (or all) of the following to finish the job:

>> Use the Brush in Masking to make dodge and burn local adjustments.

>> Use the Tone Curve panel to enhance contrast.

>> Adjust Clarity, Texture, and/or Dehaze.

>> Use the Color Grading panel to add color to the highlights and shadows.

>> Use the Effects panel to darken or lighten the edges or add grain.

The best way to know when you're done is to roll up your sleeves and experiment. The wonderful thing about Lightroom Classic is that none of these adjustments alters the pixels in your original images. You can always go back. Using the Snapshots panel to preserve key states in the development process or even virtual copies to branch out into multiple versions gives you a lot of room to move.

Adding color to shadows and highlights

A common use of the Color Grading panel — the panel stuck right under the Color Mixer (or B&W) panel (and formerly known as Split Toning) — is to add a hint of a color tint to black-and-white images. Of course, you can and should try using it with color photos, too! Color Grading allows you to add a color tint to the highlights, midtones, and shadows (or any combination of the three), with Hue, Saturation, and Luminance sliders for each tonal region.

The panel opens, displaying a color wheel for each tonal region, which is called *3-way view* (see Figure 10-8). Across the top are icons that allow for switching from 3-way to view a larger color wheel for just one tonal region at a time, as shown in Figure 10-9 for the Shadows. Within a color wheel, you can click-and-drag to dial-in a specific hue and saturation value for the desired tint. The tint is applied to that tonal region in real time, so what you see is what you get. When viewing a single tonal range, you can click the disclosure triangle to reveal the Hue, Saturation, and Luminance sliders, which can also be manipulated to fine-tune the look you want.

FIGURE 10-8:
The Color
Grading panel
allows for
creative and
practical color
adjustments.

The Hue and Saturation sliders control the color of the tint, whereas the Luminance slider allows you to control the brightness of the corresponding tonal range. Because you can apply a tint only to pixels that are not pure white, it can be helpful to use the Luminance slider to darken the highlights to better see the applied tint to that region. When in 3-way view, the Luminance slider appears below each color wheel. The Eye icon below each color wheel allows you to hide the effect of the corresponding color wheel when clicked.

At the bottom of the panel, you'll find the Blending and Balance sliders. Blending controls how much mixing of tints happens between the tonal ranges, so if set to 0, there would be no mixing of tints, whereas if set to 100, there would be maximum mixing of the applied tints. The Balance slider can shift the tonal ranges that are considered highlights or shadows. If Balance were set to 100, it would force the tint applied to the highlights across

FIGURE 10-9:
The Color Grading panel, showing just the controls for adding color to the shadows.

almost all pixels in the entire image, and a setting of −100 would force the shadow tint across almost all pixels. I suggest applying a strong tint to the shadows and an opposite tint to the highlights, and then experiment with different Blending and Balance settings to see how they work.

TIP

To learn even more about Color Grading, check out my tutorial on Lightroom Killer Tips: https://lightroomkillertips.com/introducing-color-grading.

The Devil's in the Details

Working your way down the right side of the Lightroom Classic interface, your next stop is the Detail panel, which is the place for getting up close and personal with your photos. I think you'll agree with me that sometimes you need to zoom to the 100% view to see what's happening in your photo. In fact, the only way you can really see the adjustments made in the Detail panel is when you're in at least 100% zoom level (or greater). To make that easier, the folks at Adobe added a nice little Preview window to the Detail panel, which you can see in Figure 10-10. You can click-and-drag inside the Preview window to view different areas of the photo or click the squarish crosshair to the left of the window and then click on the photo in the content area to focus the Preview window on that

FIGURE 10-10:
The Detail panel, showing the Preview window and Sharpening controls.

section of the photo. If you want to zoom closer, you can right-click inside the window to choose either the 100% or 200% zoom level from the contextual menu that appears.

Applying capture sharpening

Sharpening can't correct an out-of-focus image, but it can increase the perception of detail in a properly focused image. Lightroom Classic has come a long way in regard to sharpening. You can find output sharpening to use in both Print and Web modules, as well as in the Export dialog. In addition, you can even selectively apply sharpness using Masking for more creative and localized sharpening applications. When all of these tools are put together in a sharpening workflow, you can apply the sharpening in the Detail panel as it was originally intended, which is simply to compensate for the inherent softness in raw captures. This is referred to as *capture sharpening*.

Sharpening is a powerful adjustment, and, as with most powerful tools, you should never use more than the minimum required to get the job done. Increasing sharpness can bring details to life, which can translate into a greater visual impact. Increasing sharpness too much can make a photo appear crunchy and overprocessed and cause viewers to have a negative reaction to the image. You want your sharpness setting to be *just right* — if anything, you might want to err on the softer side.

One key trait that humans find pleasing to the eye is the separation of edges (*sharpening*) around certain details. The human eye is drawn to this edge detail, and sharpening can be used to draw a viewer in closer. Lightroom Classic's sharpening controls are all about edge detection and enhancement. The controls are described in this list:

>> **Amount:** This is simply the amount of sharpening being applied. An increase in the amount translates to an increase in sharpening.

>> **Radius:** This determines how far that sharpening amount extends from the edges being sharpened. The higher the radius, the farther the reach from the edges.

>> **Detail:** This determines how much of the finer detail between the prominent edges has sharpening applied to it. The higher the setting, the more the finer detail edges are sharpened.

>> **Masking:** This control provides a means to protect areas of the image from having sharpening applied. No Mask means all areas have sharpening applied to them. A high Masking value means that only the most defined edges are sharpened.

By default, all raw photos have a moderate amount of sharpening applied. However, you may want to move beyond the defaults, depending on the subject matter of your photos. One of the best ways to understand how this panel was intended to be used is to examine the settings contained in the two sharpening presets against the default sharpening settings. Table 10-1 compares the default values against the values found in the presets Sharpen–Scenic and Sharpen–Faces (found in the Presets panel on the left side of the Lightroom Classic interface under the Classic–General group, which is the same group we restored in Chapter 8 to use the Punch preset).

Here's what the Adobe folks were thinking when they came up with a Scenic preset and a Faces preset. In a typical scenic photo, you see a lot of details. In fact, overall detail is a favored trait. You *want* to see details. Detail draws in the eye. Now think about a portrait. Detail is certainly important, but only in certain places. Sharpness of the eyes is vital. Showing every pore and wrinkle in sharp relief is not important.

TABLE 10-1   **Comparison of Preset Sharpening Settings**

Settings	Default	Scenic	Faces
Amount	40	40	35
Radius	1.0	0.8	1.4
Detail	25	35	15
Masking	0	0	60

Looking at the settings of the Scenic preset, you see that the amount is set to 40, compared to 35 in Faces. Not a huge difference, but not surprising that scenic landscapes would get a greater amount of sharpening. I come back to Radius at the end, but for now, I want to move on to the Detail setting. The Scenic Detail setting is 10 points higher than the default, whereas the Faces setting is 10 points lower than the default. This, too, makes sense because you definitely want to bring out the finer detail in a landscape, but not in a person's skin. Now, as you compare the Masking setting of 0 for Scenic versus 60 for Faces, you can see that sharpening is being applied to all areas of the landscape image, but only on the most defined edges of the portrait. This high Masking value also explains why the radius was slightly bumped up in the portrait image to thicken the edges of the most defined features, knowing that the finer detail would be left unsharpened.

So ask yourself the following question: Is your photo more like a portrait, where only the most defined edges should be sharpened, or is your photo more like a landscape, where even the finest detail needs a boost? With that determination in mind, I suggest applying the appropriate preset even if you just use it as a new starting point over the default.

To see how all this works in tandem with the Detail panel, follow along as I walk through one example. Grab a portrait photo of your own because it's easier to see the effect of the Detail panel settings on your screen than in the limited reproduction ability of the book.

1. **Click the eye (or an equally important detail) to zoom into 100% view.**

You can see the effects of the sharpening only when you're zoomed to 100% or looking at the 100% Preview in the Detail panel.

2. **In the Presets panel on the left side of the Lightroom Classic interface, apply the Sharpen–Faces preset.**

In many cases, you can stop right there, but for the sake of explaining the process, I want you to see whether you can finesse this starting point. If you don't see the Classic–General preset group, refer to the Chapter 9 section about managing your presets to make it visible.

3. **Increase the Amount setting and then dial back the setting until you see nice edges with no jagged pixels or white halo along the edges.**

Hold the Option key (or Alt on Windows) while dragging the slider to see your photo in black-and-white. Sharpening is applied only to the luminance (brightness data), not to the color data, so seeing the photo in black-and-white provides another way to see what exactly is happening to the photo.

4. **Leave the Radius at its default.**

By making the decision about which preset to apply, you're already in the ballpark. If anything, you may want to dial back Radius, but your energy is better spent on the other three adjustments.

5. **Hold the Option key (or Alt on Windows) and increase the Detail slider until you can see unwanted detail appear, and then dial back the slider until only the key edges are visible.**

By using the Option (or Alt) modifier with this adjustment right from the start, you can truly focus on just the detail. I typically dial up Detail until I can see pores on the skin and then dial it back until those pores are diminished. Keep in mind that by applying the Faces preset, you already have a high Masking amount being applied, which limits the areas being sharpened.

6. **Increase the Masking amount as necessary to compensate for increases made to the Detail setting.**

The Option (or Alt) modifier works with this slider, too! In this case, you see the mask itself. Areas of white in the mask are the areas where sharpening will be applied. Black areas will have no sharpening.

7. **Check other areas of the photo at 100% to evaluate the level of sharpening applied.**

At the end of that process, the settings I preferred were not far from the Faces preset. Would anyone notice that difference in a normal viewing environment? Not likely. When you're processing tens, hundreds, or thousands of photos, you don't want to spend this kind of time finessing the capture sharpening on a photo–by–photo basis. Get a good feel for what the sliders can do, create your own presets (or use the existing ones) that suit your needs/tastes, and apply those presets in batches to your photos.

Dealing with noise

The bottom section of the Detail panel deals with noise reduction — no, not that acoustic paneling stuff. In terms of digital photography, *noise* is simply random electrical signals recorded by the camera's sensor that can degrade the quality of the photo. In the absence of light, these random signals are more visible because the sensor records less actual data, which is why noise issues are common in underexposed and high-ISO photos.

REMEMBER

I cover the new AI-powered Denoise option for noise reduction in Chapter 7 — if you want to learn about the manual noise reduction controls, read on. Typically, you'd use one or the other, but not both.

Lightroom Classic's Manual Noise Reduction options are simple (refer to Figure 10-11 to see the noise-reduction controls in the Detail panel), but they can be effective when it comes to reducing minor noise issues.

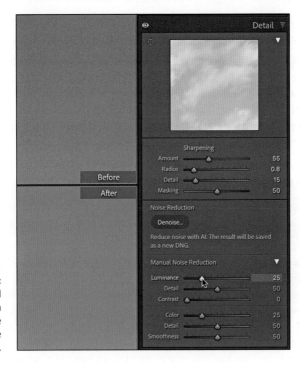

FIGURE 10-11: A Before and After view of a luminance noise correction.

You have one set of sliders for dealing with luminance noise reduction, and another set of sliders for reducing the effects of color noise. After you figure out how to differentiate between the two, it's simply a matter of adjusting the respective set of sliders just enough (and no more) to solve the problem. Here's my handy guide to discerning luminance noise from color noise:

>> **Luminance noise tends to look like the more familiar *grain* you see in film.** You have fluctuations in brightness levels, whereas color remains essentially consistent — common in areas of blue sky.

» **Color noise can be recognized by the presence of multicolored pixels (like Christmas tree lights).** It's typically present in the shadow areas.

With luminance noise, the most likely place you encounter that headache is in blue skies. Figure 10-11 shows a Before and After (at 300% zoom) example of a blue sky with the typical grainy signs of luminance noise. To counteract the noise level in the Before image, I adjusted the Luminance slider until the tones in the sky smoothed out. (Try increasing the Masking slider above to avoid sharpening noise and you may find that you don't need to apply any noise reduction.) Use the Detail (helps preserve areas of minute detail when set to higher value) and Contrast (sets amount of edge detection used to identify noise) sliders to fine-tune results.

Figure 10-12 shows a Before and After (at 300% zoom) example of a color noise reduction on an ISO 4000 photo. The default setting of Color=25 is usually good enough for most lower-ISO photos. If color noise is still visible, continue to increase the Color slider until you've neutralized as many of the random multi-colored pixels as you can. Use the Detail slide (same as with Luminance, above it) and the Smoothness slider (helps reduce color mottling artifacts at higher ISOs) to fine-tune its application.

FIGURE 10-12:
A Before and After example of a color noise correction.

The main issue to watch for with any type of noise reduction is the loss of detail. Too much noise reduction can turn your photo into a mush of pixels resembling a watercolor painting. Having a little noise and more detail rather than less noise and pixel mush is usually better.

Correcting lens distortions and vignetting

The Lens Corrections panel has two tabs, labeled Profile and Manual. I review the options on the Profile tab first because that's often the only one you need. With the introduction of lens profiles several versions back, correcting lens distortions (where straight lines bend outward or inward due to the nature of the lens used) became as easy as selecting a check box — the Enable Profile Corrections box, to be specific. Figure 10-13 shows Before and After views for a correction of the common barrel distortion (lines bend outward) found in wide-angle lenses. When you select that check box, Lightroom Classic automatically applies the correct lens profile by reading the photo's metadata to determine the camera and lens combo used, which will correct lens distortion and lens vignetting (darkening of the edges). Lightroom Classic has a list of supported lenses, which grows with every update.

FIGURE 10-13: Before and After views of applying a lens profile to correct barrel distortion.

If your lens isn't automatically found, you can select the make and model of your lens, which opens a list of all profiles for that lens that you can choose from. Check here for the complete list of supported lenses and resources for creating custom lens profiles if your lens isn't supported: `https://helpx.adobe.com/camera-raw/kb/supported-lenses.html`.

After you apply a profile, you can use the Distortion and Vignetting sliders in the Amount section at the bottom to turn down the adjustment (and bring back some distortion or vignetting). You'll most commonly leave these at the default settings, but sometimes it's nice to bring back some natural lens vignetting instead of adding it in the Effects panel.

If the barrel or pincushion distortion wasn't completely corrected, an additional Distortion slider on the Manual tab can be used to fine-tune the correction (see Figure 10-14). Move the Distortion slider to the right to further correct barrel distortion and to the left to correct any remaining pincushion distortion. At the bottom of the Manual tab, you find a manual control for further fine-tuning the vignetting correction, if needed.

FIGURE 10-14:
The Manual tab of the Lens Corrections panel.

The Remove Chromatic Aberration check box at the top of the panel is an easy one-click correction aimed at what is called *lateral chromatic aberration,* which can appear as a colored fringe in the corners of some images. All you need to do is select the check box to remove it. For ideas on dealing with the more challenging axial chromatic aberration, see the next section.

Reducing chromatic aberration

Axial chromatic aberration, when present, most commonly appears throughout the photo in the form of a reddish or greenish fringe along high-contrast edges. You can also sometimes encounter purplish fringing around specular highlights (bright highlights, like sun glinting off metal), which is called *sensor blooming.* All these forms of fringing can be reduced using the tools in the Defringe section of the Manual tab within the Lens Corrections panel, as shown in Figure 10-15.

FIGURE 10-15: Before and After views of a chromatic aberration correction.

Within the Defringe section of the panel, you find the following tools:

» **Fringe Color Selector:** This one can be used to select the range of hues contained within the fringe area and set the Defringe Amount and Hue sliders with a single click on the fringe. It works best when zoomed to 100%.

» **Amount:** The purplish color of the top Amount slider is the giveaway that this controls the amount of correction applied for removing reddish-purple fringe.

» **Purple Hue:** These sliders control the range of reddish-purple hues that will be affected by the Amount slider above them. The range can be shifted and expanded as needed to make the desired correction.

» **Amount:** The greenish color of this Amount slider is the giveaway that this controls the amount of correction for removing greenish-blue fringe.

» **Green Hue:** These sliders control the range of greenish-blue hues that will be affected by the Amount slider above them. The range can be shifted and expanded as needed to make the desired correction.

The basic idea is that if you see reddish-purple fringing appearing in your photo, you can increase the corresponding Amount slider until the fringe is removed and adjust the Purple Hue slider to hone in on the exact hue of the fringe in question. Likewise, if you see a greenish fringe appearing along high-contrast edges, use the corresponding green Amount slider and Green Hue sliders to remove that fringe from your photo. Figure 10-15 shows Before and After views of just this type of correction. You may find it helpful to zoom to even greater than 100% to better see and correct the fringe.

TIP

If you find that your Defringe correction accidentally removes color from objects that should be that color, you can use the Masking Brush configured with a negative amount of Defringe to paint over that region and remove the Defringe correction to restore the color.

Transforming perspective distortions

Perspective distortions are caused by how you hold the camera relative to the subject. A common example is when you tilt the camera backward to take in the top of a tall building. Because the camera is no longer perpendicular to the building, you've introduced a perspective distortion that makes it appear as though the building is leaning backward. You may also encounter the dreaded crooked horizon caused by not holding the camera level. Many versions ago, Adobe added the Upright tools, as shown in Figure 10-16, to the Develop module.

FIGURE 10-16:
Transform panel options.

Upright consists of a set of functions that can analyze the photo and perform the needed correction or at least a better starting point.

>> **Guided Upright Tool:** Located in the upper left corner of the panel; see the Guided description in this list.

>> **Off:** Turns off all Upright adjustments.

>> **Auto:** Automatically performs a leveling adjustment combined with a vertical and horizontal perspective distortion correction; usually provides a more natural-looking correction.

>> **Guided:** If none of the one-click fixes provided by the other Upright buttons does the trick, choose this Guided button or click directly on the Guided

Upright Tool to manually draw out two (or more) guides along edges of objects (like buildings) that should be perfectly horizontal or perfectly vertical, and a corresponding correction is applied. The guides can be manually tweaked, nudged, and adjusted if not placed correctly the first time. A magnified loupe appears alongside the cursor to help you pinpoint guide placement.

>> **Level:** Useful for fixing crooked horizons.

>> **Vertical:** Performs the same leveling adjustment as the Level button, combined with vertical perspective correction.

>> **Full:** An option to be saved for the most severe distortion problems. If your photo suffers from horizontal and vertical perspective distortion, along with a crooked horizon and possibly a need to be rotated horizontally, the Full button is worth a click.

As powerful and accurate as the Upright functions can be, they sometimes need a little nudging to make the result look natural. You can further refine the adjustments made by the Upright functions using the manual controls within the Transform section (if needed):

>> **Vertical:** Correct or tweak vertical distortion problems.

>> **Horizontal:** Correct or tweak horizontal distortion problems.

>> **Rotate:** Use to fine-tune a leveling correction; similar to the Angle slider in the Crop tool.

>> **Aspect:** Can be dragged to the left to squish the photo or dragged to the right to stretch the photo to make objects in it appear more normal after a perspective distortion correction. See Figure 10-17 for an example.

>> **Scale:** Makes the photo larger (or smaller) within the existing canvas, which can be useful if empty pixels remain in the photo after a perspective correction and you want to keep the photo at its original pixel dimensions.

>> **X Offset:** Can be used to reposition the photo on the canvas along the x-axis (horizontally).

>> **Y Offset:** Can be used to reposition the photo on the canvas along the y-axis (vertically). The X and Y Offset controls are useful for tweaking the position of the photo on the canvas after a distortion correction to ensure that the important part of the photo remains visible.

>> **Constrain Crop:** Select this check box to let Lightroom Classic automatically crop the image to hide empty areas of pixels after a distortion correction. This reduces the overall pixel dimensions of the photo.

FIGURE 10-17:
Before and
After views of
a perspective
distortion
correction.

For example, if you look at the Before view of the photo in Figure 10-17, you can see that the building appears to be slightly leaning backward, which was caused by the fact that I pointed my camera upward to capture the photo. After trying the Auto, Full, and Guided upright options, I felt that the Full adjustment did the best job of correcting the perspective distortion. However, it did result in the building appearing to be stretched taller than it should be, so I moved the Aspect slider in a negative direction to squish the building down slightly to make it appear less stretched.

REMEMBER

All these adjustments are nondestructive and can be easily reset, so feel free to click every button and move every slider to see how it works.

Creative Effects

If you've ever wanted to add or enhance the appearance of lens blur or simulated film grain or creatively add a vignette into your digitally pure photographs, the Lens Blur and Effects panels are the places to go. Lens Blur is one of the newest features added to Lightroom Classic, so I'll show you that one first and then move on to the Effects panel.

Creative blur applications

Though you typically strive for sharp and in-focus photographs, what can make a sharp subject truly stand out is a nicely blurred background. Often, photographers pay top dollar for a lens with a wide aperture (like f/2.8) so that they can take photos with a shallow depth of field and a sharply focused subject. The new Lens Blur panel, as shown in Figure 10-18, provides you with a new set of tools to add or enhance the blur in the backgrounds of your photos beyond what exists in the original image. When you first open the panel, it appears grayed-out because no settings are applied until you click to select the Apply check box.

FIGURE 10-18: The Lens Blur panel with a blur applied.

Once selected, the panel comes to life and Lightroom Classic uses AI to analyze the photo and create a depth map, which it uses to apply the simulated lens blur. A more clearly defined subject yields better results. The photo shown in Figure 10-18 already had some background blur due to the aperture of the lens used (and the distance between the camera and the subject and between the subject and the background), but you can creatively use this tool to add more blur and enhance that blur to mimic different types of lenses. Let's take a closer look at the controls:

» **Blur Amount:** This slider controls the amount of blur being applied.

» **Bokeh:** Hover the cursor over each bokeh type to see which type of lens it represents.

- » **Cat Eye:** A characteristic of some lenses, increasing this slider can result in the out-of-focus highlights taking on a swirling, crescent-shaped look.

- » **Boost:** Use this option to adjust the brightness of out-of-focus light sources in the photo.

- » **Focus Range:** These tools fine-tune the areas that are in focus and blurred.

- » **Visualize Depth:** Select this check box to see a color-coded visual of what is in focus to what is blurred, with yellow representing in-focus and dark purple being blurred.

- » **Brush Refinement:** Click the disclosure triangle to access brush tools for manually adding focus or blur areas to the photo to finesse the final result.

For a deeper dive into what this panel can do, check out my tutorial, Lightroom Killer Tips, at `https://lightroomkillertips.com/exploring-the-new-lens-blur-panel`.

Creative vignette applications

The Effects panel, shown in Figure 10-19, has two sections:

- » **Post-Crop Vignetting:** Reach for this tool whenever you want to add a vignette for creative effect. Not only do you have multiple sliders to refine the effect, but it works equally on the cropped and uncropped versions as well (meaning that the effect automatically conforms to the edges of the photo after it has been cropped).

- » **Grain:** Reach for this tool whenever you want to add filmlike grain for creative effect.

FIGURE 10-19:
The Effects panel.

The Post-Crop vignette controls were added years ago after the explosion in popularity of adding a vignette as a creative effect. The goal here isn't to remove a vignette but rather to apply one! Applying a *vignette* is a simple way to create a framing effect that draws the eye into the photo. As with any creative effect, you can easily overdo it, but I really enjoy the effect all the same. Another great thing about the Post-Crop vignette is that it reapplies the vignette settings to the cropped version of the photo, should you use the Crop tool after having already applied a creative vignette. You can play around with five separate sliders in the Post-Crop section:

- » **Style:** This drop-down menu contains three options — Highlight Priority, Color Priority, and Paint Overlay — that control how the vignette blends with the colors in the photo. Highlight priority is the default and usually the best option. Color Priority is similar to Highlight, but it tries to avoid shifts in hue around the affected area (use this if you see color shifts in the vignette). Paint Overlay simply applies a black or white (depending on the Amount slider setting) overlay along the photo's edge.

- » **Amount:** As you might expect, this slider controls the amount of the added vignette. Move to the left to darken and to the right to brighten.

- » **Midpoint:** This slider increases or decreases the area at the center unaffected by the vignette. Moving the slider to the left reduces the midpoint and by extension maximizes the range the vignette can extend into the center of the photo. Moving the slider to the right has the opposite effect.

- » **Roundness:** Increasing the Roundness value results in a more circular vignette, whereas decreasing roundness produces a more elliptical result.

- » **Feather:** This slider controls the amount of fade applied to the edge of the vignette into the midpoint. A feather setting of 0 results in a hard-edged solid border, whereas a feather setting of 100 results in the most gradual transition from the midpoint to the edge of the photo.

- » **Highlights:** This slider is used to apply a different level of processing to the brighter areas of the photo affected by the vignette when Highlight or Color Priority styles are used.

There's no right or wrong way to apply a vignette; it's completely a matter of personal taste. To see an example, check out Figure 10-20, where I attempt to mimic an old-postcard look by adding a white frame (positive Amount) around the photo along with a grainy texture.

Creative grain applications

Due to photography's roots in film, digital photography often attempts to emulate certain film stocks. Although film stock colors can be mimicked with a Profile, the Effects panel is where you go to add simulated film grain. The addition of grain is also an entirely personal choice, and, as such, you may never venture this far down the panel. That said, file this information away because it may come in handy down the road. You can adjust the following three sliders (refer to Figure 10-19):

- » **Amount:** Use this to control the overall strength of the grain effect.

FIGURE 10-20:
An example of a creative vignette that adds a white border around the photo.

> >> **Size:** The larger the grain, the softer and less pronounced the edges of the grain.

> >> **Roughness:** Think of this as the way to control the frequency of the grain (from coarse to fine).

TIP

Check out the preinstalled Grain and Vignetting preset groups to see some sample settings you can use as starting points.

Modifying the Calibration Settings

The Calibration panel, possibly the least-visited panel, provides the ability to change the *process version* used on your photo and the legacy controls for changing the baseline rendering of colors in raw photos. The process version is the underlying algorithm used to render the raw data in your photographs. Over the years, Adobe has improved on that algorithm to do a better job of reducing noise, sharpening details, and basically making the most of the data captured by your camera.

The only reason you'd ever need to visit this panel is to change the process version. The Shadows, Red Primary, Green Primary, and Blue Primary sliders have been made obsolete by all the new profile options made available with the latest version of Lightroom Classic.

At the time of this writing, Process Version 6 is the latest and greatest. However, it's likely that the process version (PV) will be updated again in the future, and at that time the new PV will become the default PV to enable access to whatever new features/improvements are dependent on the updated PV. As a result, existing photos using the older PV will need to be updated to the latest PV if you want to use the new features that are tied to the new PV.

The updating process has become much more seamless, so much so that you may not even notice it happened. For example, if I grab an old photo set to PV 3 and bring it to Develop, all I need to do is move the new Texture slider (or any feature dependent on the latest PV) and Lightroom Classic quietly updates the PV for me. Occasionally updating the PV can come with a slight visual change to the photo as Lightroom Classic translates the edits to the new PV, but this is rare. For more on updating process version, check out this tutorial I wrote at Photofocus: `https://photofocus.com/software/lightroom-faq-updating-process-version`.

If you select a photo in Develop that is set to an older PV, a Lightning Bolt icon appears in the lower right corner of the Histogram panel to indicate that it's an older PV. You can click that icon to manually update the PV, or you can change the PV in the Calibration panel.

4

Sharing Your Work with the World

IN THIS PART . . .

Exporting copies of your photos and using external editors

Creating books and slideshows

Printing your photos

Making a web gallery for your photos

Chapter **11**

Exporting Copies and Using External Editors

Throughout this book, I make a big deal about the fact that your photos are never actually "inside" Lightroom Classic, which does beg the question, "If the photos are never in Lightroom Classic, why does exporting sound an awful lot like you're getting them out?" Good question! In Lightroom Classic, the export process could be called "creating copies of your photos while applying your Lightroom Classic adjustments," but that doesn't quite roll off the tongue the same way as "exporting" does. However, that is what's really happening here. If you're familiar with Photoshop, you can think of exporting as using the Save As command on steroids. No matter how you think about it, the essential point is that this is how you apply your Lightroom Classic edits to copies of your source files. You export images for many reasons, and here are a few of the most common — you want to email photos to someone, upload to a social media site, or upload to an online print service or your website.

In each case, you have a specific output destination with specific file requirements, which is what will drive the choices you make when you configure the export settings. The first part of this chapter takes a closer look at choosing the best export settings for the job, and then it wraps up with a look at exporting to an external editor (like Adobe Photoshop).

Exploring the Export Dialog

Before I dig into all the ways to access the Export dialog, shown in Figure 11-1, and the overall workflow involved with the export process, I want to introduce you to what you'll find there so that you have a sense of what's involved as you move forward:

FIGURE 11-1:
The Export
dialog.

>> **Preset section:** A consistent Lightroom Classic feature is the capability to save a collection of settings as a preset to make it faster and easier to use those same settings again in the future. The left side of the dialog is reserved for the creation and management of export presets.

>> **Plug-in Manager:** *Export plug-ins* are third-party scripts that extend Lightroom Classic export functionality by allowing you to perform additional tasks, such as sending photos to a third-party application or uploading files to photo sharing sites, as part of the export process. You use the Plug-in Manager to find and install new export plug-ins. Be sure to check out the installation and user instructions provided by the developer of the plug-in you want to install.

>> **Export To:** The topmost section in the main part of the dialog is used to choose where you'll export your photos. You have three default options: Email, Hard Drive, and CD/DVD, which are accessible from the drop-down

menu. If you install export plug-ins, they also appear on the drop-down menu. Note that directly below the drop-down menu, you see the number of photos (and, potentially, videos) selected for export.

- >> **Export Location panel:** Continuing through the panels, the Export Location panel is for choosing where you want the exported copies saved. No matter what may happen with the photos after the export is complete, they first need to be saved to a location on your disk.

- >> **File Naming panel:** Because exporting always involves creating copies, Lightroom Classic provides you with the opportunity to decide how those copies are to be named. The File Naming panel displays all the filename templates you may have created earlier (during import or while working in the Library module) and provides access to the Filename Template Editor, used to create new templates.

- >> **Video panel:** Choose the format and quality settings for the video copies that will be created (if exporting video).

- >> **File Settings panel:** Here you choose which file format you want the copies saved as; you can also configure any file-specific settings here, such as *color space* (the gamut of colors it contains) and *bit depth* (the amount of data it contains), depending on the file format you choose.

- >> **Content Credentials:** This is a new method for attaching attribution, history, and edit information to your photos. This early-access version may change in the future.

- >> **Image Sizing panel:** This panel provides the ability to resize JPEG, JPEG XL, AVIF, PSD, TIFF, PNG, or lossy DNG files created during export.

- >> **Output Sharpening:** You can apply additional sharpening to the copies based on where these they'll be viewed (either onscreen or in print).

- >> **Metadata panel:** Control how much metadata (ranging from camera-generated shooting information to keywords) is included with the exported copies.

- >> **Watermarking panel:** You can choose to add a simple textual watermark or a graphical watermark to JPG, PNG, AVIF, PSD, and TIFF copies.

- >> **Post-Processing panel:** When saving files to disk, you can have Lightroom Classic open your exported copies in another application (such as a file browser or another image editor) to facilitate moving to the next stage of your workflow.

TIP

I highly recommend confirming the number of files to be exported before you click the Export button. The number appears right above the configuration panels. (In Figure 11-1, for example, this text reads *Export 32 Files.*) I have discovered on more than one occasion that I accidentally selected more photos than I intended to export. Believe me, the last thing you want is to find that you just exported several thousand more images than you needed! Fortunately, Lightroom Classic provides a Cancel button, too.

REMEMBER

Panels are collapsible and expandable. Click a panel label to collapse or expand that panel. Use ⌘+click (or Ctrl+click on Windows) on any panel label to collapse or expand all panels. Use Option+click (or Alt+click on Windows) on any panel label to enable or disable Solo mode (meaning only one panel can be expanded at a time). When a panel is collapsed, you see a summary of its settings displayed in the panel's header. When you eventually install export plug-ins (and I suggest that you do so), you'll find that they add several configuration panels to the dialog; therefore, using Solo mode reduces the need to scroll and allows you to see all settings at a glance. Nice!

Okay, enough of the introduction. Time to take a step back and look at all the steps involved in the export process, and then I'll drill down deeper into the settings used in each export panel.

Creating Copies of Processed Photos

After you process your photos (like a pro!), you're ready to send them out into the world. That means it's export time! The humble Export dialog contains a great deal of power, and with a little practice, you can harness all it has to offer.

Employing an export workflow

Lightroom Classic (as you've probably figured out by now) is a workflow application, and within the larger workflow of taking your photos from input to output, there exist many smaller workflows within workflows. Export is no exception. Here are the basic steps:

1. **Select the images you want to export.**

2. **Initiate the Export command.**

3. **Configure settings as required to meet your output needs.**

4. **(Optional) Save settings as a preset for reuse.**

   In some cases, you may not need, or want, to create a preset for every export.

The following sections provide a closer look at each step in the workflow. I follow up that discussion with a real-world example for saving an export preset.

Step 1: Selecting the images you want to export

The photos you select for export are determined by your needs at the time. You can export images from within any Lightroom Classic module, but the Library module gives you the greatest access to your entire portfolio, and exporting from there usually makes the most sense. So if you're not there already, press G to jump to the Library's Grid view. From there, you have access to all your folders and collections, as well as the Library Filter bar, so you can go ahead and track down the images you want. (Go ahead — take your time.)

After you locate the images you want to export, you can select them by using any of the following methods:

» Press ⌘+A (or Ctrl+A on Windows) to select all photos within a folder or another grouping of photos.

» Click the first image in a series, hold down the Shift key, and click the last image in the series to select all images in between.

» Hold the ⌘ key (or Ctrl key on Windows) and click each image individually to make a noncontiguous (not adjoining) selection.

Step 2: Initiating the Export command

After you select the images, you can initiate an export from any module (except where noted) by the following means:

» **Choose File ⇨ Export.** Launches the Export dialog.

» **Choose File ⇨ Export with Previous.** Skips the Export dialog and simply exports selected files by using the settings from the previous export.

» **Choose File ⇨ Export with Preset ⇨ Select Preset.** Allows you to select a preset and export without additional configuration of the Export dialog.

» **Press ⌘+Shift+E (or Ctrl+Shift+E on Windows).** The keyboard shortcut that launches the Export dialog.

» **Press ⌘ +Option+Shift+E (or Ctrl+Alt+Shift+E on Windows).** The keyboard shortcut for Export with Previous.

» **Right-click a selected photo and choose one of the previously mentioned export options from the contextual menu that appears.**

» **Click the Export button at the bottom of the left panel in the Library module.** Visible only in the Library module, but comes in handy.

TIP

I encourage you to use the keyboard shortcuts in your export workflow as soon and as often as possible. They'll become second nature before you know it, and they're useful time-savers.

Step 3: Configuring settings to meet your output needs

Okay, okay — I admit it. The broad overview of the Export dialog's panels I provide earlier in this chapter is helpful, but we'll need to drill deeper to understand how each panel works. So get ready for the gory details.

The first choice you'll make is if you plan to export to your hard drive, to a CD/DVD burner (if you even still have one!), to an email, or to some random export plug-in you've installed. Your most common choice will be Hard Drive. From there, you configure all the panels relating to the choice you made. Although additional panels will appear with different export plug-ins, they're too specific and varied to be covered here; I focus only on the panels that come with the Hard Drive option, because that covers the most options.

THE EXPORT LOCATION PANEL

The Export Location panel, shown in Figure 11-2, is used to configure where you want to save a batch of copies on your hard drive.

Export Location
Export To: Desktop
Folder: /Users/rsylvan/Desktop
☐ Put in Subfolder:
☐ Add to This Catalog
Existing Files: Ask what to do

FIGURE 11-2:
The Export Location panel, expanded.

Where you choose to save the files is driven by two factors: how you manage your files and what you determine your output needs to be. The Export To drop-down menu provides a few options for designating a location:

>> **Specific Folder:** When you select this option, you can point Lightroom Classic to any folder on your disk. Just make sure it has enough free space to hold all the new copies. Click the Choose button and navigate to the folder you want to use.

>> **Same folder as original photo:** This option does exactly what it describes, which is to put your exported copies back into the same folder as the original.

>> **Choose folder later:** This option is useful when you're creating presets and don't want to hard-code a specific location into the preset. When you use a preset, Lightroom Classic prompts you to provide a location.

>> **User Locations:** At the bottom of the drop-down menu is a list of common user locations, like Desktop, Documents, Home, Movies, and Pictures folders, to make it easy to select.

After you choose the location for the export, you have a few additional options to consider:

>> **Put in Subfolder:** You can create a subfolder within the designated export location. Select the check box and enter a name for the subfolder in the corresponding text field.

>> **Add to This Catalog:** Think of this one as the Automatic Import option. After your copies are exported, they appear inside Lightroom Classic without your having to use the Import dialog.

>> **Add to Stack:** Stacking is a function that allows you to arrange groups of photos under a single thumbnail for organizational purposes. This option is available only when you're exporting copies back to the same exact folder as the originals (and not putting them in a subfolder). When selected, the exported photos appear *stacked* with the source photos when you view that folder in Lightroom Classic.

Because you may export photos into a folder that already contains other photos, you must tell Lightroom Classic how to handle situations where your exported copies have the same name and are the same file type as the existing photos. You have four options under the Existing Files drop-down menu:

>> **Ask what to do:** This option is the safest option and the one I recommend using. If such a situation occurs, Lightroom Classic prompts you for further instructions and then you choose one of the other three options. I like having the reminder.

>> **Choose a new name for the exported file:** In this case, Lightroom Classic simply appends a new sequence number to the end of the exported file, so you end up with two copies of the same file but with unique names.

>> **Overwrite WITHOUT WARNING:** This one does what it says (and even uses all caps on the drop-down menu). Choose this option only if you're *certain* that its' what you want to do. Note that Lightroom Classic doesn't allow you to

overwrite the source photos, so don't choose this option in the belief that you can export copies with Lightroom Classic adjustments and save over the existing source files — it won't work.

>> **Skip:** If you choose this option, no new copy is created (that is, Lightroom Classic skips the file) when an existing file with the same filename is encountered.

THE FILE NAMING PANEL

In many cases, you'll want to maintain name consistency between your source files and your exported copies. By simply choosing the Filename template, you can achieve just that. At other times, you may want to use custom names that are completely different or perhaps some variation of the original name, as shown in Figure 11-3. In any case, because you're always creating copies, you must tell Lightroom Classic how you want them named, and just as when you use the Import command or rename files in the Library module, Lightroom Classic uses filename templates to do it.

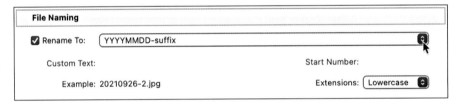

FIGURE 11-3:
The File
Naming panel.

Click the Template drop-down list and choose one of the installed templates, or you can click Edit and create a custom filename template using the good ol' Filename Template Editor. See Chapter 4 for more information about creating filename templates.

THE VIDEO PANEL

If you have a video file selected for export, you need to select the Include Video Files check box to access the (limited) format options for video, as shown in Figure 11-4:

>> **DPX:** A lossless format suited for sending to professional video editing tools (like Adobe Premiere). This format includes the option to set the quality to 24p, 25p, or 30p. (The "p" is for progressive video, which displays the odd and even scan lines simultaneously.) Choose DPX only if you know that it's required.

>> **H.264:** Good for exporting compressed video files for viewing and sharing. A description of each quality setting appears under it when selected. I recommend this option for most people.

>> **Original, unedited file:** Produces an exact copy of the original.

Video	
☑ Include Video Files:	
Video Format: [H.264 ⊕]	Source: 2304x1296, 20.000 fps
Quality: [Max ⊕]	Target: 1920x1080, 23.976 fps, 22 Mbps
As close to source as possible.	

THE FILE SETTINGS PANEL

Choose a file format based on your output needs (such as choosing JPEG for photos being displayed on a website). Some formats require additional settings. Here's a list of the formats and their options:

>> **JPEG:** When you choose the JPEG (or JPG) format, you also need to choose the level of compression to be applied to each JPEG file. You make this selection by using the Quality slider, as shown in Figure 11-5. The higher the quality value, the less compression — and the larger the file size. JPEG compression is always a trade-off between file size and image quality. If you're not too concerned about file size, leave it set around 90. The Limit File Size To option is useful if you need to achieve a specific file size in bytes, but keep in mind that you may need to also reduce the pixel dimensions (see "The Image Sizing panel," later in this chapter) when exporting large files.

File Settings	
Image Format: [JPEG ⊕]	
Quality: ●━━━━━━○━━ [80]	☐ Limit File Size To: [100] K
Color Space: [sRGB IEC61966-2.1 ⊕]	Bit Depth: [8 bits/component ⊕]
☐ HDR Output ☐ Maximize Compatibility	

- » **JPEG XL and AVIF:** These two new open-source file formats offer higher bit-depth support and smaller file sizes than the traditional JPEG format — helpful choices when sending photos to web galleries or utilizing the new HDR output option.

- » **PSD:** PSD is Photoshop's native file format. You can choose between 8- and 16-bit.

- » **TIFF:** TIFF is a widely supported format. Use the panel's Compression drop-down list to pick one of the lossless compression options. The None option is pretty straightforward; ZIP and LZW reduce the file size, but the length of time to open and close the file increases. (Note that not all image editors can open compressed TIFF files. Also note that only the Zip compression option is available with 16-bit files.) If your photo contains transparent pixels and you want to keep them in the exported copy, select the Save Transparency check box.

- » **PNG:** This one is useful for web graphics, but can also work well as an alternative to JPG.

- » **DNG:** This is Adobe's open format for *raw* (unprocessed by the camera) photos. (See Chapter 7 for more on DNG.) Note that the Use Lossy Compression option is occasionally useful for situations in which you want to keep the exported copy as a DNG file while also reducing its pixel dimensions by using the options in the Image Sizing panel.

- » **Original:** Selecting Original from the drop-down list results in the creation of an exact copy of your source image. (Raw and DNG photos include Lightroom Classic edits in the photo's XMP metadata.) No additional file settings are available with this option.

Two additional options — which appear only when you choose JPEG, JPEG XL, AVIF, PNG, TIFF, and PSD formats — warrant a separate discussion (raw files are always 16-bit and have no color space):

- » **Color Space:** A photo's color space is what determines the range of possible colors it can contain. You need to decide what color space you want these copies converted into during the export process. Your choice of color space is determined by the reason you're exporting these copies to begin with and where they will be used. You can find a more in-depth discussion of color spaces in Chapter 3, but, for now, here's a look at your choices:

  - *sRGB:* This color space contains the narrowest range of colors and is the standard for exporting photos destined for the web. It's also used by some print services.

- *Display P3:* This wide-gamut color space (contains colors on the more saturated end than sRGB) can be a good choice if your copies will be displayed on devices that you know support Display P3.

- *AdobeRGB (1998):* This option contains a wider range of colors than sRGB and is most often used when additional editing or printing is the next destination for your files.

- *ProPhoto RGB:* This one contains the widest range of colors and should be used only with 16-bit files. (I discuss bit depth in the last entry in this list.) This is the best option when you want to retain all the color information that was in your source files — not recommended when delivering copies destined for the web or anyone not used to working with ProPhoto color space.

- *Rec. 2020:* This even wider-gamut color space than Display P3 comes from the video world and is intended for next-generation HDR and wide-gamut displays.

- *Other:* Whereas the previous options in this list are the most common, you may also face advanced situations where you need to convert your files to a custom color space for printing purposes. Consult your print service to see whether it provides or requires custom profiles, and it will help you get them installed. When you choose Other, the Choose Profiles dialog opens, and you can select a color profile.

>> **Bit Depth:** *Bit depth* determines the amount of data a file contains. The higher the bit depth, the more data is contained in the file (which also means its file size will be larger, too). If you're working with raw files, you're working with 16-bit files. If you're working with JPEG files, you're working with 8-bit files. During export, you have the option to save PSD and TIFF files as 16-bit. If you choose JPEG, bit depth is grayed out, but know that JPEGs are all 8-bit by default. Saving files in 16-bit makes sense only when both the source files were originally 16-bit and when the output needs require this original data (such as when you plan to archive the exported copies to DVD or edit them in another image editor). In all other situations, 8-bit is the more common choice.

A new addition to the bottom of the File Settings panel is the HDR Output check box and the associated Maximize Compatibility check box. See Chapter 7 for more on HDR, but know that you'd select the HDR Output check box if you used Lightroom Classic's new HDR Mode editing capabilities and wanted the exported copies to be displayed as HDR on supported displays. These are the early days of HDR display support, but we are promised more vivid and lifelike renderings of high dynamic range scenes and more saturated colors. To stay up-to-date, check out Adobe's resource on HDR edit and export: `https://helpx.adobe.com/lightroom-classic/help/hdr-output.html`.

THE CONTENT CREDENTIALS (EARLY ACCESS) PANEL

Adobe occasionally includes beta or early-access features to give customers a chance to test-drive the feature, even though it isn't a final version. At the time I wrote this chapter, it was still considered early access, but the situation may change by the time you read it, so be sure to click the Learn More link in the panel to get the latest scoop from Adobe. The goal of content credentials is to give creators a new way to associate edits, history, and attribution to work shared on the web. As web users increasingly see images created by using generative AI-based tools, it can be advantageous to have a means to associate the origins and creator with your photos. Currently, it works only with JPEG selected as the file format.

THE IMAGE SIZING PANEL

Sometimes you need to save your exported copies in a different size from the source photos, such as when you want to email them or put them on a web page. To do so, you use options in the Image Sizing panel (see Figure 11-6). Lightroom Classic can make the exported images smaller or larger than the original images — a process known as *resampling*.

FIGURE 11-6:
The Image
Sizing panel.

These are the five options for resizing your exports:

» **Width & Height:** The values entered for width and height define the maximum amount each side can be resized to fit while maintaining the original aspect ratio.

» **Dimensions:** This option resizes exported images to fit within the entered dimensions while maintaining the aspect ratio. When this option is selected, height and width are no longer associated with the values fields. You just enter the maximum dimensions you want the images resized to fit, and Lightroom Classic does the rest regardless of orientation.

» **Megapixels:** If you need to resize to a specific total number of pixels (width times height), this is your option.

» **Long Edge** and **Shortest Edge:** These options function in the same manner. You set the maximum value for the edge in question and Lightroom Classic resizes all images to fit.

>> **Percentage:** This option is useful when you want to create exported copies that are a certain percentage smaller than the original.

Select the Don't Enlarge check box to prevent an image from being resampled larger than its original pixel dimensions. (This option is grayed out when Resize to Fit is deselected.)

If your output needs require your photos to print at a specific size and at a specific number of pixels per inch (PPI), you can set the *resolution* value — the metadata tag used by software to determine how big the printed file appears. For example, the value of 300 PPI is commonly requested by print services, in which case you would enter 300 and choose pixels per inch. The 300 PPI value is always a safe choice, but if your photos are destined only for the web, this value is meaningless and can be ignored.

THE OUTPUT SHARPENING PANEL

I love having the ability to add sharpening tailored for the specific output destination as part of the export process. The Output Sharpening panel, shown in Figure 11-7, is where you choose and configure the output sharpening settings. This list describes when to use the output settings:

>> **Screen:** When your photo's final viewing destination will be on a computer screen (that is, on a web page)

>> **Matte Paper:** When you're sending your photos to be printed on a type of photo paper that has a matte (nonshiny) finish

>> **Glossy Paper:** When you're sending your photos to be printed on a type of photo paper that has a glossy (shiny) finish

FIGURE 11-7: The Output Sharpening panel.

After you identify the output you're sharpening for, you can set the amount of sharpening to apply; your choices here range from Low (almost none) to High (often too much), with Standard in the middle (just right).

THE METADATA PANEL

The Metadata panel, shown in Figure 11-8, allows you some level of control over what metadata is included in the exported copies.

FIGURE 11-8:
The
Metadata
panel,
expanded.

Metadata
Include: [All Except Camera Raw Info ▼]
☑ Remove Person Info ☑ Remove Location Info
☐ Write Keywords as Lightroom Hierarchy

Clicking the Include drop-down menu offers the following options:

>> **Copyright Only:** Only the metadata entered into the Copyright field of the Metadata panel is applied to copies.

>> **Copyright & Contact Info Only:** This is the same as the previous option with the inclusion of any contact information you applied via the Metadata panel (or a metadata template).

>> **All Except Camera Raw Info:** Camera Raw Info means the actual slider values dialed into Lightroom Classic, written as part of the metadata (the adjustments themselves are applied to the pixels regardless of any of these settings). So this option builds on the previous option and then includes all other metadata except the slider values (Camera Raw Info).

>> **All Except Camera & Camera Raw Info:** This option does everything the previous one does but leaves out the camera-generated EXIF metadata and the Camera Raw Info.

>> **All Metadata:** Nothing is left out. All EXIF metadata created by the camera, plus everything added in Lightroom Classic, is applied to copies.

The Metadata panel has three additional check boxes:

>> **Remove Person Info:** If you used People view to tag photos with the names of the people shown, you can select this check box to avoid writing that information into the metadata of the exported copies.

>> **Remove Location Info:** If your photos have GPS information in them, you can select this check box to avoid writing that information into the metadata of exported copies.

>> **Write Keywords as Lightroom Hierarchy:** *Keywords* are the descriptive terms you assign to your photos in the Library module. When you enable this

option, and use keywords with parent/child relationships (meaning that the keywords are in a hierarchical structure), the exported copies retain that same keyword structure. This feature is useful for photos that will be imported into another Lightroom Classic catalog or managed with Adobe Bridge. (Chapter 6 explains Lightroom Classic's use of keywords.)

THE WATERMARKING PANEL

You can apply one of three types of watermarks to exported copies. Select the Watermark check box (see Figure 11-9) to enable the drop-down choices. The most basic is Simple Copyright Watermark, which pulls the information from the Copyright field of each file's metadata and renders it as a watermark in the lower left corner of each exported copy. This type of watermark has no configuration options.

FIGURE 11-9:
The
Watermarking
options.

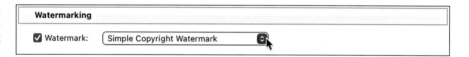

For greater control, choose Edit Watermarks to enter the Watermark Editor, where you can create either a text-based or graphical watermark with more control and save it as a preset for easy reuse. (See Chapter 15 for a closer look at the Watermark Editor.)

THE POST-PROCESSING PANEL

This is an optional panel, but it can provide a nice productivity boost to your output when you know that your photos will be opened in another application after they have been created (such as for additional image editing or viewing in your file browser). The Post-Processing panel (with the After Export drop-down list expanded) is shown in Figure 11-10. With the help of the options in this panel, you can tell Lightroom Classic to hand off your exported images to another application — in effect, having Lightroom Classic perform what's commonly referred to as an *export action* on your photos.

The After Export drop-down list includes the following preinstalled options:

>> **Show in Finder (or Show in Explorer on Windows):** This option automatically opens the folder containing the exported images in your file browser.

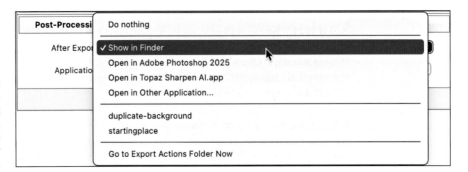

FIGURE 11-10:
The Post-
Processing
panel,
expanded to
show After
Export options.

>> **Open in Photoshop:** If you have Photoshop installed, you have the option to open the exported images in Photoshop after they're saved to the export location.

>> **Open in Additional Editor:** If you configured an additional external editor (covered later in this chapter, in "Configuring Your External Editors"), you see it listed here as an option.

>> **Open in Other Application:** Selecting this option gives you the opportunity to designate another application (such as an email client, an alternative image editor, or an FTP client) that will be invoked at the end of the export. Lightroom Classic attempts to open the exported photos in that application; just keep in mind that not every application can accept images this way. Click the Choose button and navigate to the application you want to send your photos to.

At the bottom of the After Export drop-down list is the Go to Export Actions Folder Now command. Selecting this option opens Finder (or Windows Explorer on Windows) with Lightroom Classic's Export Actions folder selected. You can place either an executable file or an alias (it's *shortcut* on Windows) to an executable file in the Export Actions folder to include it as an option in the After Export drop-down list the next time you start Lightroom Classic. This is another way to set things up so that you can send your photos to a specific program or a Photoshop droplet with one quick command.

TECHNICAL
STUFF

"What's a droplet?" you say? A *droplet* is a Photoshop action that you manage to turn (with Photoshop's help) into a tiny executable file. After you create a droplet, you can literally drag-and-drop photos on top of it to run the photos through the action automatically — a powerful way to run a batch of images through a favorite action, such as applying a specific Photoshop filter, converting to an alternative color space, or applying a custom watermark. By including the droplet as an export action, Lightroom Classic automatically runs the exported copies through the droplet after they're created.

Saving settings as a preset for reuse

Presets are such an awesome time-saver! Just think about it: You get to save scads of commonly used settings and then access them anytime you want to — directly from the Export with Preset menu (choose File ⇨ Export with Preset). Sweet!

Refer to Figure 11-11 to see the Preset panel — it's there on the left side. You get four preinstalled presets to start you off, right under the Lightroom Presets heading — presets that can't be ditched or updated, by the way.

FIGURE 11-11:
Selecting multiple export presets for a batch export.

The presets are described in this list:

>> **Burn Full-Sized JPEGs:** Sets JPG as the file format with the least compression and no resizing and then adds burning the exported images to a disc as an After Export step.

>> **Export to DNG:** Sets DNG as the file format, which essentially means you're set to convert to DNG on export. Note that using this preset makes sense only when your source files are in raw format.

>> **For Email:** Sets JPG as the file format with JPG compression set to 60 and resizes all images to limit the long edge to 500 pixels. This option tells

Lightroom Classic to pass exported copies to your default mail client when you export them.

>> **For Email (Hard Drive):** Sets JPG as the file format with JPG compression set to 50 and resizes all images to fit within 640 x 640 pixels. Note that this preset doesn't actually pass files to your email client; it just configures the export to an email-friendly size and saves the files to a location of your choosing on your hard drive.

I'm the first to admit that the preinstalled presets aren't incredibly sophisticated, but they can make good starting points and can help you see the possibilities. For example, I like to email photos to friends and family, so I took the For Email preset as a starting point and customized it to my liking. Here's how I did that:

1. **Click the For Email preset to load its settings into the Export dialog.**

   When selecting a preset, click the preset's name to load its settings. The check box to the left of the preset name is for batch exports, which is covered next.

2. **Expand the File Settings panel.**

   I prefer a higher Quality setting, so I set mine to 70.

3. **Expand the Image Sizing panel.**

   I prefer a larger pixel dimension, so I set mine to 1,000 pixels.

4. **Expand the Output Sharpening panel.**

   I selected the Sharpen For check box and selected Screen at a Standard amount.

5. **Leave the settings in the remaining panels as they are.**

   This is up to you, of course, but the remaining settings work well for me, so I didn't need to change them.

6. **Click the Add button at the bottom left of the Preset panel.**

   This opens the New Preset dialog.

7. **Enter a descriptive name in the Preset Name field.**

8. **(Optional) Create a new folder in the process of saving your preset.**

   TIP

   You can click the Folder drop-down list and choose an existing preset folder or create a new one. I find that keeping presets organized in folders makes it easier to find the one I'm looking for.

9. **Click the Create button to complete the process and add the preset to the Preset panel.**

WARNING

You can delete custom presets and folders by highlighting them and clicking the Remove button. Note, however, that removing a folder deletes any presets inside it!

You can update custom presets with new settings by adjusting the settings as you want, right-clicking the preset, and then choosing Update with Current Settings. To close the Export dialog without creating copies, click Done.

Creating a batch export

As I mention previously, if you want to load the settings of a single preset into the Export dialog, just click the preset's name. The check box to the left of each preset is for when you want to apply the settings of more than one preset to the photos being exported. Why might you want to do that? What if you need to deliver copies to someone who requested a full-size TIF and a JPG that's resized downward for social media sharing? Or maybe you need to export the same photo in a range of sizes? You could perform the export in separate instances, but with the batch export function, you can create multiple versions of the copies in one fell swoop!

The first step in the process is to create the presets to match the desired export purposes. In my example (refer to Figure 11-11), I have selected the check box next to the preset for the full-size TIF and the check box next to the resized JPG. As soon as you select the first check box, the panels on the Export dialog are set to read-only (meaning you can't change the settings further for this export). Once you've selected the boxes for each preset you want to apply to this batch, click the Batch Export button to advance. If your presets included the Choose Folder Later option (from the Export Location panel), you'll be presented with a dialog for choosing the folders for where these copies will be saved; otherwise, it uses the export location included in the preset. From there, click Export to begin the process of creating the copies based on the selected settings.

Configuring Your External Editors

Sending a photo to an external editor is basically a specialized type of export, so let's take a closer look at what's involved. I go over the External Editor settings in Chapter 3 — along with all the other preference settings — but I want to remind you of them here because this is where you actually use them. Because Lightroom Classic is an Adobe product, it does play favorites with Photoshop. Lightroom Classic reserves the primary (default) external editor slot for Photoshop and automatically recognizes it if it's installed. Although you can't manually configure the default editor, you can choose any other image editing application as the secondary editor (and save the settings as a custom preset).

Here's how to set up your primary external editor settings, as shown in Figure 11-12:

1. **Choose Lightroom Classic ⇨ Preferences (or Edit ⇨ Preferences on Windows) from the main menu.**

The Preferences dialog appears.

FIGURE 11-12:
External
Editing
preference
settings.

2. **In the Preferences dialog, click the External Editing tab.**

3. **Choose a default file type from the File Format drop-down list.**

PSD and TIFF file formats are, for all intents and purposes, equal to the task of supporting anything you can imagine doing in Photoshop. TIFF is a more widely supported format outside the Adobe family, whereas PSD is Photoshop's native file format. I tend to lean toward TIFF, but you can't go wrong either way.

4. Choose a default color space from the Color Space drop-down list.

Your choices here are ProPhoto RGB, Adobe RGB, Display P3, and sRGB. If you've configured your camera to save photos in raw format and you want to maintain as much of the original color as possible throughout the editing process, choose ProPhoto RGB. If you've configured your camera to save photos in JPG format, you've already made a color-space choice in your camera settings, so you may as well choose that same color space here to be consistent.

5. From the Bit Depth drop-down list, choose a default bit depth.

This option goes hand in hand with color space. If you chose ProPhoto as your color space, choose 16 bits/component. (ProPhoto is a 16-bit color space.) If you didn't choose ProPhoto, choose 8 bits/component. The important difference is that a 16-bit file contains much more data than an 8-bit file, which is helpful for editing but does come with a greatly increased file size.

6. (Optional) If you selected the TIFF file format, you can also choose a compressed (ZIP) or uncompressed (None) TIFF in the Compression drop-down menu.

You get the same data either way, but compressed TIFF takes longer to open and save, whereas uncompressed TIFF files have a larger file size. I favor uncompressed because I prefer the speed benefit over the size cost.

Note that a Resolution field exists, where you can change the default 240 PPI to something else, but it's only a metadata tag written into the Resolution field of the copy sent to the external editor. It has no effect on actual pixel dimensions. It's merely a convenience if you want to set that resolution tag now rather than change it later.

With the primary external editor configured, you can move on to setting up an additional external editor. Do you need one, though? Well, whether you need one or not is entirely up to you and your workflow. You may not have Photoshop installed, or perhaps you prefer another image editor for certain tasks. Lightroom Classic just provides you the option. Here's how to set up an additional external editor:

1. Click the Choose button in the Additional External Editor section of the External Editing Preferences dialog (refer to Figure 11-12).

2. In the dialog that appears, navigate to the application file you want to use, and then select it and click Choose.

On a Mac, look in the Applications folder. On a PC, you find the application files in the Program Files folder. In both cases, Lightroom Classic should open the correct folder by default, but if it doesn't, you have to navigate to the right

TIP

place. After you've selected the application and clicked Choose, you return to the External Editing dialog with your application choice displayed.

3. **Configure the File Format, Color Space, and Bit Depth options as desired.**

The choices you make here depend on the image editor you choose (not every application supports 16-bit files, for example), but be consistent with the settings you choose for your primary editor.

4. **Choose Save Current Settings as New Preset from the Preset drop-down menu.**

Doing so launches the New Preset dialog. This step is optional but recommended. By saving the Additional Editor settings as a preset, you can actually configure more than one additional editor, which gives you more options for how you want to edit your photos. You can even save different configuration settings for the same application.

5. **Give the preset a descriptive name and click Create.**

The preset names appear on the Photo ⇨ Edit In menu when you choose to send out a photo for additional work, so give it a name that tells you the name of the application and, possibly, hints at the settings. Doing so makes life easier for you when you want to use the preset.

TIP

After you create that preset, you can go back to Step 1 and repeat the process to configure additional applications. At any point in the future, you can return to this dialog and add new editors. Note that certain third-party image editors create presets here when installed.

6. **Close the Preferences dialog.**

REMEMBER

When Lightroom Classic creates a copy of your source photo to send to an external editor, it needs to give that copy a new name — technically, just a variation on the source photo's name. The naming convention you want Lightroom Classic to use when it creates these copies is the last option in the External Editing Preferences dialog. By default, Lightroom Classic appends –Edit to the end of the filename. (You can see an example to the right of the Edit Externally File Naming heading.) If that works for you, you don't need to do anything else. If you want to customize how edited files are named, you can choose Edit from the Template drop-down menu and configure a naming convention of your choice in the same Filename Template Editor I cover in Chapter 4.

TIP

If you choose to work with the PSD format, open Photoshop's preferences and turn on Maximize Compatibility. Choose Photoshop ⇨ Settings ⇨ File Handling (or Edit ⇨ Preferences ⇨ File Handling on Windows) from the main menu and set Maximize PSD and PSB File Compatibility to Always. Doing so enables Lightroom Classic to import your layered PSD files without any problems.

Chapter **12**

Designing a Book

Photo books are a helpful way to showcase your work as they make excellent gifts and can even be made available for sale. The Book module in Lightroom Classic gives you the tools to design a book from scratch using the photos you've already selected and edited in your workflow. Adobe has partnered exclusively with Blurb.com to provide seamless upload and purchase right from within Lightroom Classic. You can choose from a variety of book sizes, paper types, and page templates to create eye-popping photo books with ease.

Exploring the Book Module

I'd like to take a moment to reinforce that each Lightroom Classic module is structured in essentially the same way, which means the interface behaves the same no matter where you are! You can show and hide, and collapse and expand, panels as needed to maximize your work area, and display only the controls you need (refer to Chapter 1 for a refresher on the entire interface).

The module-to-module consistency is an asset to improving your efficiency as you move through your workflow, but as you read about the various modules, keep in mind that each has its own set of panels, tools, and menus devoted to the task at hand. This chapter helps you get oriented to the Book module workspace.

Getting to know the panels and tools

As is typical of all Lightroom Classic modules, the organizational and preview panels are on the left side of the content area, whereas the right side holds the configuration panels. The Filmstrip is across the bottom, and the Module Picker is across the top. Specific to each module are the tools provided for completing the task. Here's a brief introduction to the Book module interface (minus the repeating elements I cover throughout this book), from left to right, as shown in Figure 12-1:

>> **Preview:** Displays a preview of the selected page of the book.

>> **Collections:** Provides access to all the collections you've created as well as the controls to add new ones that retain all the Book settings. (Refer to Chapter 6 for a Collections refresher, if needed.)

>> **Filmstrip:** Displays thumbnails of the active source of photos. The Filmstrip can be used to drag-and-drop photos onto photo cells within a page of the book.

>> **Content area:** Displays an updating and fully interactive preview of your Book layout.

>> **Toolbar:** Provides controls for accessing various views of the book and navigating between pages.

>> **Book Settings:** Lets you choose a book type, book size, cover type, and paper type and estimate the cost of printing the book at Blurb.

FIGURE 12-1: The Book module interface.

- >> **Auto Layout:** Lets you quickly lay out an entire book with a few clicks.

- >> **Page:** Lets you choose from a variety of page templates, add page numbering, and add new pages to your book.

- >> **Guides:** Enables or disables various visual guides to help lay out your book.

- >> **Cell:** Controls cell padding and photo borders.

- >> **Text:** Provides controls for Photo Text and Page Text.

- >> **Type:** Formats the font used when text appears within the book.

- >> **Background:** Lets you customize the page backgrounds in your book.

Becoming familiar with the menu options

The Lightroom Classic (Mac only), File, Edit, View, Window, and Help menus remain largely consistent throughout Lightroom Classic. Unique to the Book module is the Book menu, which contains commands for creating a saved book, navigating between pages, updating metadata-based captions, and accessing your book preferences, as shown in Figure 12-2. The Book Preferences dialog allows you to configure default options for photo zoom (whether a photo is set to fill a photo cell or simply fit within the cell, maintaining its current aspect ratio), specify whether to start a new book by automatically filling the layout, and use the text box options. There are no wrong answers here, but once you start creating books, you might want to customize these settings to fit your needs.

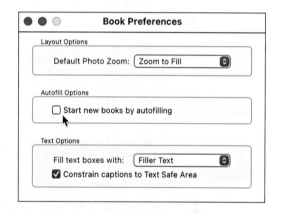

FIGURE 12-2:
The Book Preferences dialog.

TIP

Leave the Constrain Captions to Text Safe Area check box selected in the book preferences to ensure that you don't accidentally move a caption outside the printable margins of a page.

The Create Saved Book command (notice the button above the content area with the same name) allows you to create a special type of collection containing all the photos in the Filmstrip as well as the settings you've dialed into the Book module. This special collection appears in the Collections panel, and double-clicking its icon returns you to the Book module with all settings loaded. (I explore this topic in the "Employing a book workflow" section, later in this chapter.)

Setting Up a Book

Lightroom Classic is all about workflows, and designing a book is no different. Here's a high-level overview of the process:

1. **Bring your photos to the Book module.**

2. **Configure your book settings.**

3. **Select page layout templates to use as a starting point for Auto Layout.**

4. **(Optional) Save your settings and photos as a saved Book collection.**

5. **Customize the order of photos in the book.**

6. **Customize the design of each page.**

7. **Edit the front and back covers.**

8. **Output the book.**

In the next few sections, I take a closer look at each of the steps in the bookmaking process.

Step 1: Bring your photos to the Book module

The Library module is the most likely place you'll begin to gather your photos before moving to the Book module, because it provides the greatest access to your portfolio and contains tools for finding, organizing, and grouping. Whether you select a folder or a collection, or create a grouping based on keywords or metadata, you need to identify and select the photos you want to include in the book (refer to Chapter 5 for a refresher on viewing and finding photos).

TIP

One of the best ways to begin the process is to use a collection because it can contain photos from every corner of your imported portfolio. The other benefits of using a collection are

> » You can manually control the order in which the images appear in the book before you begin the layout.

TIP

>> You can create an infinite number of collections and sort them independently.

You can do a manual sort only when you're working within a single folder or a single collection. If you want to manually sort images that are across a range of folders (or collections), you need to put them into a single collection and then sort. Lightroom Classic refers to this sort order as *Custom Order*. After you're in a single folder or a collection, grab the image, not the border, and drag-and-drop in the order you want, as shown in Figure 12-3. You can do this from Grid view of the Library module, the Filmstrip in any module, or in Grid view of the Secondary Display when enabled. The order in which your photos appear in the Filmstrip is the order in which they're added to the book using Auto Layout (described a little later).

FIGURE 12-3: Manually sorting images within a collection from the Filmstrip.

After you've collected your photos for the book, it's time to bring them into the Book module. Notice that the image grouping you created in the Library module is still displayed in the Filmstrip. If needed, you can further refine your image grouping with the filtering options provided in the Filmstrip (above thumbnails). For example, you can filter your grouping to only images with a rating of three stars or greater by clicking the third star above the thumbnails. (Click the word Filter in the Filmstrip to reveal the filters if you don't see the stars.) The other filtering options (flags, color labels, and so on) work the same way (refer to Chapter 6 for a refresher on filtering).

Step 2: Configure your book settings

You'll want to start in the Book Settings panel to choose the type of book (Blurb Photo Book, Blurb Magazine, Blurb Trade book, PDF, or JPEG) from the Book drop-down menu, as shown in Figure 12-4. The choice you make for the book determines the size of your book as well as which other options are available to customize.

FIGURE 12-4:
The Book Settings panel.

Although you can choose PDF or JPEG from the Book menu, which would result in your being able to export the book as a PDF or series of JPG files, respectively, I focus on describing how to create a Photo Book, because that's the most common choice. Be sure to visit Blurb.com to learn more about each of the book types and paper choices, and how to create a free Blurb account to expedite the purchasing process when your book is complete.

Once you've selected a book type, you'll need to make choices on the following aspects of your book:

>> **Size:** You must choose from one of the available sizes for the type of book you choose.

>> **Cover:** Choose from the available types of covers for the book type.

>> **Paper Type:** Each book has a selection of paper options to choose from. Visit Blurb.com to learn more about each paper type.

>> **Logo Page:** Only photo books offer the option to add a page with the Blurb logo at the back of the book to receive a discount on the book price. Choosing to have it On results in a discount on the base price of the book. I recommend leaving it on for your first book.

These settings form the basis of the book you create. If you change the book size later, Lightroom Classic will have to change the format and lay out your book again, so it's good to finalize this one before you begin.

Step 3: Select page layout templates to use as a starting point for Auto Layout

By default, when you enter the Book module for the first time, it automatically lays out your book based on the preset selected in the Auto Layout panel. Earlier, I mention the book preferences under the Book menu (refer to Figure 12-2), and one of the options there is to start new books by autofilling, which is selected by default. I recommend deselecting that option so that you have time to choose your own layout preset first, and then you can trigger the Auto Layout command manually from the Auto Layout panel.

If your book was laid out automatically and you want to start over, just click the Clear Layout button. To customize your own Auto Layout preset, click the Preset drop-down menu and choose Edit Auto Layout Preset to open the Auto Layout Preset Editor, as shown in Figure 12-5. Here you can choose from all the various page templates to configure what you want used on the left and right pages of your book. You can further customize individual pages any way you want later on, but setting up Auto Layout with a desired preset gets you off to a fast start. Once you've configured the layout options, click the Preset drop-down at the top of the dialog and choose Save Current Settings as a New Preset to preserve it for the future. Click Done to exit the editor, and then click the Auto Layout button in the panel to put it into action. Note that Auto Layout is limited to 240 pages when printing via Blurb (PDF-only books have no page limit).

FIGURE 12-5:
The Auto
Layout Preset
Editor.

Step 4: Save your photos and settings as a special collection

When you create a saved Book collection in the Book module, Lightroom Classic saves all photos in the Filmstrip and your Book settings to a special collection with the icon of a book. Here's how it works (the process is the same in the Slideshow, Print, and Web modules):

1. **Click the Create Saved Book button above the content area.**

This opens the Create Book dialog, as shown in Figure 12-6.

2. **Give the book a meaningful name and configure as desired.**

These special saved creations can be put inside regular collections or collection sets. These are the only form of collections that can exist inside another collection. Because they're collections, you can also use this opportunity to fill them with virtual copies (not typically done), set one as the target collection (makes it easy to add more photos later), or sync them with the cloud-based Lightroom. If you save the book before including all photos in the layout, you see an option to include only used photos in this dialog. If that option is selected, any photos not yet included in your layout will be left out of the saved book (I'd leave it deselected).

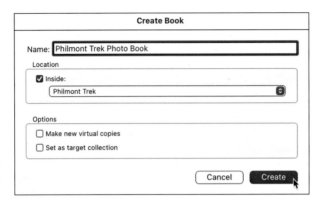

FIGURE 12-6:
The Create
Book dialog.

3. **Click the Create button to complete the process.**

   This creates a new collection from the photos used in the book and the Book settings. This continuously updates as you work, so you need to do this only once. (The button vanishes after you create a saved Book collection.)

The new collection appears in the Collections panel, and you can quickly jump back into this book double-clicking the special icon representing the saved creation. Each module has its own icon representing that module.

Step 5: Customize the order of the photos in the book

Now that Auto Layout has run, you're ready to start customizing the order of the photos. Even if you took the time to arrange the photos in a desired order before entering the Book module, you may find that, when looking at the actual layouts of individual pages, some photos work better next to each other than others. Perhaps the story flows better with a few tweaks to the order, maybe the colors in two photos clash when placed side by side, or perhaps you decide to add new pages and new photos after creating the initial layout. Whatever the reason, the fix is simple: You can drag-and-drop photos from one cell to another to swap them on a layout, or you can drag-and-drop photos from the Filmstrip into any photo cell you want.

REMEMBER

Note that a number appears at the top of each thumbnail in the Filmstrip to indicate how many times that photo appears in the book. A photo with no number at the top doesn't appear in the book, so be sure to keep an eye on the Filmstrip as you continue to edit your book.

You can view your book in a few ways as you work through it. Located on the left side of the Toolbar (refer to Figure 12-1) are three buttons for switching between views (the same options and their keyboard shortcuts are visible under the View menu, too). From left to right, they are

» **Multi-Page View:** Best for viewing all the pages at one time, and useful for dragging-and-dropping pages into a new order. Click a page to select it; then click the yellow border to move the page to a new location in the book. The Thumbnails slider at the other end of the Toolbar changes the size of the page thumbnails.

» **Spread View:** Useful for viewing a two-page spread close-up. This view is helpful when you want to move photos between pages in a spread or just see how pages look side by side in the book.

» **Single Page View:** The best view for customizing a single page or just wanting to see one page up close; useful when adding text to a page.

You can zoom in even closer using the buttons on top of the Preview panel, or you can choose View ⇨ Zoomed Page View. Press the I key to show/hide the Info Overlay that appears in the upper left corner of the content area.

Step 6: Customize the design of each page

This is where the real work begins. Auto Layout gives you a good place to start, but you have the tools to take your book to the next level by varying the page layouts, adding text, changing the background, and more. Generally speaking, the panels on the right side are arranged in a logical top–down order, but in the Book module, you're likely to skip around and choose a panel based on the task at hand. In the following sections, I take a deeper dive into what you can do in each of the remaining panels.

Page panel

The first option to consider in the Page panel is whether to include page numbers in your book. Select the Page Numbers check box to include them in your book and access the options for where they will be placed. These options are all WYSIWYG (*what you see is what you get*), so experiment with various location and display options to see what works best.

You can also add new pages based on one of the page templates or add a new blank page that you can customize yourself by using the relevant buttons at the bottom of the panel. Clicking the Page Picker, shown in Figure 12-7, reveals all the preinstalled templates as well as any custom pages you have created. To change the template used on a given page, simply select that page and choose a new template via the Page Picker in the Page panel or the Page Picker that appears at the bottom of the selected page.

FIGURE 12-7:
The Page panel, showing the contents of the Page Picker.

As you explore all the preinstalled templates, you may find a few that you want to mark as Favorites for easy access in future book projects. To mark a template as a Favorite, simply move the cursor over the template in the Page Picker and click the small, round button that appears in the upper right corner of the template thumbnail. Doing so adds that template to the Favorites section at the top of the Page Picker dialog. Clicking that same small button a second time removes that template from Favorites.

You can also customize a preinstalled template or customize a blank page from scratch by adding new cells, removing existing cells, arranging cells on the page, and resizing cells as you want. Here's how to start with a blank page, add a new photo cell, resize the cell, reposition the cell, and save it as a custom page for reuse:

1. **Select a page in the book where you want to add the new page, and click Add Blank.**

   It can be helpful to work in Single Page view for this step. I also recommend showing all the guides as you begin a custom page and starting with Grid Snap set to Grid (refer to Figure 12-9).

2. **Right-click an empty area of the page and choose Add Cell ⇨ Photo from the contextual menu, as shown in Figure 12-8.**

This places a photo cell on the page. This cell is active, and the resize handles are visible for easy resizing. Reposition the cell by clicking-and-dragging the center yellow handle. Resize the cell by using any of the resize handles along the outside edge of the cell. Use the guides to assist in placing the cell precisely where you want it to go. You can use that same contextual menu to add more cells or remove cells. Continue customizing the page until it meets your needs.

3. **Right-click anywhere on the page and choose Save as Custom Page from the contextual menu.**

This saves your page for reuse and stores it under the Custom Pages section of the Page Picker. Note that you can also mark custom pages as Favorites.

Guides panel

Having visual guides when creating a page layout can be incredibly helpful (and sometimes annoying). Expand the Guides panel, as shown in Figure 12-9, to see visual aids at your disposal. You

FIGURE 12-9:
The Guides panel.

can show (or hide) them all at once by selecting (or deselecting) the Show Guides check box. I recommend starting with them all selected; then turn them off one by one to see which you find helpful as you work. Hover the cursor over each one to see a tooltip with a short description of what it does.

At the top of the panel is the Grid Snap drop-down menu. You can choose from three options: Off, Cells, and Grid. These are useful when you're placing or moving a photo or text cell around on a page. If you want help aligning a cell to the page grid (select Page Grid under Show Guides to see it), choose Grid from the Grid Snap drop-down menu. If it's more helpful to have a cell snap to another cell in the layout, choose Cells instead. Turn it off if it gets in your way.

Cell panel

You need to select a cell to enable the options in the Cell panel, shown in Figure 12-10. Padding controls how much space (padding) appears around a photo or text within the boundaries of the cell. Be sure to click the disclosure triangle next to Padding and turn off Link All to set the controls for each side independently (if desired). Quite often, padding is set to 0 for all sides.

FIGURE 12-10:
The Cell panel.

If you want to place a border around the photo cell, you can select the Photo Border Color check box to enable it and then use the Width slider to adjust how far the border extends from the edge of the cell outward. Click the associated color swatch to set the border color.

Text panel

There are two types of text cells you can add to a page (or cover):

>> **Photo Text:** Associated with each individual photo on a page. Because Photo Text is connected with the photo that appears within the Photo Cell, you can configure Lightroom Classic to populate the text field with metadata from the photo itself (such as its Title field or Caption field) by using text templates (covered in Chapter 13) or simply type directly into the field. The cell can be anchored above, over, or below the photo with the buttons in the panel. The Offset slider allows you to position the text relative to where it's anchored.

>> **Page Text:** Associated with the entire page. Type directly in the field to add text. The cell can be anchored at the top or bottom of the page, and the offset slider allows you to tweak positioning relative to its anchor.

You can add or remove Photo Text by selecting a photo cell and selecting or deselecting the Photo Text check box in the Text panel (see Figure 12-11). Page text can be added or removed by selecting the page and selecting or deselecting the Page Text check box.

FIGURE 12-11:
The Text panel.

Type panel

You can use the controls in the Type panel, shown in Figure 12-12, to format the text you enter into either a Photo cell or Page Text cell. Start by selecting the text within the cell you want to format and then configure the attributes of the text you want to change. You'll mostly be focused on choosing a font and its color, but you can expand the disclosure triangle next to the Character color swatch to reveal additional text options. Hover the cursor over each option in the panel to reveal a short description in a tooltip. Once you configure a set of attributes that you want to preserve for reuse, click the Text Style Preset drop-down menu at the top of the panel to save current settings as a new preset.

FIGURE 12-12:
The Type panel.

Note that you cannot preview the fonts within the Book module in any way other than applying the font to the text in your book. You may want to preview fonts ahead of time in another application (such as Photoshop) or your operating system's font viewer for ease of selection. The fonts available in the Book module are simply the fonts installed on your system.

Background panel

When it comes to the background of the pages of your book (has no effect on the cover), you have a few options to consider (aside from leaving it a blank white page):

>> **Add a Graphic:** You can add a graphic to the background of the pages of your book in two ways. You can click the Background Graphic Picker, as shown in Figure 12-13, and choose one of the preinstalled graphics found under the Photos, Travel, or Wedding categories inside the picker. You can change the color of one of the preinstalled graphics via the color picker next to the Graphic check box. Or you can select any photo in the Filmstrip and drag it to the place that says Drag Photo Here (right-click that area and choose Remove Photo to clear the photo). After choosing either type of graphic, you can adjust its opacity via the slider.

>> **Change Color:** Whether you add a graphic or not, you can also change the color by simply selecting the Background Color check box and then clicking the associated swatch to access the color picker and choose the desired color.

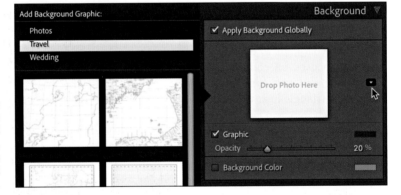

FIGURE 12-13: The Background panel, showing the preinstalled graphics.

If you want the background to be applied to all pages in the book, select the Apply Background Globally check box at the top of the panel before making your selection. If you want to apply the background to only selected pages, select the pages first and then choose the graphic you want to add (leaving Apply Background Globally deselected).

Step 7: Edit the front and back covers

There's no reason to edit the cover last except that by this time in the process, you will have spent a lot of time looking at the photos used in this project, and you may have new ideas for what you want to do with the cover. Feel free to do this at the start of the bookmaking process because you can always update it as you go. Assuming that you ran Auto Layout at the start, it will have populated the cover photo cells right out of the gate. You can replace those photos by using drag-and-drop, just as you do on the inside pages.

Depending on the type of book you chose at the start, you may have one choice or a few choices for your book cover. For example, a Blurb Magazine has only a softcover option. Keep in mind that it's only possible to add text to the spine of a hardcover book or softcover book with 70 or more pages, depending on paper type (114 pages for standard paper). You can add text for a title, subtitle, author, and other relevant information by using any combination of Photo Text and Page Text, and the same controls you used for formatting text on the inside pages.

Adding text to the spine of a book can be fidgety, as shown in Figure 12-14. I find it helpful to zoom to 1:1 view (by using the button on the Preview panel) and then hover the cursor over the spine until I see the text cell highlight. Then I simply single-click the cell and start typing. Make sure that the font size is small enough for the text to fit on the spine by using the controls in the Type panel.

FIGURE 12-14:
Entering text on the spine of a book.

Step 8: Output the book

Congratulations! You've completed all your layout tweaks and you're ready to print. A good practice before clicking the Send Book to Blurb button is to click the Export Book to PDF button (located at the bottom of the left panel group). After you click the button, Lightroom Classic prompts you to enter a filename for your book and choose where you want it to be saved. After you specify your choices, click Save (and keep an eye on the progress bar as it can take a while to complete).

After the PDF is complete, open it up in any PDF reader software and verify that the layouts look the way you want, text appears where it should, and everything is as you designed it. (Note that the cover exports as a separate PDF file due to its different dimensions than the pages of the book.) Check Blurb's Help docs if you see any error messages during the output process.

When you're ready to complete the process and have the book printed, click the Send Book to Blurb button (located at the bottom of the right panel group). This is where having already created an account (when you visited Blurb.com earlier to learn about book and paper types) comes in handy. You're asked to sign in to your Blurb account (though you can create a new account now by clicking the Not a Member link in the Purchase Book dialog). You also see the cost of the book and a summary of the book options you chose in Book Settings, as shown in Figure 12-15. From here, the book is rendered and uploaded to the Blurb servers in the background.

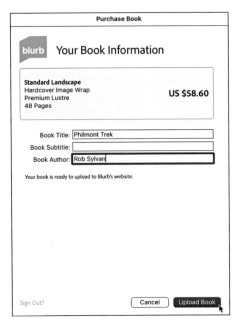

FIGURE 12-15:
The Purchase Book dialog.

Some guidance to keep in mind

I want to close out this chapter with some tips to keep in mind as you begin making your own books. The first thing people ask about is whether they can soft-proof a book in Lightroom Classic before uploading to Blurb, and the answer is no. Blurb does provide a profile for people using other software to create books, but you can't use that profile in Lightroom Classic.

When the book is uploaded to Blurb, all the file conversions, color space conversions, and output sharpening happens behind the scenes without user input. That means you can build your books with any photos in the Lightroom Classic catalog and let the Book module handle things on the back end.

TIP

I recommend making a small, square, 7x7 book with your chosen paper type, and maybe 20 pages of photos, before making a bigger book. Treat it as a test run, and work with Blurb's customer support team if you have any problems uploading or printing. If all is well, go forth with that knowledge in making larger books. Keep an eye out for discounts on Blurb books; the site seems to always run some sort of deal. Working in Lightroom Classic's Book module has different options from Blurb's own bookmaking software, so if you find that you're lacking in options, you can always export photos as JPGs (refer to Chapter 11 for more details on exporting copies) and bring them into any other bookmaking software.

Chapter **13**

Producing a Slideshow

The Slideshow module offers a flexible interface for creating simple yet professional presentations of your photos. Slideshows are useful not only for sharing your images with clients, peers, family, and friends but also as a practical tool for reviewing your own work. You have relatively few settings to configure, and the changes update in the main workspace area while you work, so you'll be displaying your images in no time at all!

You can create a slideshow from any grouping of images you can dream of pulling together. Whether the images are a folder, a collection, or an on-the-fly assemblage of images based on dates, keywords, and/or metadata, if you can group them, you can show them. You don't need to be in the Slideshow module to play a slideshow either. Press ⌘+Return (or Ctrl+Enter on Windows) from within any module to run an impromptu slideshow, which uses the last configured settings from the Slideshow module to run a show with the active images.

Exploring the Slideshow Module

An important point that bears repeating: The consistency of Lightroom Classic's interface across modules is a key strength as a workflow tool. That's true as far as it goes — otherwise, I wouldn't say it — but be aware that each module performs a unique set of tasks, which means that each module requires a specialized set of panels, tools, and menus. You have to be acquainted with each set.

Getting to know the panels and tools

Before showing you around the Slideshow module, I want to remind you that you can show and hide, and collapse and expand, panels as needed to maximize your work area and display only the controls you need. Refer to Chapter 1 for a complete rundown of the interface controls.

Okay, time to dive in! The left panel contains the organizational and preview panels, whereas the right panel is where the adjusting, tweaking, and modification panels are found. Each module has its own specialized toolbar, but the images always take center stage. Here's a brief introduction to the Slideshow interface (minus any elements that appear across modules), as shown in Figure 13-1:

>> **Preview panel:** This panel displays a preview of each slideshow's layout while you move the cursor over the templates listed in the Template Browser.

>> **Template Browser (or template organizer):** This is where you find the preinstalled templates as well as all your saved templates.

>> **Export PDF and Export Video buttons:** These buttons provide an alternative output option for your slideshow. Clicking the PDF button creates a single PDF document, and clicking the Video button exports an MP4 file you can play in any video playback software. Hold down the Option (or Alt on Windows) to change the Export PDF button to Export JPEG and export a series of still JPEGs of your slideshow.

FIGURE 13-1:
The Slideshow interface.

>> **Options panel:** Control the look of the photo's border and drop shadow and the way the photo appears within the layout guides.

>> **Layout panel:** Determine the size and location of the photos on the slide.

>> **Overlays panel:** Control the look of the overlay elements (such as identity plate, text, and ratings) that you can add to enhance a slideshow.

>> **Backdrop panel:** Configure the look of the *backdrop,* which is the part of the slide not covered by the photos.

>> **Titles panel:** Add optional intro and/or ending slides to your slideshow, which provides a nice finishing touch to any slideshow.

>> **Music panel:** Add, arrange, and remove music tracks to play with your slideshow.

>> **Playback panel:** This is where you configure slide timing, balance audio in video files with music, control pan and zoom effects across slides, and choose playback screens (if using multiple monitors) and other playback settings.

>> **Preview and Play buttons:** Clicking the Preview button plays the slideshow within the Content area, and clicking the Play button controls the start of the full-screen show.

>> **Content area:** Display a live preview of the active image (or the *most selected* image) within the slide layout.

>> **Toolbar:** This element contains the controls for navigation, designation of which photos to use in the show, playback, rotation of the overlay elements, and addition of text overlays.

Becoming familiar with the menu options

The Lightroom Classic (Mac only), File, Edit, View, Window, and Help menus remain largely consistent throughout Lightroom Classic. The menu commands unique to the Slideshow module are related to creation and playback, as described in this list:

>> **Slideshow menu:** Here you find the commands for creating new templates and template folders; exporting a slideshow to PDF, JPEG, or video; adding text overlays; and rotating an image within the slide. The Create Saved Slideshow command allows you to save the current settings and photos as a special collection (the same as the button of the same name above the content area).

>> **Play menu:** This menu contains commands for playing, ending, and navigating within a slideshow. The Content command provides the option to choose which photos within the active image grouping end up being displayed in the show (the same task as the Use drop-down menu on the Toolbar).

Creating a Slideshow and Employing a Workflow

Your photos, your intended audience, your reason for showing these images, and your own creativity drive the look of your slideshow. These are some of the questions you should think about before you begin:

>> Who is my intended audience, and what story am I telling them?

>> What image order will make the most sense and impact?

>> Would any supporting information (such as captions, titles, camera-generated data like f-stop and shutter speed, and so on) make this presentation stronger or more targeted to this audience?

>> How much time do I have?

>> Would the addition of an audio component make this slideshow stronger?

With the answers to these questions in mind and knowing that new questions will emerge, you can enter your slideshow workflow on the right footing.

Lightroom Classic is all about workflows. To me, *workflows* are ways to build efficiencies into the repetitive tasks required to reach a desired outcome. Creating a slideshow presentation is no different. The creation of every slideshow follows the same basic steps. Here's an overview of the process:

1. **Select your photos and switch to the Slideshow module.**

2. **Select a template for your starting point.**

3. **Customize the slideshow as desired.**

4. **(Optional) Save your settings as a new template for reuse.**

5. **(Optional) Save your settings and photos as a special slideshow collection.**

The next few sections take a closer look at each of these steps in the process.

Step 1: Bring your photos to the Slideshow module

The Library module is your organizational hub. You've already spent time putting photos into a folder structure, embedding keywords in them, and organizing them into collections. You have an array of camera-generated metadata that can also be used to refine your image groupings further. All these options are accessible from the Library module, and that's why the first step in slideshow creation starts there.

One of the best ways to begin the slideshow process is to use (or create) a collection because it can contain photos from every corner of your portfolio (as I did in Figure 13-1). The other benefits of using a collection are the following:

>> **You can manually control the order in which the images appear in the slideshow.**

   You can do only a manual sort when you're working within a single folder or a single collection. So, if you want to manually sort images that are across a range of folders (or collections), you need to put them into a single collection and then sort. Lightroom Classic refers to this sort order as *Custom Order.*

>> **You can create an infinite number of collections and sort them independently.**

With your photos in hand (so to speak), bring them into the Slideshow module by clicking Slideshow in the Module Picker. Notice that the image grouping you created in the Library module appears in the Filmstrip of the Slideshow module.

Step 2: Select a template for your starting point

A Lightroom Classic template is simply a way of saving unique combinations of settings for reuse. The preinstalled templates are helpful for seeing possibilities but also serve as useful jumping-off points for creating your own, custom slideshows. You can see a thumbnail layout of any template in the Preview panel by moving the cursor over its name. The five preinstalled templates, shown in Figure 13-2, are listed under the Lightroom Templates heading.

This list describes the key settings used in each:

>> **Caption and Rating:** This one displays the contents of the Caption field from each image's metadata as well as its star rating (if applied).

>> **Crop to Fill:** Layout guides are maximized to fill the screen, and the Zoom to Fill Frame option is enabled (I go over this setting in the next section), which results in images appearing full screen.

>> **Exif Metadata:** This setting also includes an identity plate but adds several text overlays, which display creator and capture data pulled from each file's EXIF *metadata* — the information recorded with each photo by the camera, as in f-stop, shutter speed, and similar items.

>> **Simple:** This setting makes use of an *identity plate* (a personalized graphical or text element) and a black background.

>> **Widescreen:** The layout guides are maximized to fill the screen, but the Zoom to Fill Frame option is disabled, so images are resized to fit within the layout frame without being cropped or distorted.

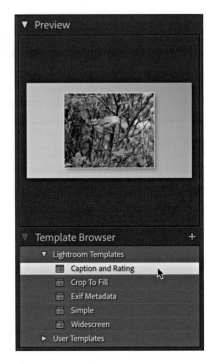

FIGURE 13-2:
The Template Browser and Preview panel, displaying the Caption and Rating template.

Step 3: Customize the slideshow

The right-side panels are where the rubber meets the road when customizing your slideshow. The panels are arranged with an efficient workflow in mind, so start at the top and work your way down. At the beginning of this chapter, I give you a brief introduction to all the panels, but to get you up to speed on how you actually use them, I need to drill down further. In the sections that follow, I go over the key controls within each panel.

Options panel

You find three controls in this panel, as shown in Figure 13-3. All three function independently to determine the appearance of the photo on the slide.

Here's what they do:

>> **Zoom to Fill Frame:** When the Zoom to Fill Frame option is enabled, the aspect ratio of your images is ignored in favor of the *frame* created by the

layout guides (see the later section "Layout panel"). In other words, photos appear zoomed in and cropped if they don't have the same aspect ratio as the frame. With this option disabled, the aspect ratio of each image is respected, and the image is sized to fit within the frame accordingly. Figures 13-4 and 13-5 show the difference this setting can have on the same portrait-oriented image.

FIGURE 13-3:
The Options panel.

FIGURE 13-4:
Zoom to
Fill Frame
disabled.

FIGURE 13-5:
Zoom to
Fill Frame
enabled.

WARNING

With Zoom to Fill Frame enabled, all photos are centered in the image area and zoomed until the frame area is filled from edge to edge. If a photo appears cropped, you can adjust its position within the frame by clicking-and-dragging the image to reposition it.

>> **Stroke Border:** A stroke border can be used to set the image off the background. Select the check box to enable the stroke and then click the color swatch to choose a color. The width of the stroke can range from 1 to 20 pixels. Note that the stroke appears inside the layout frame, so increasing the width of the stroke decreases the size of the photo.

Cast Shadow: The ability to add a drop shadow to each image is another way to set it off from the background. You can adjust the shadow's visibility with the Opacity setting, its distance from the photo with the Offset setting, the hardness of its edges with the Radius setting, and its direction with the Angle setting. Note that the drop shadow appears outside the layout frame, so if the layout frame reaches the edge of the slide, a shadow may not be visible. Likewise, if the background color is set to black, you don't see the shadow.

Layout panel

Use the controls in the Layout panel to determine the size and placement of the photos on the slide by adjusting the left, right, top, and bottom guides. The guides create the frame that defines the area within which the photos appear and are easier to adjust when visible. Click the Show Guides box to toggle their visibility on and off. In Figure 13-6, the guides are visible. Note that they never appear when the slideshow is playing.

FIGURE 13-6:
The Layout panel.

TIP

Guides can be adjusted in tandem or individually, depending on the configuration of which link boxes (the white, square buttons next to each guide) are enabled.

Here are the three ways to adjust the guides:

» **Click and drag the guide.** When the cursor is placed over a guide in the content area, the cursor changes to a double-sided arrow. Click the guide and drag to adjust its position.

» **Use the sliders.** Click-and-drag the sliders in the Layout panel to move the guides in big increments. Place the cursor over the number field, and it changes to a small, scrubby slider. Click and drag to move the guides in small increments.

» **Change the numbers.** Click the number field and enter a pixel amount. This number represents the distance in pixels from the edge of the slide. When the number field is active, you can use the up- and down-arrow keys to increase and decrease that number.

The Aspect Preview drop-down menu lets you see how the slideshow appears on different aspect-ratio displays. Choose Screen if the slideshow will display on the same monitor you're using now, or choose the correct aspect ratio for where the slideshow will play from the list.

Overlays panel

Although photos should definitely take center stage in a slideshow, you still have a lot of room to add supporting cast members, such as an identity plate, rating stars, and text. You can add and modify these supporting elements in the Overlays panel, as shown in Figure 13-7.

Here's a closer look at each overlay element:

» **Identity Plate:** Identity plates can be used to brand your slideshows. Selecting the Identity Plate check box causes the default identity plate to appear on the slide. You can reposition the plate anywhere on the slide by clicking-and-dragging it into position. Note that when you drag the identity plate across the slide, you see anchor points along the slide or

FIGURE 13-7:
The Overlays panel.

guide edges connecting to the nearest Resize handle on the identity plate, as shown in Figure 13-8. These anchor points appear with every overlay element and can be useful in aligning elements on the slide.

FIGURE 13-8:
Anchor points aid in aligning overlay elements on the slide.

You can choose a saved identity plate or create a new one by clicking the Identity Plate drop-down arrow. (Check out Chapter 5 for more on creating identity plates.) You can override the color of your identity plate — without affecting the saved identity plate — by selecting the Override Color check box and clicking the color swatch to choose a new color. You can adjust the visibility of the identity plate with the Opacity slider. This is a helpful way to turn an identity plate into a low-opacity watermark for exported slideshows.

Identity plates can be resized by using either the Resize handles on the object or the Scale slider. Selecting the Render Behind Image check box causes the identity plate to become a background element and display behind the photo, stroke, and shadow.

>> **Watermarking:** Similar to an identity plate in some ways, a watermark can be customized text or a graphic that appears on a photo. You can employ your saved watermarks from here, in the Web module, in the Print module, and when exporting copies. The process to create one is the same in all cases. See Chapter 15 for more on watermark creation.

>> **Rating Stars:** Select the Rating Stars check box to display the ratings overlay element on the slide. If you haven't applied ratings, you don't see the rating element on the slide. You can apply a rating to the active image while in the Slideshow module by pressing the 1 to 5 number keys on the keyboard,

respectively (even while the slideshow is playing). You can go back to the Library module and uncheck Auto Advance under the Photo menu if you don't want to switch to the next photo after applying a rating.

You can change the color of the rating stars by clicking the color swatch. The Opacity and Scale sliders work the same as for the identity plate, and the element can be repositioned similarly as well.

>> **Text Overlays:** Although there can be only one identity plate and rating element per slide, you can use any number of text-overlay elements in your presentation. Figure 13-9 shows a caption and a date text element centered below the photo. A customized identity plate appears at the top.

FIGURE 13-9:
Multiple
text overlay
elements
in use.

You can add a new text overlay by clicking the ABC button on the Toolbar or the Slideshow ➪ Add Text Overlay menu. You can configure the textual content from the Toolbar by clicking the ABC drop-down menu and selecting an existing text template or choosing Edit from the bottom of the menu to create your own text template with the Text Template Editor. (I walk you through a step-by-step example of the Text Template Editor shortly.) If you choose the Custom Text template, an input field appears on the Toolbar. Just enter your text and press Enter.

REMEMBER

Any text overlay you add appears on every slide. If you want the contents of the text overlay to change with each photo, choose a text template that displays the title or caption or some other information that is pulled dynamically from each photo's own metadata (refer to Chapter 6).

Because multiple text overlays can be used in a slideshow, they each need to be adjusted independently. After you select a text element, the dotted border and Resize handles appear. You can adjust the text element's color, opacity, and font by using the controls in the Overlays panel. Text elements can be resized only by using the Resize handles and are repositioned in the same manner as the other overlay elements. To remove any overlay, select it and press Delete.

TECHNICAL STUFF

>> **Shadow:** Before digging into how this setting works, I need to point out that this is one of the few areas where there's a difference between the Mac and Windows versions of Lightroom Classic. If you're a Windows user, you don't see the Shadow section in the Overlays panel (sorry!). I hope the engineers can overcome whatever operating system obstacle stands in the way of including this feature on Windows in a future version, but it has been this way since the beginning. (If you're a Windows user, feel free to skip ahead.)

The purpose of this control is to add a drop shadow to an overlay element. You enable the Shadow option by clicking an overlay element to make it active and then selecting the Shadow check box. While the overlay element is active, you can adjust the opacity, offset, radius, and angle of the drop shadow in the same manner as the Cast Shadow control in the Options panel. Note that the opacity setting of the overlay element also affects the opacity of the element's shadow, so if the element itself has a low opacity setting, you'll need a high opacity setting to see the shadow.

You can create custom text templates that will be available to be used in the Slideshow module, as well as the Print, Web, and Book modules. The process starts with clicking the ABC button and choosing Edit from the drop-down menu that appears. From there, follow these steps:

1. **Delete any tokens that appear within the Text Template Editor, as shown in Figure 13-10.**

2. **Add tokens by clicking the desired token's Insert button.**

    This adds the token to the editing field, so the order in which tokens are added is important. You can also type directly into this field to include elements such as punctuation between tokens.

FIGURE 13-10:
The Text Template Editor.

3. **Click the Preset drop-down menu to save your template for reuse.**

You can also use that menu to manage your templates over time. Saved templates appear in all modules where they can be used.

Backdrop panel

A good background supports and frames your photos but doesn't compete with them. The Backdrop panel, shown in Figure 13-11, offers three ways to adjust the look of the area behind your photos. I don't mind telling you that I wish the controls were arranged differently, and after I show you how to use them, I think you'll agree.

FIGURE 13-11:
The Backdrop panel.

Here's how the controls work in the order, in which I use them:

» **Background Color:** Select the Background Color check box to enable it, and click the color swatch to choose a color. Keep in mind that your perception of color is influenced by surrounding colors. Because of this, you see black or neutral gray as the most common background color choices. Of course, you can use any color you want, if that's what fits with your goals for a particular audience. Know the rules and then break them when it suits you!

» **Background Image:** As an alternative, you can add a background image to the slide. Select the Background Image check box to enable it, and then drag a photo from the Filmstrip to either the slide background or the Background Image box in the Background panel, as shown in Figure 13-12. After the

FIGURE 13-12:
Adding a background image to the slide.

background image is in place, you can adjust its opacity via the slider.
Note: When you decrease the opacity of the background image, the

background color increasingly shows through. Different background colors affect your background image in different ways.

>> **Color Wash:** Each of the earlier options can be further enhanced by applying a color wash, which is why I use this control last. You use it to add an additional color, in the form of a gradient, across the background. You can adjust the opacity and angle of the gradient wash by using the respective controls.

As you can see, these controls can be used alone or in tandem to offer an almost unlimited variety of creative background possibilities!

Titles panel

The Titles panel, shown in Figure 13-13, offers a simple bit of polish to your slide-show presentation by providing a means to add a nonphoto beginning and ending screen to your show.

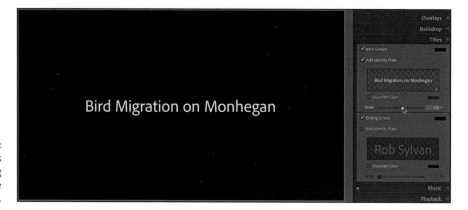

FIGURE 13-13:
The Titles panel, showing the title on the slide.

The Intro Screen appears before the first photo slide, and the Ending Screen appears after the last photo slide. These screens are entirely optional and function independently, meaning that you can add an Intro without an Ending and vice versa. The Titles panel is divided into two sections, with the Intro options on top and Ending options below. However, the type of controls for each screen are the same, as described in this list:

>> **Enable Screen check box:** Each screen type is enabled by selecting the check box at the top of each section.

>> **Color swatch:** Click the color swatch to set the color of that screen.

» **Add Identity Plate check box:** Select this check box to add an identity plate to either screen. This is the only means to add text or a graphic here.

» **Choose/Create Identity Plate:** After you've selected the check box to add the identity plate, you can choose to use an existing one or create a new one specifically for this purpose by clicking anywhere in the box with the checkerboard pattern and choosing from the menu that appears.

» **Override Color:** This control allows you to override the actual color of a textual identity plate without having to alter the identity plate itself. In other words, if you have a custom identity plate that uses black text but want to add it to a black Intro screen, you can simply override the original color with this option and change it to white without affecting your custom identity plate. Make sense?

» **Scale:** This adjusts the size of the identity plate.

Click and hold the handle on the Scale slider to see a preview of the screen in the content area.

Music panel

The way to add music to a slideshow has evolved over the years, and the current incarnation is the best so far. You can add as many as ten music tracks (though that can be a very long total playing time) using .mp3, .m4a, or .m4b music files. The process is simple:

1. **Toggle the switch in the panel header to the Up position to allow music to be added.**

2. **Click the plus sign (+) icon, navigate to the music file you want to add, and select it.**

   The track is added to the slideshow. The duration of the track is displayed alongside the filename. A running total duration appears at the top as you add more music tracks.

You can reorder the tracks by dragging and dropping them within the panel into the order you want. You can remove a track by selecting it and then clicking the Remove Music (−) icon at the top of the Music panel.

REMEMBER

Music isn't included in JPG or PDF outputs.

Playback panel

After you design the look and sound of your slideshow, you're ready to configure how it plays. The Playback panel, shown in Figure 13-14, is divided into the seven sections (or six, if you have only a single monitor):

>> **Slideshow Mode:** When set to Automatic, playback follows the settings configured in the Duration section. When it's set to manual, you advance each slide manually with the arrow keys, and unsupported options are hidden from the panel.

>> **Slide Duration:** Unless you have a one-photo slideshow (unlikely!), you should set the slide length and transition timing. The Slide Length slider controls how long each photo appears, and the Crossfades slider controls the duration of the transition from one photo to the next. If your slideshow includes music, try selecting the Sync Slides to Music check box, which disables the previously mentioned sliders and tells Lightroom Classic to set the transitions based on the beats in the music. (Note that selecting Sync Slides to Music disables the playing of video within the slideshow.) Clicking Fit to Music tells Lightroom Classic to adjust the slide length so that the duration of the slideshow is the same as the duration of the combined audio.

FIGURE 13-14:
The Playback panel, showing two-monitor setup.

>> **Audio Balance:** If your slideshow includes video clips (with audio), you can use the Audio Balance slider to adjust the volume of the audio in the video clip so that it can be either silenced (move the slider toward Music) or easily heard over the music (move the slider toward Video).

>> **Pan and Zoom:** Commonly known as the Ken Burns effect, when Pan and Zoom are enabled, they can add some movement to your stills by automatically panning and zooming into and out of each slide. The higher the setting, the more movement you see. (Use them in moderation to prevent motion sickness in your audience.)

>> **Repeat / Random Order:** These two are pretty straightforward.

>> **Playback Screen:** If you have only one monitor hooked up to your computer, this section doesn't appear in the Playback panel. If you have multiple monitors, you use this section to choose on which monitor to run the slideshow. Click the icon representing your monitor choice, and the Play symbol appears on the icon. Select the Blank other screens check box to black out the screen not running the show.

>> **Quality:** The options on the Quality drop-down menu — Draft, Standard, and High — control the quality of the previews used in the slideshow. The higher the quality, the longer it takes to build the previews. Use Draft when you tweak the presentation, and switch to High when you show it to others. If you run the slideshow through on High by yourself, the previews should be ready to go when you're in front of your audience. (You don't want them to sit in front of the Preparing Slideshow progress bar.)

TIP

If you see an exclamation point next to an audio file, Lightroom Classic can't play it, and you'll need to select a different track.

Step 4: Save your settings as a template for reuse

You don't need to rely solely on the preinstalled templates after you get your feet wet. As you begin to customize slideshows to your liking, I recommend saving your preferred settings as templates. Here's how:

1. **Choose Slideshow⇨New Template Folder to create a new template folder.**

Give the folder a descriptive name and click the Create button.

TIP

Keeping your templates organized can increase your efficiency by providing order to your template collection. The Template Browser displays template folders and individual templates in alphanumeric order, right below the *Lightroom Templates* heading. Note that you cannot create template folders within folders.

2. **Go to Slideshow⇨New Template to create a new template from the settings you specified.**

Give the template a descriptive name, assign it to your desired folder, and click the Create button.

Step 5: Save your photos and settings as a special slideshow collection

Special collections, sometimes referred to as *saved creations,* are first covered in Chapter 12 (refer there for the steps), which covers creating books. In the Slideshow module, creating a saved slideshow collection saves all photos in the Filmstrip and your slideshow settings to this special collection with the icon for slideshows.

Playing the Slideshow for Your Audience

Showtime! Now, before you head onstage to show your work, do a few dress rehearsals to check your timing and make sure everything flows as it should.

Playback

To aid you in test-driving your show, Lightroom Classic can play the show directly within the content area. Click the Preview button below the Playback panel. You'll hear the music (if it's enabled) and see the show just as it would play if you had it full screen, but you can also watch the progression of photos in the Filmstrip. Consider this a preflight check to ensure you're ready for prime time. Click the content area or press Esc to stop the preview.

If you have a dual-monitor setup, you get to choose which monitor you want to run the show on by selecting its icon in the Playback panel. If you have a single-monitor setup, the choice is made for you. To start the show, click the Play button, sit back, and enjoy!

TIP

Lightroom Classic provides three keyboard shortcuts worth memorizing for running a slideshow:

>> Press Enter to start the show.

>> Press the spacebar to pause the show.

>> Press Esc to quit the show.

Export

Having options is nice. When you can't bring your computer to your audience or bring your audience to your computer, you can send your slideshow to your audience. Lightroom Classic's slideshow Export function can save your slideshow to a series of JPEG files or a single multipage PDF file, or as a video. The good news is that anyone with a simple image viewer can see JPEGs: The free Adobe Acrobat Reader is in such wide use that almost anyone can view a PDF, and every computer has a default video player installed. The thing to keep in mind is that music isn't included in JPEG or PDF exports, and the transition times are fixed in PDF, so if music is important, choose the video option.

First, here are the steps to export your show to PDF:

1. **Click the Export PDF button at the bottom of the Left Panel group.**

   The Export Slideshow to PDF dialog appears.

2. **Navigate to the location on your computer where you want to store the PDF.**

3. **Enter a name in the Save As field.**

4. **Choose a quality setting for the JPEG compression applied.**

   The higher the quality setting, the less JPEG compression, which results in a better-looking image but a larger file size.

5. **Choose the width and height of the exported file.**

   This value should be based on the resolution of the monitor the presentation will be viewed on. The Common sizes drop-down menu can help you pick a size.

6. **Select the Automatically show full screen check box.**

   When the PDF file is opened, it appears full screen and begins the slideshow. Warn the people you deliver the file to that this will happen so that they know what to expect. Also tell them to press the Esc key to exit when they're done.

7. **Click the Export button.**

When Lightroom Classic's progress meter is complete, the file is ready to test (always test everything). If you're sending the file by email, check the final output size of the PDF and resave with either higher JPG compression or smaller pixel dimensions (or both) if the file is too large.

The Export JPEG Slideshow menu (under the Slideshow menu) functions essentially the exact same way (right down to the dialog), with one logical difference: There's no Automatically show full screen box. With the Export JPEG function, Lightroom Classic simply saves each slide out as a separate JPEG file. How the slides are viewed depends on which application the viewer uses to open them. That said, the most common export option for a slideshow is as a video. Here's what that looks like:

1. **Click the Export Video button at the bottom of the Left Panel group.**

   The Export Slideshow to Video dialog appears.

2. **Navigate to the location on your computer where you want the file saved.**

3. **Enter a name in the Save As field.**

4. **Choose a video preset based on where the video is destined to be played.**

   A helpful description appears at the bottom for each preset size to help you gauge the best choice for your intended purpose.

5. **Click the Export button.**

When Lightroom Classic's progress meter is complete, the file is ready to test. Double-click the video to open it in your computer's default player. Video files are much larger than PDFs or JPGs, so I don't recommend delivering them via email. Look into a free cloud-based file sharing service (such as Dropbox) to help facilitate the sharing of large files.

TECHNICAL
STUFF

Lightroom Classic's video export is intended to be played on a computer or mobile device. If your intention is to play in a DVD player, you must find software for authoring a DVD (that you can import this video into) and a device to burn the DVD (because optical media is fading from common use and isn't typically included on new computers), all of which are outside Lightroom Classic's skill set.

IN THIS CHAPTER

» **Getting to know the print interface**

» **Establishing a print workflow**

» **Customizing print layouts**

» **Creating templates**

» **Working with your printer**

Chapter **14**

Printing Your Work

The goal of Lightroom Classic's Print module is to facilitate putting your digital work to paper in a color-managed environment with a high-quality output. (Say that three times fast.) Although originally geared toward sending data to a local inkjet printer, Lightroom Classic also makes it possible to save your print layouts as a JPEG (I prefer the shorter JPG) file that you can deliver to a print service.

Can I tell you what I think is one of the greatest aspects of printing from Lightroom Classic? It's that you can create a print right from your raw image data without first having to save a TIFF, PSD, or JPG copy of the original (most printing applications are unable to print raw files). Gone are the days of having to create and manage multiple versions of each file cropped, optimized, and prepared for each print size! Of course, you might need to render TIFF, PSD, or JPG versions of your raw files at times, and that's fine, but it sure is helpful when you don't have to bother!

Exploring the Print Module

I'd like to take a moment to reinforce that each Lightroom Classic module is structured in essentially the same way, which means the interface behaves the same no matter which module you're working in. You can show and hide, and collapse and expand, panels as needed to maximize your work area, and display only the controls you need. For a look at the Lightroom Classic interface as a whole, refer to Chapter 1.

WARNING

This statement is more of a heads-up than a dire warning, but the Print module is a place where minor visual differences exist in the interface depending on the operating system being used. Most of my screen captures throughout this book are from a Mac, but I do include Windows captures when needed to call out those differences. Assume that figures are showing the Mac interface unless the caption indicates that they show Windows.

Getting to know the panels and tools

As is typical of all Lightroom Classic modules, the organizational and preview panels are on the left side of the content area, and the right side holds the configuration panels. The Filmstrip is across the bottom, and the Module Picker is across the top. Specific to each module are the tools provided for completing the task.

A unique aspect of the Print module is that it contains three different layout possibilities (Single Image/Contact Sheet, Picture Package, and Custom Package), and although I go into each layout in detail, I want to point out that your choice of layout controls which configuration panels are available on the right side. To illustrate the difference, Figure 14-1 shows the Print module interface with the Single Image/Contact Sheet layout selected, and Figure 14-2 shows the Picture Package layout (Custom Package's panels are the same as Picture Package). It's like having three Print modules for the price of one!

FIGURE 14-1:
The Print module interface, showing the Single Image layout selected in the Layout Style panel.

An embarrassment of riches? Wait until you see the plethora of tools and panels Lightroom Classic lays at your feet. Admittedly, you never see all these panels at the same time, but I thought it would be a good idea to list all of them for easier reference:

FIGURE 14-2:
The right side of the Print module, showing the Picture Package panels.

>> **Preview panel:** Displays a preview of each template layout as you move the cursor over the items listed in the Template Browser.

>> **Template Browser:** Provides controls for creating new templates — and managing existing ones.

>> **Collections panel:** Provides access to all the collections you've created, as well as the controls to add new ones that retain all the print settings. If needed, refer to Chapter 5 for a collections refresher.

>> **Page Setup button:** Launches the Page Setup (or Print Setup on Windows) dialog for choosing your printer and paper size. This is how Lightroom Classic communicates with your *printer driver,* which is the software that installs with your printer for the purpose of configuring printer settings and running printer maintenance. It's a vital part of the printing pipeline. In Windows, you click the Properties button in this dialog to access advanced printer settings. (I explain this topic later in this chapter, in the "Setting Up a Print Job" section.) You might need to pull out your printer manual if you're not familiar with configuring its settings.

>> **Print Settings button (Mac only):** Launches the Print dialog for configuring your printer settings. The options in this dialog vary based on your printer model; it's not a Lightroom Classic dialog. You might need to pull out your printer manual if you need guidance on configuring its settings.

>> **Layout Style panel:** Provides access to the three types of layout options:

  ● *Single Image / Contact Sheet:* Create print layouts using a grid model, where each cell in the grid has the same dimensions. You can print different photos on a single layout (a different photo in each cell, but the cells are all the same size).

  ● *Picture Package:* Create print layouts using cells of various dimensions, but only one photo can appear on a single layout (the same photo in each cell, but the cells can be various sizes).

- *Custom Package:* Create print layouts using cells of various dimensions and put different photos in each cell (different photos in each cell and the cells can be various sizes).

» **Image Settings panel:** Contains settings that affect the look of the photos appearing in the layout.

» **Layout panel:** Specific to Single Image; provides options for creating the desired grid layout to be used.

» **Guides panel:** Specific to Single Image; provides options for the visibility of these particular layout aids.

» **Rulers, Grid & Guides panel:** Specific to Picture Package and Custom Package; provides options for the configuration and visibility of these particular layout aids.

» **Cells panel:** Specific to Picture Package and Custom Package; controls the addition and configuration of new cells to a layout.

» **Page panel:** Allows for an identity plate, watermark, and supporting photo info text to be added to the print layout for output. Note that photo info text isn't available to either package style.

» **Print Job panel:** Controls output settings for sending data to a printer or saving it as JPG.

» **Toolbar:** Provides controls for navigating between print jobs containing multiple pages, an indicator of how many pages will be printed, and the Use controls for designating which photos will be used in the layout.

REMEMBER

The layout style you choose determines which panels appear and the available options within panels for a given style. I continue to reinforce the differences as I cover the workflow throughout this chapter.

Becoming familiar with the menu options

The Lightroom Classic (Mac only), File, Edit, View, Window, and Help menus remain largely consistent throughout Lightroom Classic. You soon discover, though, that a couple of print options are located on the File menu. The Print command (same as the Print button) sends the current layout directly to the printer, using the existing settings without opening the printer driver — a helpful command to have when you're set up and you just want to print. You also have access to other print-related submenus — Printer, Page Setup, and Print Settings (Mac only) — that function just the same as the previously mentioned buttons of the same name. Take note of the keyboard shortcuts!

The Print menu contains commands for creating new templates and template folders, navigating between pages in a multiple-page print job, and rotating the photos. The Create Saved Print command (note the button above the content area with the same name) allows you to create a special type of collection containing all the photos in the Filmstrip as well as the settings you've dialed into the Print module. This special collection appears in the Collections panel, and double-clicking its icon jumps you right to the Print module with all settings loaded up.

Setting Up a Print Job

Waiting to see a print for the first time can be a little bit like opening a birthday present — a mixture of hope and anticipation that it will be just what you want while bracing for disappointment if it isn't. Unless you're buying your birthday presents, you can't do much about that, but you can ensure that the best possible print emerges from your printer.

Employing a print workflow

Although the three layout styles have some distinct differences and options, they still fit within the same place in the larger print workflow. I do my best to address their individual quirks and foibles, but for now, I just want to give you the big picture:

1. **Bring your photos to the Print module.**
2. **Configure the page setup.**
3. **Select a layout style for your starting point.**
4. **Customize the layout as desired.**
5. **Configure the output settings.**
6. **(Optional) Save your settings for reuse.**
7. **(Optional) Save your settings and photos as a saved print collection.**
8. **Print the layout.**

Step 1: Bring your photos to the Print module

The Library module is the most likely place you'll begin to gather your photos before moving to the Print module because it provides the greatest access to your portfolio and contains tools for finding, organizing, and grouping. Whether you select a folder or a collection, or create a grouping based on keywords or metadata, you need to identify and select the photos you want to print before you can print them.

TIP

One of the best ways to begin the process is to use a collection because it can contain photos from every corner of your imported portfolio. The other benefits of using a collection are

» You can manually control the order in which the images appear in the layout.

» You can create an infinite number of collections and sort them independently.

After you collect your photos for printing, you're ready to bring them into the Print module. Notice that the image grouping you created in the Library module is still displayed in the Filmstrip.

Step 2: Configure your page setup

Before you dive into creating your layout, you need to tell Lightroom Classic a few things about the page you want to create. Click the Page Setup button below the Collections panel or press Shift+⌘+P on a Mac (or Shift+Ctrl+P on Windows) to launch the Page Setup (the dialog box is named Print Setup on Windows) dialog, as shown in Figure 14-3.

FIGURE 14-3:
The Mac Page Setup dialog (left) and the Windows Print Setup dialog box (right).

These are the three steps you want to take here:

1. **Select a printer.**

2. **Select a paper size.**

3. **Select a paper orientation.**

Click OK to close the dialog. Lightroom Classic uses this information to determine how the page displays in the content area as well as the document size and the minimum margins. Choose View⇨Show Info Overlay (if it isn't already showing) to enable the display of a nonprinting indicator that shows you key information about your setup. You can also press the I key to toggle this overlay on or off. Keep Info Overlay on while you get familiar with Lightroom Classic to serve as a reminder of what you've configured.

Step 3: Select a layout style for your starting point

Expand the Layout Style panel (refer to Figure 14-1) and choose the style you want to use. Many of the panel options stem from this choice. Before I dig into the details, I want to clarify the differences between these three layout styles so that you know which will best suit any given job:

>> **Single Image / Contact Sheet:** This style uses a grid to divide the paper into equal-size cells. The more cells you add, the smaller each cell becomes (because the paper size remains constant). This layout style is for when you want to print different photos on a single page within equal-size cells (although it's possible to fill every cell on a page with a single photo), or you can use it to print a single photo, which requires just a single cell. The photos in the Filmstrip automatically populate the print cells based on the Use drop-down menu setting in the Toolbar.

>> **Picture Package:** You use this style to create a layout for printing a single photo in a range of sizes on one or more pages. Think school portraits, where a single pose can be purchased in a package that includes prints from 8 x 10 down to wallet size, and in various quantities. This is a useful feature for anyone needing to produce a set package of prints quickly. Just keep in mind that you can't create a single-page picture package that includes more than one photo. You can apply the same Picture Package layout to multiple photos, but each photo requires its own page. The photos in the Filmstrip appear in each package layout based on the Use drop-down menu setting in the Toolbar.

>> **Custom Package:** This style provides the most flexibility in that you can use it to create cells of various sizes and then fill those cells with the same photo or a variety of photos. You can even overlap the cells to create poster-like layouts. The configuration options are basically the same as Picture Package, but many people use this option for all prints because it can print a single photo (one cell) or multiple different photos (multiple cells of various sizes) on a single page. Drag and drop photos from the Filmstrip to the layout.

Step 4: Customize the layout as desired

This is the fun part! The rest of the panels on the right side of the window are arranged with an efficient workflow in mind, so keep working your way down. As I've said, you'll see some differences in the options available, depending on the layout style you choose. With Single Image, you have the Layout and Guides panels. With Picture Package and Custom Package, you have the Rulers, Grids & Guides panel and the Cells panel.

The rest of the panels appear in all styles, aside from a few minor differences in the Image Settings and the Page panels. In the next few sections, you get up close and personal with each configuration panel.

IMAGE SETTINGS

The controls in the Image Settings panel, shown in Figure 14-4, affect what happens inside each photo cell, regardless of the layout style used.

FIGURE 14-4: The Image Settings panel with Single Image layout selected (left) and Picture Package selected (right).

Here's what the various controls do:

>> **Zoom to Fill:** When this option is deselected, your entire photo fits within each cell. If the aspect ratio of the cell is different from the aspect ratio of the photo, the photo doesn't fill the entire cell. When Zoom to Fill is selected, the photo is sized to fill the entire cell. If the aspect ratio of the cell is different from the aspect ratio of the photo, the photo appears cropped. Zoom to Fill doesn't appear in Custom Package because the photo always fills the cell, regardless of the cell's aspect ratio. Note that if your photo does appear cropped, you can reposition it within the cell by clicking-and-dragging while in Single Image layout or by holding down ⌘ on a Mac (or Ctrl key on Windows) and clicking-and-dragging while in Picture Package or Custom Package.

>> **Rotate to Fit:** Select this check box to have Lightroom Classic automatically rotate each photo to best fit the orientation of the cell. This is handy when

printing a sheet of both portrait- and landscape-oriented photos and you want each photo to fill as much of the cell as possible.

>> **Repeat One Photo per Page:** This pretty much does what it says — fills every cell on a single sheet with the same photo. This option doesn't appear in Picture Package or Custom Package.

>> **Stroke Border:** This control adds a stroke around each photo. Click the color swatch to choose a color. Keep in mind that the stroke remains inside the cell, so increasing the stroke decreases the size of the actual photo. In Picture Package and Custom Package, this option is called *Inner Stroke*.

>> **Photo Border:** Control the width of the border around each photo in a Picture Package or Custom Package layout. The color of this border can't be changed and is always white. The option doesn't exist in Single Image.

>> **Inner Stroke:** Add a stroke around each photo in Picture Package or Custom Package. Click the color swatch to choose a color. Keep in mind that the stroke remains inside the cell, so increasing the stroke decreases the size of the photo. In Single Image, this option is named *Stroke Border*.

LAYOUT

The Layout panel, shown in Figure 14-5, appears only when the Single Image / Contact Sheet style is active because all the controls affect the layout of the grid on the page.

The Layout panel has four sets of controls:

>> **Margins:** The Margins sliders function independently and control the edge of the printable area on the page. The smallest margin amount is determined by the printer driver settings, so if you want to print borderless, be sure to enable borderless printing in your printer driver (via the Page Setup button) before trying to zero out the margins. (Borderless isn't an option for every paper size and printer.) Set all margins to the same value to create centered prints.

FIGURE 14-5:
The Layout panel.

>> **Page Grid:** Control the number of cells in the layout. Rows are horizontal, and columns are vertical.

>> **Cell Spacing:** Adjust the amount of spacing between cells. This option is grayed out when the grid consists of a single cell.

>> **Cell Size:** This control determines the size of the actual printed photo. Maximum cell dimensions are determined by the size of the paper, the margins, and the number of cells being used. Keep in mind that all cells in the grid are the same size. If you're interested in creating square cells, select the Keep Square check box, and the Height and Width sliders will be set to the same value and linked to each other when moved.

GUIDES

The Guides panel, shown in Figure 14-6, is also unique to the Single Image style. It contains a set of layout guide tools (under Show Guides) that can be enabled by selecting their respective check boxes. When the guides are enabled, you see them appear in the content area. Placing the cursor over any one of the guides and clicking-and-dragging allows another means to make layout adjustments. You can modify margins, cell size, and spacing this way. Selecting the Dimensions check box displays the cell size dimensions as an overlay in each of the cells.

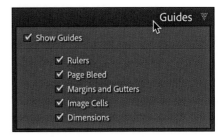

FIGURE 14-6:
The Guides panel.

RULERS, GRID & GUIDES

The Rulers, Grid & Guides panel, shown in Figure 14-7, is specific to Picture Package and Custom Package.

It provides the following layout aids for creating your package layout:

FIGURE 14-7:
The Rulers, Grid & Guides panel.

>> **Ruler Units:** This one allows you to choose the unit of measurement.

>> **Grid Snap:** You might find it helpful to turn on snapping to Cells or Grid as you move the cells on the page. This way, you feel a "snap" whenever you

encounter either the background grid or another cell. Set it to Off if it gets in your way. I find that snapping to cells helps prevent cells from overlapping each other when aligning them tightly.

>> **Show Guides:** This check box toggles all the visual guides on or off. Underneath it you can control each one individually:

- *Rulers:* Toggle the rulers on or off.

- *Page Bleed:* Toggle the shaded area showing the unprintable margin on or off.

- *Page Grid:* Toggle the layout grid on or off.

- *Image Cells:* Toggle the cell border on or off.

- *Dimensions:* Toggle the display of the cell dimensions within each cell on or off.

The problem with overlapping cells is that one photo will print on top of the other and cost you money in wasted paper and ink. Lightroom Classic warns you if two or more cells overlap in Picture Package by displaying an exclamation point inside a black circle in the upper right corner of the layout, as shown in Figure 14-8. Click the Auto Layout button in the Cells panel (see the next section) to have Lightroom Classic rearrange the cells correctly.

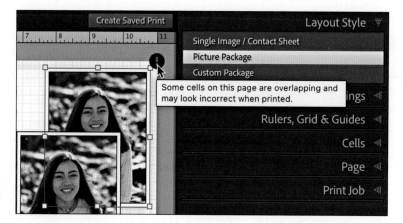

FIGURE 14-8:
Cell overlap
warning.

CELLS

The Cells panel, shown in Figure 14-9, is also specific to Picture and Custom Package. As the name of the panel indicates, all the controls contained here are for the creation and modification of Package cells.

In the Add to Package section, you find the following controls:

>> **Cell buttons:** You use the cell buttons to add new cells to your layout — just click the button representing the size you want to add. The six buttons represent the default cell sizes, but you can click the drop-down arrow next to any button and choose a different cell size or click Edit to enter a custom cell size. Every button click adds a new cell. Additional pages are added to the package as needed to accommodate new cells.

>> **New Page button:** As you might expect, clicking this button adds a new page to the package. You can create multiple new, blank pages before adding cells and then drag-and-drop cells between pages to create your layouts. Note that Lightroom Classic automatically adds a new page when you add a cell that requires a new page to fit in the layout.

FIGURE 14-9:
The Cells panel.

REMEMBER

As soon as you have more than one page in a package, Lightroom Classic displays a black Delete Page button in the upper left corner of each page, as shown in Figure 14-10. Click that button to delete that page (and any cells it contains) from the package.

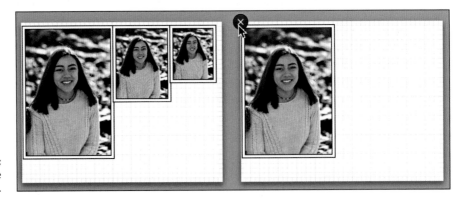

FIGURE 14-10:
The Delete
Page button.

>> **Auto Layout button (not available on Custom Package):** Click this button to arrange the cells to make the most efficient use of paper by rearranging cells in the layout across all available pages.

>> **Clear Layout button:** Remove all cells from the layout.

TIP

After you add a cell to the layout, you can click-and-drag a resize handle to change the dimensions of the cell, or you can make height and width adjustments using the Adjust Selected Cell sliders. You can reposition a cell in the layout by clicking-and-dragging the cell to a new location, or even move cells between pages. To delete a cell, select it and press Delete on a Mac (or Backspace on Windows). To duplicate a cell, hold the Option key (or the Alt key on Windows) while clicking and dragging a cell.

TIP

Keep in mind that each cell is simply a frame in which to place a photo. Your photo has a particular aspect ratio, but you could potentially create multiple cells with a range of aspect ratios. For example, a typical aspect ratio of an uncropped photo is 2:3 (also known as 1:1.5). A 4-x-6 print has an aspect ratio of 2:3. Therefore, if you place a photo with a 2:3 aspect ratio in a 4-x-6 cell, it should fill the entire cell without being cropped. Now, if you also want to include a 5-x-7 print in that package, you need to do some cropping because the 5-x-7 cell would have a 1:1.4 aspect ratio. However, you don't want to crop the source photo itself because then it wouldn't fit the 4-x-6 cell!

Here's where that Zoom to Fill check box comes in handy. After you select that check box, you see the photo in the 5-x-7 cell appear to grow larger and fill the available space in that cell; the 4 x 6 remains the same because it was already filling the cell. Now you can print a full 4 x 6 and a full 5 x 7 from the same source photo, and yes, the 5-x-7 print will be cropped, but the source photo will remain unchanged. You also can move your photo within that 5-x-7 cell to improve the default placement. Press and hold the ⌘ key on a Mac (or the Ctrl key on Windows) and click-and-drag the photo within the cell for better placement.

REMEMBER

Note that you encounter a few minor differences when you use Custom Package. One is that there's no Auto Layout button because (I suppose the assumption is that) in Custom, you put the cells where you want them. You'll find a Rotate Cell button for flipping the orientation of the cell. And finally, there's a Lock to Photo Aspect Ratio check box that keeps the cell's aspect ratio locked but allows you to resize the cell as needed.

PAGE

The Page panel contains the controls for background color (does what you expect), the identity plate, and watermarking, as well as a few additional layout-style–specific overlay elements. Figure 14-11 shows the contents of the panel when each layout style is active, though the contents are the same for both Picture Package and Custom Package.

FIGURE 14-11:
Page panel
contents with
Single Image/
Contact Sheet
(left) and
Picture/Custom
Package (right).

Consider the Identity Plate section first because it functions the same way in all styles. The purpose of the identity plate is to provide a means to add either a textual or graphical element to your printed page. This could be your graphical logo or simply a textual copyright notice and your name. You can apply it on each image or place it on a blank area of the page.

The identity plate appears in many places throughout Lightroom Classic. Here are the basic steps for using identity plate in the Print module:

1. **Click the Identity Plate check box to toggle it on.**

2. **Choose Edit from the Identity Plate drop-down menu.**

   Choosing Edit launches the Identity Plate Editor. If you previously created a custom identity plate, you'll see it listed on the menu, and you can (obviously) choose it.

3. **In the Identity Plate Editor, select either a styled text or graphical identity plate.**

4. **Customize as desired.**

   Chapter 5 has bunches more info on customizing your identity plate.

5. **Choose Save As from the Custom drop-down menu if you want to save your customized identity plate for future use.**

   Doing so launches the Save Identity Plate As dialog, where you can name this identity plate and click Save.

6. **Click OK.**

TIP

The identity plate appears in the content area. Click-and-drag the identity plate to reposition it. You can adjust opacity and size as desired with the provided sliders. The Override Color option allows you to change the color of a textual identity plate temporarily without permanently altering your saved identity plate. You can rotate the identity plate by clicking the rotation amount indicator (starts at 0 degrees) in the upper right corner of the panel. Choose the amount and direction of rotation you require.

TIP

Select the Render on every image check box if you want to use the identity plate as a watermark for all images in the layout. Just keep in mind that when this option is enabled, the identity plate will be "rendered" to the center of each photo. You can still adjust its rotation, scale, and opacity, but it cannot be repositioned off the center.

Render behind image is a little-used option that places the identity plate behind your photos. This can be used when you want your identity plate and photos to overlap but don't want the identity plate to print on top of the photos.

Further down the right side of the screen, you encounter Watermarking options. I provide more in-depth coverage of watermarking in Chapter 15 because you're more likely to use it in a web gallery. However, you can select the Watermarking check box to access your saved watermarks or create a new watermark from the Watermarking drop-down menu. Just remember that the placement of the watermark is based on how you create the watermark in the Watermark Editor. From here, the remaining options are unique to each layout style. In Single Image, you have

>> **Page Options:** Allows for the addition of page numbers, page information, and crop marks to be printed on the page with your photos. Page information includes

   - *Sharpening Setting:* The amount of sharpening you choose in the Print Job panel

- *Profile Used:* The color-management setting you choose in the Print Job panel

- *Name of Printer:* The name of the printer you use

» **Photo Info:** Provides the ability to include a limited amount of textual information about the photos being printed. Click the check box to enable this option, and then click the drop-down menu to choose a text template to apply, or click Edit to create a new text template. You can adjust the size of the font via the Font Size drop-down menu. You cannot change the font face and positioning.

In Picture Package and Custom Package, Cut Guides provide a printed visual to aid in cutting the photos after printing. Choose either Lines or Crop Marks.

Step 5: Configure the output settings with the Print Job panel

After you finalize your layout, as outlined in the previous sections, you're ready to prepare the data for output. This is the phase where you prepare Lightroom Classic to hand off the image data to the printer (or a JPG file to a print service).

The prep work here involves configuring a few settings in the Print Job panel and/or tweaking settings in the printer driver — if you're printing locally. The most critical component of this hand-off process is the color management of the image data. The next few sections take a closer look at each setting involved.

The Print Job panel, as shown in Figure 14-12, is where you configure your output image data so that it meets the specifications for the job at hand.

The options are the same for both the Grid and Picture Package layout engines:

» **Print To:** The Print To drop-down menu is where you choose whether you want to send your output to a printer or save it as a JPG file.

FIGURE 14-12:
The Print Job panel.

» **Draft Mode Printing:** When Draft Mode Printing is selected, Lightroom Classic uses the image data from its preview cache instead of re-rendering image data from your source files. The benefit of this strategy is purely speed. The trade-off is quality. The quality of the image data in the preview cache is usually good enough for thumbnails on contact sheets, which is when *I* am most likely to use Draft Mode printing. When in Draft Mode print resolution, the Print Sharpening and Color Management configuration options are disabled. The Color Management setting is set to Managed by Printer.

» **Print Resolution:** When this option is selected, you can set the resolution value for Lightroom Classic to use when it renders the image data you want delivered at output. Here's why I tend to leave it deselected: If enough pixels exist in my source photo so that the native resolution is 180–480+ Pixels Per Inch (PPI), I don't worry about it.

TIP

Here's an easy way to see the native resolution at a given print size:

1. *Select a photo.*

2. *Choose the Single Image layout style from the Layout Style panel.*

3. *Create a cell that matches your desired print size in the Layout panel.*

4. *Check the Dimensions box in the Guides panel.*

5. *Deselect Print Resolution in the Print Job panel.*

6. *Look at the Dimensions overlay in the cell.*

   This little trick works in both layout engines, but I just picked Single Image for this example. The key is to have Dimensions selected and Print Resolution deselected. Lightroom Classic displays the print size in the selected units as well as the native resolution for that print size.

If you're in the 180–480 PPI window, you're good to go. However, if this setting makes you the least bit uneasy, go with the default setting of 240 PPI. If you're printing to a JPG and you're not sure what your print service requires, the safest setting is 300 PPI.

» **Print Sharpening:** Adobe worked with the group of folks who wrote the book on print sharpening to create the sharpening algorithms that are applied to your image data. Now, you won't see any change in the content area, because this sharpening is applied only after you click the Print button, when Lightroom Classic renders the image data from the source file and applies all your Lightroom Classic adjustments. The proof lies in the print, so I strongly suggest that you produce a set of test prints on each type of media you use with each sharpening setting to gain a sense of which you prefer. Here's how you do that:

1. **Select the Print Sharpening box.**

2. **Choose an amount (Low, Standard, or High) from the Print Sharpening drop-down menu.**

3. **Choose either Matte or Glossy (depending on the paper type you're using) from the Media Type drop-down menu.**

You can also apply sharpening when saving your output in JPG format — you determine the settings the same way as when you're printing to your attached printer. Don't be surprised by how the image looks if you open it in Photoshop; the proof will still be in the print.

» **Color Management:** This is possibly the most important setting in this module, simply because a bad Color Management setting can singlehandedly ruin your output (and possibly your day). The goal of color management is to literally manage the conversion of colors between Lightroom Classic's working color space and the color space of the output device. The method for achieving the best output is to let Lightroom Classic manage the conversion. The alternative is to let the printer manage the colors (which arguably has improved greatly in recent years).

When the print job is configured to let the printer manage colors — select Managed by Printer from the Profile drop-down menu — Lightroom Classic sends the image data using its color space and leaves it up to the printer driver to convert those colors to the output color space correctly. The problem is that not all printers know how to handle ProPhoto RGB data and, therefore, are unable to convert the colors correctly. Feel free to test the Managed by Printer option, but know that older printers may not handle this as well as newer ones. That said, if you want to try it, here are the steps:

1. **Choose Managed by Printer from the Profile drop-down menu.**

2. **Configure the other Print Job settings as desired.**

   These settings might be deselecting Draft Mode Printing, setting the resolution (or not), and applying sharpening.

3. **Click the Printer button and do the necessary stuff in the Print dialog.**

   This stuff includes opening Advanced Settings and turning on the printer driver's color adjustment setting, setting paper type and print quality, and then clicking Print to send the job to the printer.

If the colors look good, your printer can handle the data that Lightroom Classic is sending. If you see a color cast, or if the colors look washed out, your printer can't handle the data Lightroom Classic is sending and you need to have Lightroom Classic manage the color.

You may be wondering why Managed by Printer is the default setting for Draft Mode printing. The reason is that, with Draft Mode printing, the image data is sent from the preview cache in Adobe RGB space, which most printers can handle.

To let Lightroom Classic manage the colors, you need to have installed the ICC profiles for the paper-and-printer combination you're using. The manufacturer of the paper (which can also be the same company that makes the printer) typically provides these profiles. Go to the paper manufacturer's website and download the latest profile available for the specific paper and printer model you're using. After installing the profile with the directions provided by the supplier, do the following:

1. **Choose Other from the Profile drop-down menu.**

   The Choose Profiles dialog appears (see Figure 14-13).

FIGURE 14-13: The Choose Profiles dialog.

2. **Select the check box next to the profile for the paper you'll use and then click OK.**

   Lightroom Classic returns to the Print module.

3. **Click the Print Settings button (or Page Setup on Windows) at the bottom of the left panel, go to the Printer Options section of the printer driver (on Windows, click the Properties button in the Print dialog box and go to the Main tab and then locate the Color/Intensity section), and click Color Matching to make sure color adjustment is disabled (on Windows, select Manual, and then click Set, and on the Matching tab choose None).**

   This step is absolutely critical, or else the printer driver also attempts to manage the colors, which typically results in light prints with a magenta cast. Access to these settings varies with each operating system and printer. Depending on your printer driver, look for a color management setting that appears disabled or reads Off, No Color Adjustment, or No ICM. Consult your printer manual if you're unsure where this setting is on your system. Figure 14-14 shows the location of this setting for a Canon Pro-1000 on Mac Sonoma and Windows 10.

FIGURE 14-14: Location of color adjustment setting on Mac (left) and Windows (right).

4. **In the printer driver, select the correct Media Type (based on the paper you're using) and desired Print Quality settings, and then click Save (or OK on Windows).**

   Lightroom Classic returns to the Print module.

After you return to Lightroom Classic, you still need to choose a rendering intent. "What's that?" you ask. Well, when Lightroom Classic is set to convert colors to the output space by using the ICC profile you choose, it needs for you to tell it how to handle colors that are beyond what the printer is capable of printing. In other words, it needs for you to tell it what your "rendering intent" is. It gives you two choices:

- *Relative:* Keeps all the colors that are within the gamut of the output color space and clips those outside it to the nearest reproducible color.

- *Perceptual:* Remaps all colors in the source space to fit within the destination space. The downside is that colors within the gamut can appear desaturated, but the upsides are better gradation between colors and overall better color detail when many out-of-gamut colors are present.

REMEMBER

Keep in mind that the goal of both rendering intent options is to preserve the original color appearance. For a rule of thumb, if a photo contains many out-of-gamut colors, try Perceptual; otherwise, go with Relative, but I would encourage you to make a few test prints to get a feel for any differences.

>> **Print Adjustment:** When the Print Adjustment check box is selected, you have the ability to control the brightness and contrast of the print. As with print sharpening, you don't see anything change in the content area. These adjustments are applied to the image only during output. One of the most common complaints in the early days of Lightroom Classic were of getting prints that were too dark, which were often caused by the monitor being set too brightly. Adobe's solution for people who just couldn't get good prints from traditional color-management workflow techniques was to just increase the Brightness slider to compensate. If this sounds like you, you need to conduct a few test prints to find the right setting, but then you can just leave it that way for all future prints.

TIP

If you're a Mac user and you're printing to a printer that supports 16-bit data, you can print in 16-bit from Lightroom Classic. The benefit is improved gradations, but it might take a keen eye to spot the difference between an 8-bit and 16-bit print. If you fit these criteria, you can enable this feature by first selecting the 16-bit Output check box in the Print Job panel and then enabling 16-bit printing in the printer driver. After you have a layout and your print settings are configured, it might be in your best interest to save them for reuse. Read on to find out how to do that.

Step 6: Save your settings for reuse

This optional step in the workflow has the potential of combining all the steps to this point into a single click. You just invested all that time creating the layout and configuring all your output settings, so if there's any chance that you'd repeat those steps with the same or different photos, I strongly suggest that you save your work. Here's how:

1. **(Optional) Choose Print ⇨ New Template Folder. Give the folder a descriptive name and click the Create button.**

TIP

   This step opens the New Folder dialog, where you can enter a name for your folder. Keeping your templates organized can increase your efficiency by providing order to your template collection. The Template Browser displays template folders and individual templates in alphanumeric order, right below the Lightroom Templates default template folder. To keep my custom template folders organized, I name them with a number. Note that you can't create template folders within folders. Once you create your folder structure, you don't need to create a new folder each time.

2. **Choose Print ⇨ New Template. Give the template a descriptive name, assign it to your desired folder, and click the Create button.**

   This opens the New Template dialog, where you can enter a name for your template, and even choose a folder to place it within.

Step 7: Save your photos and settings as a special collection

We first encountered these special collections, sometimes referred to as *saved creations*, in Chapter 12 (refer to Chapter 12 for the steps). Here in the Print module, creating a saved print collection saves all photos in the Filmstrip and your settings to this special collection with the icon for Print.

Step 8: Printing the layout

It took a bit of work to reach this step, but this is the moment you've been waiting for — clicking the Printer button (at the bottom of the right panel group). Doing so launches the printer driver (again) and gives you one last chance for a preflight check of your settings. Until you feel confident in the setup and configuration of everything, I strongly recommend that you double-check the printer driver settings. It just takes a few seconds, and it can save you both time and money. If all the settings are correct, click the Print button (or OK on Windows) to complete printing (and don't forget to load paper in the printer). You'll see the message "Preparing print job" appear (briefly) above the Identity Plate, and then Lightroom Classic hands off the data to the printer to complete the job.

When you feel like you have it down and you consistently get the expected results from the printer, click the Print button to bypass the printer driver's dialog and simply send the data directly to the printer.

Putting it all together

I'd like to walk through a few examples, including the process of soft-proofing (simulating how your print will look in Lightroom Classic), to demonstrate how you'd set up a Single Image layout, a Picture Package layout, and a Custom Package layout. I'll send the Single Image layout to an online print service and send the Picture Package one to my inkjet printer just to highlight the key differences in output as well.

TIP

The workflow scenarios can be accessed by going to `https://lightroomers.com/L4D/printworkflows.pdf`.

Chapter **15**

Creating a Web Gallery

t's an online world these days. High-speed Internet and digital photography go together like peanut butter and chocolate. Lightroom Classic's Web module offers a diverse range of photo gallery styles and configurations for creating professional-looking galleries without touching a bit of code. Seamless integration between your portfolio and Lightroom Classic's built-in File Transfer Protocol (FTP) software means you can take your photos from import to web gallery to web server in a matter of minutes!

As with a book or slideshow, you can create a web gallery from any grouping of images you can pull together in the Library module. You can start from a folder, keyword search, metadata browse, or collection. If you can group them, you can put them on the web!

Exploring the Web Module

If you've been reading this book from the start, you might be tired of hearing it by now (but at least you won't forget), but each Lightroom Classic module is structured in essentially the same way to make your workflow more efficient. Here's the benefit you gain from this consistency: The interface behaves the same way no matter where you are! You can show/hide and collapse/expand panels as needed to maximize your work area, and you can have Lightroom Classic display only the controls you need. To find out more about the Lightroom Classic interface as a whole, move on over to Chapter 1.

TECHNICAL STUFF

This statement is totally unrelated to the Web module, but everyone with a Creative Cloud subscription gets a free online portfolio via Adobe's Portfolio product. Adobe Portfolio is simple to use and includes online hosting (no need to buy a domain or pay for hosting). Discussing it is outside the scope of this book, but head over to `https://portfolio.adobe.com` to get started.

Getting to know the panels and tools

Figure 15-1 shows the Web module interface. The organizational and preview panels are on the left side of the content area. The right side holds the configuration panels — the Filmstrip (across the bottom) and the Module Picker (across the top) are consistent across all modules. Keep in mind that the only elements that change from module to module are the tools and settings specific to that module. It's small comfort, perhaps, when you're first trying to take it all in, but I'll guide you each step of the way.

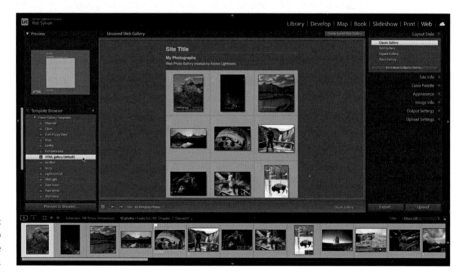

FIGURE 15-1:
The Web module interface.

Time to take a closer look and see what's here. Here's an overview of all the Web module components (minus the ones I cover in earlier chapters):

>> **Preview in Browser button:** A button you click to display the current web configuration in your default web browser.

>> **Layout Style:** Lists installed web galleries and is used to choose the active gallery. (Look at the About option under the Web menu for a description of the active gallery.) The four preinstalled gallery types are

- Classic Gallery
- Grid Gallery
- Square Gallery
- Track Gallery

>> **Site Info panel:** Contains input fields for information about the gallery. Options vary with each gallery.

>> **Color Palette panel:** Allows for changing the color scheme of certain gallery elements. Options vary with each gallery.

>> **Appearance panel:** Configures attributes that affect the structural appearance of each gallery type. Options vary with each gallery.

>> **Image Info panel:** Allows you to display information about the images in the gallery.

>> **Output Settings panel:** A panel whose main option controls the output size settings of the larger version. (Most galleries make use of a small thumbnail photo in combination with a larger version of the same photo.)

>> **Upload Settings panel:** Holds configuration and storage of your FTP settings.

>> **Export button:** A button you click to save all your gallery files to a location on your disk.

>> **Upload button:** A button you click to begin copying files to the web server you configured in the Upload Settings panel.

REMEMBER

Keep in mind that the content of certain panels changes to reflect the options available in a given layout style. All the screen captures reflect the contents of the Classic Gallery because it reveals the most options.

Becoming familiar with the menu options

The one menu option unique to the Web module is the aptly named Web menu. It contains commands for creating new templates and template folders, reloading the content area (similar to refreshing your web browser), exporting the web gallery, and previewing the gallery in your browser. The Create Saved Web Gallery command allows you to save the custom settings of the gallery and the photos as a special collection. The Content command provides the option to choose which photos — within the active image grouping — appear in the gallery. The About menu provides additional functionality details regarding the active gallery type.

Creating a Web Gallery and Employing a Workflow

The look of your web gallery is driven by your photos, your intended audience, the reason(s) you're putting these images online, and your own creativity. With that in mind, and knowing that new questions will emerge, you can enter into your web gallery workflow on the right footing.

Lightroom Classic is all about workflows within workflows! The creation of every web gallery follows the same basic steps. Here's an overview of the process:

1. Bring your photos to the Web module.
2. Select a template or layout style for your starting point.
3. Customize as desired.
4. (Optional) Save your settings as a template for reuse.
5. (Optional) Save your settings and photos as a special web collection.

Step 1: Bring your photos to the Web module

After you collect your photos for the gallery, it's time to bring them into the Web module by clicking Web in the Module Picker. Notice that the image grouping you created in the Library module is still displayed in the Filmstrip.

Step 2: Select a template or layout style for your starting point

A *template* is simply a way of saving unique combinations of settings for reuse. The preinstalled templates are helpful for seeing possibilities, but they also serve as useful jumping-off points for creating your own custom web galleries. You can see a thumbnail layout of any template in the Preview panel by hovering the cursor over its name. The preinstalled templates (refer to Figure 15-1) are grouped by layout type. Alternatively, you can select one of the gallery types from the Layout Style panel, which applies the default template for that style as your starting point.

Step 3: Customize as desired

The controls for customizing your web gallery are on the right side of the module. The panels are arranged with an efficient workflow in mind, so start at the top and work your way down.

Site Info panel

The content of the Site Info panel depends on which gallery type you choose. However, all galleries share some form of Title field. This information is displayed on the title bar of web browsers visiting your site and can be displayed within the content area of the gallery, depending on the gallery type you choose.

TIP

You can either enter the information into the fields in the panel or click the text you want to edit in the Content area and edit it right in the live gallery preview!

Only the Classic Gallery makes use of the following fields, shown in Figure 15-2:

>> **Collection Title:** Think of this field as a subtitle for your site title.

>> **Collection Description:** Enter a description of the contents of your gallery.

>> **Contact Info:** This field works hand in hand with the Web or Mail Link field below it to create a clickable link.

>> **Web or Mail Link:** Enter the link or mailto: code ("mailto:" is a code used on webpages to automatically open a new email when clicked) to accompany the data you entered for the contact Info.

Lightroom Classic remembers text you've entered in each field and provides you quick access to previous entries via the drop-down arrow above the field.

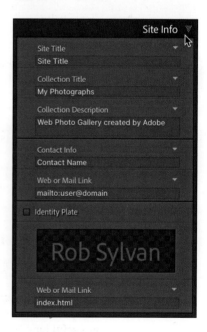

FIGURE 15-2:
The Site Info panel.

REMEMBER

Only in the Classic Gallery can you add an identity plate in addition to the site title at the top of your page, as shown earlier, in Figure 15-2. You won't see this in the Site Info panel for any other gallery type.

Select the check box to enable the identity plate. You can choose an existing identity plate or create a new one. You can make the identity plate into a clickable link by completing the Web or Mail Link field that appears below it (see Chapter 5 for more on the Identity Plate).

COLOR PALETTE PANEL

As its name suggests, the Color Palette panel holds the controls for changing the color scheme of your gallery. Figure 15-3 shows the Color Palette panel for the Classic Gallery. Although the configurable elements in each gallery type vary, the color controls work the same way in each instance.

FIGURE 15-3:
The Color Palette panel.

Click the color chip corresponding to the element you want to change to access Lightroom Classic's Color Picker (it's *cool*), as shown in Figure 15-4.

FIGURE 15-4:
The Color Picker.

You can use the swatches along the top of the Color Picker to save colors you like. Hovering the cursor over each swatch displays a pop-up tooltip instructing you how to use that swatch. Close the Color Picker by clicking the color chip on the color palette you selected to open it.

Appearance panel

The contents of this panel vary the most of any panel among the various gallery types. As you can imagine, each gallery type has a set of controls to alter its appearance. Figure 15-5 shows the Appearance panel for the Classic Gallery.

Despite the differences in the controls for each gallery, they're all rather straightforward in their purpose — you immediately see your adjustment's effects on the active gallery. For example, if you add more cells to the Classic Gallery by clicking on the grid in the Grid Pages section, the live preview automatically updates before your eyes. Note that in the case of the Classic Gallery, the controls in the Image Pages section affect the page that displays the large version of the image. Click a thumbnail in the content area to switch to an Image Page to see the effects of the controls.

Image Info panel

The Image Info panel, shown in Figure 15-6, is where you find controls for adding a caption and title to accompany the large image in your gallery. The main difference between Title and Caption is where they're located in each gallery (Title is always higher). You can display any type of textual information in either element (refer to Chapter 13 for steps to create custom text templates).

Here's how to add a caption:

1. **Select the Caption check box.**

2. **Click the drop-down menu, and either choose one of the text templates listed or choose Edit to create a custom text template.**

   After you choose a template, it immediately appears in the gallery. Note that Caption and Title appear only when viewing the large version of the photo; so if you're viewing the Classic Gallery grid, you don't see them until you click a photo to open the large version.

FIGURE 15-5:
The Appearance panel for the Classic Gallery.

FIGURE 15-6:
The Image Info panel.

REMEMBER

If you're using a Caption or Title template, you must enter an actual caption or title for each photo via the Metadata panel in the Library module. The text tokens pull that information from each photo's metadata to display in the gallery.

Output Settings panel

The Output Settings panel, shown in Figure 15-7, contains the settings that affect the large image component of the gallery:

FIGURE 15-7:
The Output Settings panel.

>> **Quality:** This control sets the amount of JPG compression applied to the large image. The more compression, the smaller the file size — though the appearance can be degraded with too much compression. I wouldn't go below 50.

>> **Metadata:** This one gives you the option to leave all metadata intact in the large JPGs (by selecting All from the drop-down menu) or strip everything but your copyright (by choosing Copyright Only).

>> **Watermarking:** The Simple Copyright Watermark just pulls the copyright data you entered into the Copyright field of the Metadata panel in the Library module and displays it as a watermark on the photo. You can also choose existing custom watermarks or create your own (which I cover next).

>> **Sharpening:** This setting applies one of three levels of output sharpening (low, standard, or high) when the gallery leaves Lightroom Classic. Standard is a good default amount.

To open the Watermark Editor (shown in Figure 15-8), click the Watermarking drop-down menu and choose Edit Watermarks.

You can also get there from any module via the Lightroom Classic ⇨ Edit Watermarks menu (or Edit ⇨ Edit Watermarks on Windows). From there, follow these steps to create a text watermark:

1. **Select the text watermark style and enter some text in the field below the photo.**

To create the © symbol, press Option+G (Alt+0169 on the numeric keypad for Windows).

FIGURE 15-8:
The Watermark
Editor.

2. **Expand the Text Options panel.**

   Select a Font from the drop-down menu; and then configure its style, alignment, and color.

3. **(Optional) Select the Shadow check box if you want to apply a drop-shadow effect to the text.**

4. **Expand the Watermark Effects panel.**

   Set the Size of the watermark first. You can use three controls for sizing a watermark:

   - *Proportional:* Enables the size slider so that you can set the watermark to a size that remains constant (in proportion to the size of the exported photos), regardless of the photo's orientation

   - *Fit:* Expands the watermark to fit the entire width (or height, depending on how the watermark is rotated), regardless of the photo's orientation

   - *Fill:* Expands the watermark to fill the width and height of the photo

   I recommend experimenting with each size setting to get a better feel for how they work. Proportional is likely to be the one used most often.

5. **Adjust the opacity with the Opacity slider.**

6. **Use the Inset and Anchor settings to control the exact placement of the watermark.**

   For example, click the lower-left-corner Anchor point; then use the Horizontal Inset slider to bring it off the left edge of the photo, and the Vertical Inset slider to bring it up off the bottom. You can rotate the watermark using the buttons to the right of the anchor.

7. **Preview the watermark on different photos.**

   At the top of the panel are left- and right-facing sets of arrows. These allow you to step through all the photos you selected before opening the editor. Go back and adjust sizing and placement as needed.

8. **Save as a preset.**

   Click the preset drop-down menu in the upper left corner and choose Save Current Settings as New Preset. Enter a descriptive name in the New Preset dialog and click Create. You can also use that same preset drop-down menu to access existing presets for editing, renaming, and deleting.

All the settings in the Watermark Effects panel work the same way for creating a Graphic style watermark, except that the Text Options panel is unavailable. Here are the key things to know about creating a Graphic Style watermark:

» Create the graphic in Photoshop before you launch the Watermark Editor.

» Only JPG and PNG file formats will work.

» If you want to maintain transparent areas in your graphic, turn off the background layer in Photoshop and save as PNG.

With that in mind and your graphic on hand, you can click the Choose button in the Image Options panel and create a new preset based on a graphic. From there, you can click the Done button to exit the editor. The next time your output needs require a watermark, you can access your presets from any output module and send out your photos in style.

Step 4: Save your settings as a template for reuse

You don't need to rely solely on the preinstalled templates after you get your feet wet. As you begin to customize web galleries to your liking, I recommend saving your preferred settings as templates. Here's how:

1. **Choose Web⇨New Template Folder to create a new template folder.**

   Give the folder a descriptive name and click the Create button.

2. **Choose Web⇨New Template to create a new template from the settings you've specified.**

   Give the template a descriptive name, assign it to a folder, and click the Create button.

Step 5: Save your photos and settings as a special module collection

I cover these special collections, sometimes referred to as *saved creations*, in Chapter 12. (For the steps, see the section "Step 4: Save your photos and settings as a special collection.") Here in the Web module, creating a saved web gallery collection saves all photos in the Filmstrip and saves your gallery settings to this special collection with the icon for a web gallery.

Web Gallery Output Options

Testing your web gallery *locally* (meaning on your computer) is standard operating procedure in web development, but the next phase is testing on a web server. Lightroom Classic has a built-in FTP utility that enables you to upload your gallery directly to your web server without ever leaving Lightroom Classic! However, you also have the option to export all the web gallery files directly to your hard drive, if you have no FTP access to your web server or you prefer to use your own FTP application.

Uploading your gallery with Lightroom Classic

To test your images on a web server, you need access to a web server. A *web server* is just a computer that serves up files over the Internet. Clearly, the professional solution is to get your own website. It doesn't cost as much as you might think (sometimes as little as a few dollars per month). Web hosting companies are a dime a dozen, so ask your web-savvy friends whom they recommend.

I'm going to assume, then, that you've somehow secured access to a server. Nicely done. Now you need to come up with three critical pieces of information to configure Lightroom Classic so that it can upload your files to your web host:

>> **Server address:** The FTP address needed to access the web server

>> **Username:** The username for your FTP account

>> **Password:** The password for your FTP account

To set up Lightroom Classic's FTP configuration dialog, follow these steps:

1. **Choose the Web module from the Module Picker and expand the Upload Settings pane.**

2. **Choose Edit from the FTP Server drop-down menu.**

    The Configure FTP File Transfer dialog appears.

3. **Enter your FTP server information in the Server field, along with the username and password you were given for that server.**

    Select the Store password in preset check box if you're the only person using that computer.

4. **Configure the Server Path field.**

    What you enter here will vary based on the web server. *Server path* refers to the folder on the web server where Lightroom Classic stores the files you upload. In some cases, you leave this field blank; in others, it might be something like `public_html/`. Ask your web hosting provider if you're unsure what to enter. Unless you're instructed otherwise, leave the Protocol drop-down menu set to FTP, the Port menu set to 21, and the Passive mode for data transfers drop-down menu set to Passive.

5. **Choose the Save Current Settings as New Preset option from the Preset drop-down menu.**

6. **In the New Preset dialog that appears, give the preset a name and then click Create.**

    You return to the Configure FTP File Transfer dialog.

7. **Click OK in the Configure FTP File Transfer dialog to close it.**

    In the Upload Settings panel, you now see the name of your preset listed as the FTP Server. Now all you need to do is decide where on your web server you want to store your gallery.

8. **In the Upload Settings panel, select the Put in Subfolder check box, enter a name in the field below it, and then press Enter.**

    The full path that appears at the bottom of the panel shows where your folder sits in relation to the Server Path field you configured in Step 4.

Do not use spaces in your folder names because spaces in links can be problematic.

This subfolder becomes part of the path or URL (Uniform Resource Locator) to your gallery. Therefore, if you're uploading a gallery of flower photos (and who doesn't have a gallery of flower photos?), you might name the subfolder *flowers,* which would result in the following path to your gallery: http://www.*yourdomain*.com/flowers/.

9. **Click the Upload button in the lower right corner of the panel.**

After the progress meter has done its thing, navigate to your new gallery in your web browser and give it a test-drive! If you make changes to the gallery in Lightroom Classic, be sure to upload it again.

Exporting your gallery

If you have preferred FTP software, or if you have no FTP access to your hosting environment, you can click the Export button, save your web gallery to your hard drive, and then upload the files outside Lightroom Classic.

Here are the steps:

1. **Click the Export button (at the bottom of the rightmost panel group, as shown in Figure 15-1).**

   It's next to the Upload button.

2. **In the dialog that appears, navigate to the location on your hard drive where you want to save the gallery files.**

3. **Enter a name for the folder that will contain the gallery in the Save As field at the top of the dialog and click Save.**

Wait for Lightroom Classic's progress meter to complete before attempting to upload the gallery to your web host. Be sure to upload the entire contents of the folder.

You can change the name of the folder holding all the files, but do not change the name of any files within the folder unless you update the HTML code within the files to reflect that change. At this point, Lightroom Classic's job is finished and it's up to you to complete the job. If you make changes to the web gallery in Lightroom Classic, you need to reexport the entire gallery.

5

The Part of Tens

IN THIS CHAPTER

» **Exploring why using these programs together is useful**

» **Dodging potential pitfalls**

» **Getting set up**

» **Syncing and sharing**

» **Keeping up with changes**

Chapter **16**

Ten Tips for Lightroom Classic and Lightroom Together

I n Chapter 1, I explain the differences between Lightroom Classic and the (newer) Lightroom ecosystem based on cloud storage, with the goal of helping you choose the right product for your needs. I still believe that Lightroom Classic offers the best combination of editing power, library management, and output options for the price, which makes it the path I recommend for most people. That said, there's a lot to like about the cloud-based Lightroom, and it makes a lot of sense for Lightroom Classic users to learn about its capabilities and how the two programs can be used together. There may even come a day when you find that the Lightroom ecosystem has all the features you want, allowing you to switch over to it completely.

WARNING

To avoid confusion, Adobe does not recommend installing the desktop version of the cloud-based Lightroom on the same computer running Lightroom Classic and then turning on the sync function between them.

Why Would You Use Them Together?

As much as I love my DSLR, I must admit that I have my iPhone with me all the time and, as a result, I use that mobile camera a lot. Regardless of whether I capture a photo with my iPhone, DSLR, drone, or point-and-shoot digital camera, I want to manage all my photos with Lightroom Classic on my computer. The Lightroom app for mobile provides me with the following:

>> **Sync with Lightroom Classic:** *Syncing* means that I can automatically share photos and edits from Lightroom Classic to my mobile device and vice versa. I explore this capability further in the later section "Syncing Collections from Lightroom Classic."

>> **Familiar Editing Tools:** You have almost the entire Develop module in your pocket (see Chapter 17).

>> **Familiar Flagging/Rating Tools:** Flags and star ratings applied to synced photos are visible in both apps (see Chapter 17).

When I sync these apps, I can designate photos in Lightroom Classic that I want to see in the mobile app, and any edits, ratings, or flags I apply to those photos (in either app) are kept in sync. Any new photos I add or capture in the mobile app are automatically downloaded (via the cloud) to my computer running Lightroom Classic. At the most basic level, I gain a portable portfolio of my work on my phone that is always in my pocket, and through Lightroom, I have an automated system for downloading all mobile photos back to my main computer for storage and backup. As helpful as all this sounds, you should be aware of some things before you dive in.

Know Before You Go

Lightroom for desktop and mobile are designed specifically to work together, and as such, all photos, videos, settings, keywords, albums, folders, and so on are kept in sync between those apps. Unfortunately, Lightroom Classic has become the local-storage-only workflow option for anyone not wanting to go all in on cloud storage, so there is a bit of a rift in how the syncing features work between Lightroom Classic and the Lightroom cloud-based apps. So be aware that some things cannot sync between Lightroom Classic and the other Lightroom apps, such as keywords, color labels, people tags, and organizational structure for grouping collections.

Setting It Up

Here's how to get your Lightroom Classic catalog to sync with the Lightroom app on your mobile device. The key to syncing is your Adobe ID, so when the time comes, you just need to be logged in with the same Adobe ID on your computer and on your mobile device. Follow these steps to enable sync in Lightroom Classic:

1. **Open the Lightroom Classic catalog you want to sync with Lightroom for mobile.**

   You can sync only one Lightroom Classic catalog, and most people have only one anyway.

2. **Click the Cloud icon in the upper right corner to open the syncing pop-up dialog.**

3. **Click the Start Syncing button.**

   Once sync has been enabled, the Start Syncing button changes to a Pause Syncing button, which you can click to pause syncing, if needed.

4. **Grab your mobile device and install the Lightroom app from the App Store on iOS or Google Play Store on Android.**

   Log in to the mobile app using the same Adobe ID and password you use on your computer. If prompted during setup, deselect Auto Add (if it's enabled) to prevent all photos on your device from importing into Lightroom at this time.

Lightroom Classic Preferences

Once you have sync enabled, you can tweak your preferences to suit your needs. In Lightroom Classic, head to Lightroom Classic ⇨ Preferences for Mac (Edit ⇨ Preferences for Windows) and click the Lightroom Sync tab. In the Location section, select the Specify location for Lightroom's Synced images check box, and then click Choose to navigate to the folder on your system where you want all photos downloaded from the cloud to be stored. This folder is where photos you take using the Lightroom for mobile camera or photos directly imported into Lightroom for mobile will be downloaded locally. You also have the option on that panel to have Lightroom Classic create subfolders based on the capture date of the downloaded photos.

Syncing Collections from Lightroom Classic

The primary vehicle for syncing photos from Lightroom Classic to the cloud-based Lightroom is regular collections. When you sync photos from Lightroom Classic, a smart preview for each synced photo is created, and it is this smart preview that gets uploaded from Lightroom Classic to the cloud. There is no way to upload full-resolution copies of your photos from Lightroom Classic to the cloud.

The upside of uploading only Smart Previews is that these Smart Previews do *not* count against your cloud storage limit. When you consider that the old standard Creative Cloud Photography Plan came with only 20 gigabytes (GB) of cloud storage (the All Apps subscription plan gives you 100GB), this is a huge benefit because it enables you to theoretically have unlimited photos synced from Lightroom Classic to the cloud. Since Adobe replaced the 20GB Photography plan with the Photography plan with 1TB for new subscribers those folks don't have to worry about filling up storage as fast.

Here's how to sync existing collections using Smart Previews:

1. **Expand the Collections panel.**

2. **Select the check box to the left of the collection name.**

   If you don't see the box to the left of the collection name, go back to the Cloud icon and enable syncing, as described in the earlier "Setting It Up" section.

Deselecting that box removes the collection from being synced, but it may leave synced photos in the All Synced Photographs collection, which I cover in the upcoming section "All Synced Photographs."

 When you create a new collection, you can sync your collection right from the start by selecting the Sync with Lightroom check box in the Create Collection dialog.

TIP

Making Collections Public

When you view a synced collection in the Library module, you may notice the button labeled Make Public in the upper right corner, above the thumbnails. Because all synced photos are stored in the cloud (even if just as a Smart Preview), you can view those photos from your web browser. Adobe refers to this as Lightroom for the Web (and it has no relation to the Web module described in Chapter 15), which is a bit of a mouthful. The core feature that we are concerned with here, though, is being able to share that link with other people so that they can view and interact with a gallery of photos.

After you click the Make Public button, a link is generated and displayed above the thumbnails. Clicking that link opens Lightroom in your default web browser, or you can right-click the link and copy it to your clipboard for easy pasting into an email or text message to share with others. You can learn more about this feature on my blog: `https://lightroomkillertips.com/lightroom-cc-webs-gallery-feature`.

All Synced Photographs

Photos synced between applications appear in a special collection found in the Catalog panel labeled All Synced Photographs, which keeps a running tally of all photos synced between Lightroom Classic and the Lightroom ecosystem. You can drag-and-drop photos from other places in Lightroom Classic into this collection to have those photos sync, although doing so can become unmanageable, because those photos may not appear in any individual collections.

You can also remove photos from being synced by selecting them in this collection and pressing the Delete key for Mac (Backspace for Windows). You see a prompt warning you that those photos will be removed from all synced devices (and all synced collections) but not removed from the desktop catalog. I use this option to remove photos from being synced because that also removes them from being stored in the cloud without removing them from my local storage. Doing so is useful for managing how much data you have stored in the cloud. You can read more about this over on my blog: `https://lightroomkillertips.com/managing-adobe-cloud-storage-space-classic-users`.

Collections or Albums?

Brace yourself for a bit of confusing lingo you need to understand. *Collections* in Lightroom Classic are referred to as *albums* in the cloud-based version of Lightroom. In Lightroom Classic, collections are organized with *collection sets*. In the cloud-based version of Lightroom, albums are organized by putting them into *folders*. To further complicate matters, collection sets cannot be synced to cloud-based Lightroom; you must manually organize your albums in the cloud-based app to group them into folders. This is one more place where the rift between Lightroom Classic and the new cloud-based Lightroom is apparent.

Lightroom for Mobile Interface

Although this app does get updated frequently with new features, and it looks slightly different on the two supported platforms (iOS and Android), the core layout appears the same across platforms, as shown in Figure 16-1:

>> **A:** Drop-down menu to access folders and albums

>> **B:** Search icon to search the entire library

>> **C:** Access app settings

>> **D:** Filter icon, to filter the current view

>> **E:** Add Photos icon, for adding photos

>> **F:** Camera icon, to launch the Lightroom camera

Be sure to bookmark the Lightroom Learn & Support page to learn more: https://helpx.adobe.com/support/lightroom-cc.html.

FIGURE 16-1:
The Lightroom for mobile interface on an iPhone.

Change Is a Constant

Adobe is clearly committed to continually evolving its products to meet the needs and technologies of the future, and it can pose challenges for users to keep up with the changes. (This is a strength and a weakness of the times we live in.) My hope is that this book provides a good foundation for you to build on — no matter what changes occur. However, if you ever encounter something in your software that doesn't quite match what you see in this book, it's most likely because something changed after the book was published. Stay up-to-date by visiting me at https://LightroomKillerTips.com.

Chapter **17**

Ten Tips for Organizing and Editing in Lightroom

C hapter 16 is devoted to getting you set up with syncing your Lightroom Classic catalog with Lightroom for mobile. This chapter builds on that chapter with a look at the top things you need to know about using Lightroom for mobile to organize and edit your photos. Keep in mind that although Lightroom Classic is the ultimate home base for all your photos in this workflow, there's still a lot you can do while on the go. I use Lightroom on my iPhone as my primary mobile camera app, but I also use it to import photos from a memory card while in the field. No matter where my photos are coming from, I can leverage all the key editing tools in Lightroom Classic's Develop module to edit those photos and have it all sync back to my Lightroom Classic catalog.

There's no way I can fit everything there is to know about Lightroom for mobile in these last three chapters of the book, so be sure to check out the resources I've provided throughout the book to keep up-to-date with new changes and to learn more. My goal here is to whet your appetite and get you started.

Note that I'm writing this chapter from the perspective of a mobile phone user because those devices are better for using the built-in camera. However, all these functions are available on mobile tablet devices — though the interface for tablet screens may look slightly different from my phone-screen captures shown in this book.

Help and Support

You can get some help in the form of FAQs, access to the Adobe support forum, and editing inspiration directly within the app itself. Tap the Lr icon in the upper left corner of the Home screen to enter the app settings. On the App settings screen, find the menu for Help & Support along with a great deal of other useful features to help you get the most out of the app. Take a moment to explore each option to see what's available. Check out the What's New section after each app update to see what was added. At the bottom of the Home screen, tap the Community icon to learn and be inspired by your peers.

All Photos and Filtering

Tapping the Lightroom icon at the bottom, and viewing the All photos album that appears at the top, gives you single-tap access to all photographs that have been added and synced with Lightroom. This includes all photos that were synced from Lightroom Classic and all photos you've captured in the app or imported from your camera roll or an attached memory card.

You can filter what's displayed by tapping the Funnel icon at the top of the screen. I find it helpful to filter what's displayed when viewing All photos, but the feature works the same in any album you're viewing. Tapping the Funnel icon displays the following (and growing) list of criteria you can use to filter your photos:

>> **Rating:** Star ratings applied here or in Lightroom Classic can be used to refine what is visible.

>> **Flags:** As with ratings, flags applied in either app can be used here.

>> **Type:** Filter by HDR, photo, panorama, raw, or video.

>> **Camera:** Filter by the camera used to create the photo.

>> **People:** If you've used the face recognition functionality within the cloud-based Lightroom, you can filter on those results. Note that people tags don't sync between Lightroom and Lightroom Classic.

>> **Location:** Photos can be filtered based on their geolocation data.

>> **Keywords:** If you've applied keywords in the cloud-based Lightroom app, imported photos that had keywords applied to them previously, or migrated a Lightroom Classic catalog (where you import an entire catalog into the

Lightroom cloud), you can filter on those keywords. Note that keywords don't sync between Lightroom and Lightroom Classic.

>> **Edited:** Filter based on whether a photo has been edited.

Segmentation and Other Options

Tap the three-dot menu in the upper right corner of the screen to access the menu for changing how the photos are *segmented* (grouped), enabling info overlays, initiating selecting multiple photos, starting a slideshow, adding more photos, and access additional app setting options. When used together, they are a set of powerful tools for displaying just the photos you want to see and how they are shown.

Adobe Sensei Search

Because all photos in Lightroom are stored in the cloud (even if just as a Smart Preview), Adobe employs its proprietary technology that uses machine learning and artificial intelligence (referred to as *Adobe Sensei*) to identify the contents of your photos and automatically tag them with relevant keywords that you can use to search within Lightroom. (Note that this functionality does not exist in Lightroom Classic.)

Using Adobe Sensei, you can search your library in the cloud-based Lightroom without having to manually add any keywords. Just tap the Search icon (it looks like a magnifying glass) when viewing the source you want to search (start in All photos to search everything), and then enter the words you want to search on. As you type, you see a list of terms (facets) — keywords, locations, camera metadata, and more — that you can tap to see the results (or just keep typing to enter your criteria). You can enter multiple facets to further refine the results. Tapping the x on any search facet removes it from the results. I expect this feature to only continue to improve in time.

Adding Photos from Your Device

If you're like me, you're bound to have a multitude of other photo editing and camera apps on your mobile device, and you probably have more than a few photos already on your phone. You can certainly keep using any other apps, but I would urge you to consider importing all important photos on your device into Lightroom to copy those photos to your computer and back them up. Here's how:

1. **Tap the blue Add Photos icon in the lower right corner of the screen.**

   The left side of the blue button is for adding new photos, and the right side opens the Camera module.

2. **Choose the source where your photos reside.**

   Your Device is the most likely location, but you may see other options based on your model of mobile device and what's connected to it.

3. **Select the photos you want to add.**

   You can single-tap any photo to select it, or tap-drag across a range of photos. The three-dot menu in the upper right corner gives you access to commands for selecting all photos and even filtering by photo, video, raw, or screen shot. Any photos that had previously been added to Lightroom display the Lr logo in the thumbnail's upper left corner. You can deselect photos by tapping them a second time.

4. **Tap the Add button that appears at the bottom of the screen to complete the process.**

You can add photos to a specific album by first entering that album and then tapping the Add Photos icon to start the process. You can import photos from a memory card from any camera in the same fashion. (You may need an adapter with a card reader, depending on your device.) The photos you add in this manner are uploaded in full resolution to the Lightroom cloud storage and count against your storage quota. Check out the article I linked in Chapter 16, in the section "All Synced Photographs," on how to manage your cloud storage space if you import photos from your device or a memory card.

TIP

That said, a new feature added to the Lightroom mobile app is the ability to use Lightroom to edit photos on your device without having to upload them to the cloud. To do this, rather than add the photos, tap the Device icon (the Gallery icon on Android) to view the photos on your device. Tap the photo you want to edit to open it directly into the editing tools. From there, just make your desired adjustments using the available tools. Tap the Share icon to save an edited copy to your device or share to another app. Tap the left-facing arrow at the top to return to Device view to select a different photo. This gives you the power of Lightroom editing without having to utilize your storage quota.

Apply During Import

Though you can't do as much from cloud-based Lightroom as from the Import window in Lightroom Classic, you can automatically add a few things to photos as part of the import process. Tap the Lr icon on the Home screen to go to the App settings screen. From there, tap Import to access its options. Here you can enable and disable the automatic adding of photos, screen shots, and videos from your camera roll (I recommend disabling all of these right away, to avoid your entire camera roll getting dumped into Lightroom), have a simple copyright statement applied to photos, and customize the Raw Default setting (learn more at `https://lightroom killertips.com/customizing-camera-raw-defaults-in-lightroom-classic`).

Creating Albums and Folders

As you add more photos to Lightroom, you may want to organize them using albums and folders. Refer to Chapter 16 to see how albums and folders map back to what you use in Lightroom Classic for organization in the Collections panel. The key thing to know here is that albums hold photos and folders hold albums.

In my case, I created a single album that I use as my working camera roll within the app, which is where I place all new photos at first, until I can review them and decide which ones I will keep. Because all photos I import into Lightroom are uploaded to the cloud and then downloaded to my computer, I don't keep *any* photos on my device's camera roll (at least not for long). This strategy has allowed me to regain a lot of storage space on my device without losing the ability to view my important photos within Lightroom. Once photos are imported into Lightroom and I've confirmed that they were downloaded to Lightroom Classic, I delete them from the device's camera roll.

Here's how to create a new album:

1. **In Lightroom view, tap the drop-down menu at the top left (it may show All photos) to access all albums.**

   This reveals all existing folders and albums, and the options for creating a new album or folder. At the top are Lightroom albums, and below that are any albums you create.

2. **Tap the Create new icon at the bottom.**

   This reveals the Create New pop-up window.

3. **In the Create New pop-up window, tap Album, enter a meaningful name, and tap OK.**

   This adds the new album.

The steps for creating a new folder are the same, except that you tap the icon for Folder instead.

REMEMBER

Be aware that folders in the cloud-based Lightroom do not sync (nor do collection sets from Lightroom Classic).

Applying Ratings and Flags

One of the first uses for the Lightroom on mobile workflow was a way to apply ratings, flags, or both to your photos while on the go. One scenario might be to import a shoot into Lightroom Classic while in the field and then add those photos to a synced collection/album. After the sync is complete, you can leave Lightroom Classic and then, while on the flight/ride home, pull out your phone, open Lightroom, and review the photos to start the flagging and rating process. (Note that data charges may apply when not on Wi-Fi.)

To start applying ratings or flags, you need to switch to Rate & Review view. Single-tap a photo to have it fill the screen, and then tap the *i* icon (for info and rating) in the upper left corner of the screen. Quickly apply a star rating by tap-dragging up or down on the left side of the image and stopping when you reach the desired star rating that appears onscreen. You can quickly change the flag state by tap-dragging up or down the right side of the photo to access the flagging options. Then swipe left or right to move to the next photo. After you have a little practice, the process moves along pretty quickly. Those settings are then automatically synced back to Lightroom Classic. You can also tap the star and flag icons below the photo to apply ratings and flags that way as well. Tap the left-facing arrow at the top to exit the info and rating screen and return to editing.

Editing Photos Anywhere

Remember that everything you can do in Lightroom Classic can be rendered correctly in Lightroom for mobile and vice versa. The differences in the interface are largely due to using a smaller, touch-based device as opposed to a keyboard and mouse — though Adobe did also rename and regroup certain adjustments with the move to the cloud-based Lightroom. As a Lightroom Classic user, I think you'll find the tools to be intuitive and familiar after I get you oriented.

To enter Editing mode, simply single-tap a photo from Device view (Gallery on Android) or Lightroom view. If you hold your device in portrait orientation, the editing tools appear along the bottom of the screen. Tapping a tool icon opens its relevant panels in the row above it. Lightroom has more tools than can appear on one screen, so you may need to scroll to see them all. If you rotate your device to landscape orientation, the editing tools vanish, and you see your photo full screen until you rotate back to portrait orientation.

Tap the Edit icon at the bottom and note that it is highlighted in blue, and that the tools it contains are shown in the row above. Most of the tools are a straightforward match with what you know in the Develop module.

Along with the Edit icon along the bottom are additional tools to get to know. From left to right, you'll find Quick actions (currently an early-access feature, which can be enabled in App settings), Presets, Crop and geometry, Edit, Masking, and Remove. Tapping each respective icon reveals its relevant controls.

Exporting Copies

After doing all the work to get your photos into the app, sort them, rate them, and edit them, you're probably ready to share them with the world. Sure, you can wait until they all sync back to Lightroom Classic and use the Export function, but there's no need to wait. You can select photos inside Lightroom and share edited copies to your favorite social media platforms, other photo editors, email, text messaging, or even your camera roll. In fact, this is the best way I've found to share photos to social media apps such as Facebook and Instagram.

If you're looking at thumbnails, do a long-press on the photo you want to select (just like when you're adding photos to albums), select any other photos you want to share, and you'll see the Share icon appear along the bottom of the screen (look for the Share label). If you're viewing a single photo (such as when you apply ratings or editing), a Share icon (a square with an upward-pointing arrow) appears in the upper right corner of the screen. Tapping the Share icon when viewing a single photo reveals options for saving copy to device, sharing to other apps, adding a border and share (currently iOS only), share to web, or sharing your edits in the Community section. The available options depend on your device's operating system and what other apps you have installed on that device. Tap Export

As to configure export settings for the copy that's created. There are fewer share options when selecting multiple photos to share in a batch.

REMEMBER

Note that if the selected photo was synced from Lightroom Classic, you'll be working only with a Smart Preview, which is limited to 2560 pixels on the long edge, so you won't be able to export anything larger than that.

This is only the tip of the Lightroom for mobile iceberg, so explore, check out the resources I've shared, and have fun.

Index

B

C

L

X

Y

Z

About the Author

Rob Sylvan is a photographer, educator, and aspiring beekeeper. He is the author of many Lightroom, Photoshop, and photography related books, e-books, and videos. Rob also authored and curated tutorials found within the Photoshop and Lightroom applications, is a Canon Product Educator, and regularly teaches at photography industry conferences such as Adobe MAX, Photoshop World, Lightroom Summit, and more.

Dedication

To Jeff Leimbach, this one's for you, buddy!

Author's Acknowledgments

The fact that you're holding this book right now is more a testament to the multitude of people who made it possible than just the person who put the words to paper.

My deepest thanks go to Pete Bauer, for not only taking me on to the NAPP/KelbyOne Help Desk all those years ago, and mentoring me, but for opening doors to new worlds of opportunity. Of course, without KelbyOne I would not be where I am today, and so I would also like to extend my thanks to Scott and Kalebra Kelby, Jean Kendra, and all the rest of the amazing staff for creating and maintaining the most amazing professional resource I have had the pleasure of being associated with. I am also grateful to all the KelbyOne members who have sent in their Photoshop and Lightroom questions over the years; you served as the voice in the back of my mind as I wrote.

My undying gratitude goes to the awesome team at Wiley. To the folks I worked with directly, Alicia Sparrow, Jennifer Yee, Tim Gallan, Becky Whitney, and Chris Main, as well as all those behind the scenes, many thanks for your patience, support, professionalism, and most of all, for making this all come together!

Thanks to the Camera Raw, Lightroom Classic, and Lightroom teams at Adobe for mixing your passion and brilliance into this fantastic tool for digital photographers.

All my love to my wife, Paloma, my son Quinn, and the rest of my family and friends for keeping the coffee flowing, putting up with late nights, making me get out of my chair at regular intervals, and generally taking such good care of me. We did it!

Publisher's Acknowledgments

Acquisitions Editor: Alicia Sparrow

Development Editor: Tim Gallan

Copy Editor: Becky Whitney

Technical Reviewer: Chris Main

Special Thanks: Jennifer Yee

Senior Managing Editor: Kristie Pyles

Managing Editor: Sofia Malik

Cover Image: © SunnyVMD/Getty Images